MONTY'S MANOR

MONTY'S MANOR

Colin Montgomerie and the Ryder Cup

Iain Carter

Yellow Jersey Press
LONDON

Published by Yellow Jersey Press 2010

2 4 6 8 10 9 7 5 3 1

First published in Great Britain in 2010 by
Yellow Jersey Press
Random House, 20 Vauxhall Bridge Road,
London SW1V 2SA

www.rbooks.co.uk

Addresses for companies within The Random House Group Limited can be found at:
www.randomhouse.co.uk/offices.htm

The Random House Group Limited Reg. No. 954009

A CIP catalogue record for this book
is available from the British Library

ISBN 9780224083317

The Random House Group Limited supports The Forest Stewardship Council (FSC),
the leading international forest certification organisation. All our titles that are printed on
Greenpeace approved FSC certified paper carry the FSC logo. Our paper procurement
policy can be found at www.rbooks.co.uk/environment

Mixed Sources
Product group from well-managed
forests and other controlled sources
www.fsc.org Cert no. TT-COC-2139
© 1996 Forest Stewardship Council

Typeset in Minion by Palimpsest Book Production Limited,
Falkirk, Stirlingshire
Printed and bound in Great Britain by
CPI Mackays, Chatham ME5 8TD

For Dad for introducing me to the game
and Sarah and Ollie for being there when I'm not

Contents

LIST OF ILLUSTRATIONS

1. Team Europe at Kiawah Island, 1991; Corey Pavin and Steve Pate wearing Desert Storm caps, 1991; Mark Calcavecchia putts, 1991 (all Getty Images)

2. Colin Montgomerie and Nick Faldo study a putt at the Belfry, 1993 (PA Photos); Bernard Gallacher jumps for joy on the final green as Europe win at Oak Hill, 1995 (PA Photos); Colin Montgomerie with European captain Severiano Ballesteros at Valderrama, 1997 (Getty Images)

3. Colin Montgomerie celebrates victory after halving the final match, 1997 (Colorsport); Team USA invade the green at Brookline, 1999 (Getty Images)

4. Colin Montgomerie celebrates beating Scott Hoch in the final day singles at the Belfry, 2002 (Colorsport)

5. Tiger Woods and Phil Mickelson are partnered at Oakland Hills in 2004 (Offside); Team USA captain Hal Sutton, 2004 (Getty Images); Colin Montgomerie raises his arms after he sinks the winning putt for Europe, 2004 (Offside); Colin Montgomerie embraces his captain, Bernhard Langer, 2004 (Getty Images)

6. Assistant captain, Sandy Lyle, and Colin Montgomerie at the K Club, 2006 (PA Photos); Colin Montgomerie putts to win his singles match with David Toms, 2006; Colin

Montgomerie celebrates beating David Toms in the final-day singles, 2006 (both Getty Images)

7. The 18th fairway is waterlogged as rain falls and play is suspended during the Friday morning fourball matches at Celtic Manor, 2010; Graeme McDowell of Europe watches his putt on the 16th green in his final-day singles match, 2010 (both Getty Images)

8. Team Europe pose with the Ryder Cup following their 14½ to 13½ victory over the USA, 2010; European captain Colin Montgomerie poses with the Ryder Cup, 2010 (both Getty Images)

FOREWORD

I would like to begin this foreword by saying that Colin Montgomerie, as well as being an outstanding competitor, has the word 'winner' in his genes. Colin is one of the greatest golfers I have ever known. If he hasn't won a major it is only because luck has not been on his side. His record in golf leaves no room for doubt, and the Ryder Cup will always have the name Colin Montgomerie engraved upon it. You only have to look at his record in this competition to see that, in singles, no opponent managed to win against him. To date he has achieved six victories and two draws. He remains unbeaten.

In my opinion, Monty has always been the player who most embodies the best sort of relationship that needs to exist between a player and his team. When you rely on a player who gets involved in such a determined way, body and soul, as Colin Montgomerie does, the rest of the team functions because he provides that special focal point. In the Ryder Cups I played with Monty, I noticed that his winning spirit was always present. His personality is his reputation. Few players in the world have the qualities that Monty possesses. In the European team his mental strength and charisma are transmitted in a decisive way to the other players. I myself was affected by this when I was his captain at Valderrama in 1997. It was obvious from Monty's performance that he was a winner. Furthermore, his character, which sometimes makes him appear grumpy or feisty, is what has helped him to develop as a brilliant golfer.

In addition, Colin's feelings and awareness of how to conduct himself make him a person who is as honest with himself as he is with others. I admire him for many reasons, not least because he has proved himself worthy of respect, both at a personal and a professional level. When I have personally needed something, Colin has always been there at my side. To give one example of his generosity, his help for me with the Seve Trophy was reflected in the first four occasions this event took place. His participation as captain of the Great Britain and Ireland team helped the Seve Trophy achieve both its reputation and financial stability. The same applies to the Royal Trophy in 2010. In Thailand Monty stood in for me as captain and achieved victory for Europe over Asia in an extraordinary match.

I want to say here and now that the sport of golf owes a great deal to Colin Montgomerie. If he never succeeds in winning a major I will continue to see him as a GREAT among GREATS; not for nothing has he been, on eight occasions, number one in the rankings on the European circuit. His record will be very difficult to beat.

The great challenge that now faces Colin, as captain of the European team, will be to take the Ryder Cup from the powerful Americans. This promises to be a complex but fascinating task, and there is no one better than Monty to teach his players how to achieve victory in Wales. Obviously I wish for this with all my heart. I am convinced that the success he will achieve for Europe will give my friend Colin Montgomerie the recognition his brilliant sporting career so much deserves.

Severiano Ballesteros
May 2010

Prologue

*'The only time I give a stuff about golf is when
the Ryder Cup is on'*
My mate Dave in the pub, early September 2010

Everything stopped.
People sat in cars, radios on. Others stood in pubs and bars, their gazes transfixed by the big screen. Unfortunate souls stuck in their offices stared at computer pages with golf in the web address. At home the next cup of tea would have to wait; so would the school run. Monday afternoons were not meant to be like this.

By their thousands, many more skipped work to be there; to roar on Europe in their quest to wrest back golf's most precious team prize, the Ryder Cup. No other golf event stirs such raw emotions in so many people.

Right now, on this sunny afternoon, it was within touching distance. An hour earlier victory looked as if it might be achieved without much drama or intrigue. Not any more. America was striving to keep its fingers on that precious trophy. Striving hard. Accomplishing astounding deeds to keep alive hope of taking it back on their return across the Atlantic.

The outcome was hanging in the balance and the options had run out for Europe.

Of all those watching, wheresoever and by whatever means,

there was one person who wanted and needed victory more than any other. He had protested that this wasn't the case; that it was about the team, about European golf, the Tour and not him.

Poppycock.

Time after time he'd had his hands taken from the game's biggest individual trophies, but he was always unbeatable on the final day of a Ryder Cup.

Well, he was as a player. What about as a captain?

This was the event that defined him; it was his manor. It provided his legend and yet it could all go to ruin at the very last. What a journey it had been. He always reserved his finest golf for autumnal jousting with the best the USA could throw at him. Rarely was he ever bounced off and if he was he would be straight back on board. They would never get him a second time.

Yet right now he was a helpless bystander watching his heritage being moulded by hands that were not his own. This could be his legacy; a loser, even in his favourite arena.

After two glorious decades representing his continent as a player, after twenty months as its captain, meticulously planning his team's strategy, and following an unprecedented four days of golf it had come to this.

It was down to the guy he had hand-picked for just such an eventuality. Would this lad from Northern Ireland – the US Open champion no less – justify the captain's faith?

All the skipper could do was watch, hope and pray. Just like everybody else, whether they were greenside, like him, or in the pub or their offices, cars or living rooms.

1

'Having played in eight Ryder Cups it doesn't really affect how I would help the European cause one way or another. I would like to help in any way, shape or form' — Colin Montgomerie

*H*is eyes were wide. He was startled. Things had changed. Rapidly. He'd been asked to leave the room. They wanted to discuss him and he had to go. Life might never be the same again. Probably wouldn't be. This might be what he had wanted for so long. But now? Was this the right time? Could be, that's what he had just suggested. Why not?

The press were waiting – his friends and foes, together in a pack outside the door. They always had been – mates one day, enemies the next; it went with the territory. Right now they were all friends because they wanted to know. He couldn't tell them. No way. This was between him and those he had left in the room. No one else, no one. He had to say something. He always did. Usually it turned into headlines. Not this time. Couldn't – that would blow it. He shut the door behind him, quickly. Had to say something. 'Not today, thank you' usually sufficed when things had gone badly. But things were going rather well, actually. Even so, this wasn't comfortable. This could be it, though. Depended on what they thought and said when he was out of the room. A lot to be said: there always was where *he was concerned. They'd be starting now. Discussing him for the job, the big job, the one he'd always wanted. Had to say something. The press had noticed who had come out of the room. Gave them a glance but not a clue. Then: 'I need to go to the toilet. Does anybody know the way?'*

It wasn't meant to happen this way. Colin Stuart Montgomerie OBE, who became Europe's most talked-about golfer, was not being spoken of as captain of his continent for the 2010 Ryder Cup. When the credits rolled at the end of the clash with the United States at Celtic Manor in South Wales in October his name was not likely to occupy the lead role. Maybe there could have been a position in the supporting cast, perhaps even a spot as a guest star, but this golfing blockbuster was never intended to be *The Full Monty*.

To be named captain of your continent to take on the United States of America for the famous Ryder Cup is to be given top billing. It is the highest honour in European golf. It is recognition for making a sustained and supreme contribution to the game, for the respect you command among your peers, for your ability to inspire, to be tactically astute, savvy in deed and word and to be a leader of men in golf's most captivating arena. It is an opportunity to secure a place in the history of the sport, to take centre stage and play that lead role. Montgomerie has been the star turn of European golf for the better part of two decades. No European has earned more money through stroking a ball into a hole in the fewest possible shots. No European has talked a better game or split opinion in quite the way the man universally known as Monty has done. To some he is a graceful, sublime golfer, an entertainer on and off the course. To others he is regarded as being boorish and bad tempered; someone who doesn't quite have the requisite temperament when the biggest prizes have been at stake. Worst of all, he is seen in some quarters as someone who crossed an unbreakable line with the rules of the game. It is impossible to be ambivalent about the man; anyone with an interest in golf has a view on Montgomerie. Fittingly for someone who is such a contradictory figure, you could find his sternest critics agreeing that he was amply qualified to lead Europe in the Ryder Cup but not even his most ardent fans had anticipated him doing it so soon.

It is one thing to play well for yourself, as pro golfers try to do the other fifty-one weeks of a Ryder Cup year; it is quite another to do so when the hopes and fears of eleven team-mates rest on your performance. Yet it was this scenario that always brought the best from Monty during the long period when he was one of Europe's leading players. Whenever his continent required a contribution he would find a way to make it and he would relish the fact that it would be at the expense of an American opponent. Montgomerie's playing record in the Ryder Cup bears comparison with any of the greats who have taken part in it. He played in eight of these matches and was on the winning side a record-equalling five times. As a partner in foursomes and fourball play and on his own during the closing day of singles matches he amassed 23½ points – a tally third only to Nick Faldo who holds the European record of 25 points and Bernhard Langer who has 24. No American was ever able to beat Montgomerie in the all-important final day one-on-one combat and overall the Glasgow-born Scot was on the winning side on twenty occasions from a total of thirty-six matches. He is justly proud of these stellar statistics.

At the height of his powers Montgomerie was Europe's

dominant golfer on tour and for a sustained period. He won more money than anyone else each season for seven straight years from 1993. After this run was interrupted in 2000 he bounced back to win another Order of Merit, the European Tour's league table of earnings, in 2005. Golfing success in the professional game is often measured by the amount of money a player wins and there was no danger of Monty disappointing the statisticians or his bank manager. But he never claimed a major title and these are the events that all golfers want to win most. The Open, Masters, US Open and US PGA are the game's Holy Grail. These are the events that always attract the best players in the world. They are the big ones, the tournaments to win more than any of the others.

Golfing greatness is measured by the majors; Monty was runner up five times at this level. He walked down the aisle many, many times but he never emerged with the ring on his finger. What do they say about finishing second? You are the first person in the tournament to have been beaten. On this basis Montgomerie could be construed as golf's biggest loser but that is a hard argument to sustain. The most telling reason is the Ryder Cup and his extraordinary exploits in this arena, one that has a capacity to turn general sports followers into golfing fanatics once every two years. It stirs emotions like no other golfing event. While polite applause and respectful cheering are the norm, at a Ryder Cup the air is filled with throaty, bellowed roars of encouragement, chanting and celebration. Galleries become crowds in a partisan atmosphere unique in the game of golf whenever Europe and the United States renew their rivalry. Monty loves it, every decibel of passion, to his core. It is ironic, given his vast earning capacity on the golf course, that this is the one part of the professional game where there isn't a penny, cent or dime at stake. His place among golf's elite has always been assured, for his eight Orders of Merit and multiple tournament victories, but most of all because of his ability to beat Americans when that little golden cup has been on the line. He was, therefore, always destined one day to become captain of his continent, but not for the 2010 match.

It just didn't seem likely to be his moment. Montgomerie had made it abundantly clear that he considered himself a shoo-in to do the job in 2014 on his home Scottish soil at Gleneagles, which is just down the road from where he lives. 'There's a wrong time and a wrong place and the right time and the right place,' he had said. 'I just hope I am in the right place come 2014 when it comes home here to Scotland.' These comments came on a Sunday morning in January 2009, two days before the decision-making process would continue and possibly conclude on who would be skipper for the following year's match. Furthermore, as speculation began to mount as to the identity of Nick Faldo's successor after Europe's 16 ½-11½ defeat at Valhalla in 2008, Monty seemed more concerned with supporting another candidate and playing himself back into the team. He showed no appetite for standing in a leadership contest.

That 2008 defeat in Kentucky had been the first Ryder Cup Montgomerie had missed since his playing debut in 1991 and he had been bitterly disappointed not to have been invited to serve as a vice-captain. Once it became clear that he would not be part of Europe's defence of the trophy, I asked him: 'Have you hit your last shot in the Ryder Cup?' This was the day after Faldo had announced Ian Poulter and Paul Casey would be the two wild-card picks who would complete his team, confirming that Monty would miss out. 'No, I don't think I have' was the unhesitating response. By definition he was setting his sights on returning to the playing fold for the 2010 match and he had said nothing to change that view in the months that followed. If he did return to the team it would be under the captaincy of someone who was yet to be announced.

The decision over who leads the continent's Ryder Cup team is made by the European Tour's Tournament Committee. It is a fifteen-strong body of current and recently retired players to which the Tour's executive reports. Since Severiano Balles-teros had taken over as captain in 1997 a different leader has been appointed for every one of these biennial matches. Bernard Gallacher had done the job for the three matches before Seve took over and before him Tony Jacklin had reigned for four Ryder Cups. Between them Jacklin and Gallacher had presided over the period in which this contest had grown into the biggest event in golf and by some estimates the third most watched sporting gathering in the world behind only the Olympics and football World Cup. Being captain had become a lucrative appointment abundant with spin-off opportuni-ties and the committee felt it right that the post should be shared around as many top names as possible. The unwritten rule that followed Gallacher's departure was that future skip-pers could only ever do the job for one match.

Making such appointments is a contentious business and a difficult balancing act. Should they go for the player who most deserves the post or the one who is most likely to win the match? This is a question that rarely surfaces in other sports but in golf there is often felt to be an obligation to reward service and achievement with positions of honour. The last time the committee had deliberated the captaincy had been in early 2005, when they felt obliged to make a double appointment. They had two former world number ones to choose from and believed that they couldn't give the job to one without giving it to the other. So Ian Woosnam, the diminutive Welshman who was the Masters champion in 1991, was put in charge for the record-equalling win at the K Club in Ireland in 2006 and Britain's greatest golfer, Nick Faldo, was allocated the away match two years later. Europe's defeat ended an unprecedented run of three consecutive victories. So when the committee gathered in Abu Dhabi on 13 January 2009 they were deliberating the captaincy issue for the first time in quite a long period. It was regarded as a heavy responsibility because wresting back the trophy was a huge priority for the European game.

As a long-established member of the committee, Montgomerie was one of the fifteen who would decide the next captain. He had given no indication that he was interested in the job and the hot favourite was Spain's José Maria Olazábal. The two-time Masters champion had been sounded out by committee chairman Thomas Björn months earlier. The Spaniard expressed hope that he would be able to play at Celtic Manor. Being a footsoldier rather than the general would be his preferred role. But few within the game believed the popular Olly would be able to sustain the quality of golf required to make it into the team. He had been a long-term sufferer from rheumatism which severely limited the number of tournaments he could play. Being able to amass substantial quantities of prize money and world ranking points over a year-long period was a prerequisite to qualify for the side. The committee believed the forty-two-year-old would come to accept this harsh reality and set his sights on leading the team rather than playing in it.

'He is going to be an absolutely outstanding Ryder Cup captain whenever it is his turn. He is different class,' said committee member Paul McGinley ahead of the meeting. The Irishman, who holed the winning putt for Europe in the 2002 Ryder Cup, had just played under Olazábal's leadership in an event called the Royal Trophy which pitted a European team against an Asian side in Thailand. McGinley clearly felt the fact that Europe had lost the match 10-6 was nothing to do with Olazábal's captaincy and team-mate Paul Lawrie agreed. 'Any player who makes José Maria's team when he's Ryder Cup captain will be lucky indeed. He couldn't do any more,' said the 1999 Open champion. Lawrie was also on the committee that met in Abu Dhabi on 13 January 2009.

Olazábal was never going to be short of support but he wasn't the only candidate. The most intriguing contender was Sandy Lyle, the only one of Europe's 'big five' never to have done the job. Lyle was at the heart of the quintet of players from the continent who shattered America's domination of events like the Masters and the Open. Seve Ballesteros, Bernhard Langer, Faldo and Woosnam were the others and all four had been rewarded with the captaincy. Lyle, who won the Open in 1985 and the Masters three years later, played in five Ryder Cups and is one of the greats of the British game. He was one of Woosnam's assistants at the K Club, but there were always doubts about whether he possessed what Europe required in a leader, especially one charged with the task of regaining the trophy.

Ironically, Lyle's biggest supporter at the Middle East meeting to discuss the captaincy was none other than Colin

Montgomerie. 'I'd choose Sandy Lyle if I had the casting vote. It would be a shame if of all that big side we had of Langer, Seve, Faldo and Woosnam, Sandy Lyle missed out,' Monty said. This support was rendered even more ironic given the major falling out between the two men that occurred later in 2009. But at the time of the meeting it appeared Montgomerie would be speaking up for his fellow Scot and there was no doubt that Lyle was very keen to do the job. 'I can't see any reason why not me. As far as available captains go there are not an awful lot around. I look like the favourable choice,' Lyle told members of the Scottish press. 'This is my last chance. I'm still fairly well in touch with the present players.' Such strident self-promotion is rare in golf and was even more surprising coming from the often self-deprecating and modest Lyle. It showed just how much he wanted to lead Europe in Wales. He said that he would appoint the German Langer as a vice-captain and play plenty of events on the European Tour to stay in touch with the players who would make up his team. In what was a public pitch for the job, Lyle also said he believed that his relationship with the American skipper, the man he would have to pit his wits against, should count in his favour as well. 'Corey Pavin and I have grown up together. He played the European Tour in the late seventies, early eighties and I've seen him on a regular basis in America. I know pretty much how he works. And I think I'll know pretty much how the American team will work as well.

'I'm sure the players feel I'm very approachable,' Lyle went on. 'You need to be laid back. It's no good seeing the captain get all red-faced and flustered. They'll think he might not be able to make the right decisions then. Forceful, decisive but also relaxed, that's what I'd want to be.' Whether the committee would share his opinion that he possessed those qualities for a 'must-win' match was another question.

Clearly Lyle was trying to steer the argument away from the fact that if he was given the job it would be seen as an appointment made mainly because it was his turn. He would be fifty-two by the time the 2010 match was played, realistically the very upper age limit for any captain who wanted still to be firmly in touch with his players. He was putting forward strategic reasons why he should be skipper, but they were destined to fall on deaf ears. Lyle felt his biggest rival for the job was Ian Woosnam. This assessment was misplaced, too. Influential figures like 2002 captain Sam Torrance had been championing Woosnam's candidacy because the match would be played in Wales. Butch Harmon, former coach of Tiger Woods, said the Welshman was surely the only man for the job, especially given his success in 2006 at the K Club. On that occasion the skipper had harnessed a tide of emotional support for the recently widowed Darren Clarke and used it to create an unstoppable European force that surged to a record-equalling win. But Woosnam was never a serious contender because the committee was keen to enforce its unwritten rule that makes the captaincy a one-off appointment.

They were also keen to appoint a continental European. To date only Spain's Ballesteros (1997) and Langer (2004) had broken the British domination of the role. A match that had originally been Great Britain against America at the Ryder Cup's 1927 inception had become an amalgam of Britain and Ireland in 1973 and only genuinely competitive when the whole of Europe came on board in 1979. The great Jack Nicklaus had suggested the move because the event was proving too one-sided. Ritual thrashings dished out by America were becoming boring and the Ryder Cup was dying at just the time when golf in continental Europe was starting to flourish. Once exciting Spaniards like Ballesteros, Antonio Garrido, Manuel Pinero and José Maria Canizares became available a kiss of life could be administered. The European influence enabled the Ryder Cup to thrive and grow and a fair few Americans took a golfing kicking along the way. But despite this seismic continental influence the European Tour remains very British-centric. Its headquarters are at Wentworth to the west of London in Berkshire and the executives responsible for its day-to-day running are almost exclusively of British or Irish origin. The vast majority of dedicated golf writers and broadcasters have the same roots and so much of the pre-meeting coverage had a predictable and parochial slant.

The make-up of the Tournament Committee, on the other hand, was more cosmopolitan and was chaired by the Dane Thomas Björn. There were four Swedes – Joakim Haeggman, Chris Hanell, Robert Karlsson and Henrik Stenson – Spaniards Gonzalo Fernández-Castaño and Miguel Ángel Jiménez and Frenchman Raphael Jacquelin around the table in Abu Dhabi. Irishman Paul McGinley, England's Richard Finch, Barry Lane and Mark Roe were there, too, along with the Scots Montgomerie and Lawrie. Northern Ireland's Darren Clarke was also on the committee but missed the meeting because he was playing a tournament in South Africa.

Björn was known to be keen for a continental European to do the job and that was one of the reasons he had already sounded out Olazábal, who had served as Faldo's vice-captain in 2008. Another Spaniard was in the picture; indeed, ahead of the meeting Miguel Ángel Jiménez was a better bet than either Lyle or Woosnam. Jiménez is a hugely popular figure among his peers and with golf fans across the continent, and in a twenty-seven-year career had played in three Ryder Cups and won fifteen times on Tour. He always plays with a smile on his face; a fat cigar and glass of the best red are never far away. His bunched ponytail is not the expected hairstyle of a golfer in middle age, but somehow he carries it off. He is undoubtedly one of the game's most distinctive figures. But Jiménez has never made much commitment to becoming fluent in English and his heavily accented delivery makes him hard to understand whenever a microphone is nearby. The game may have moved into previously uncharted territory in a period of massive global expansion, but English remains the golfing language in Europe. He would have needed to address these issues if he were to become captain and would have needed plenty of persuasion to do so. This inevitably counted against him and strengthened further the hand of his Spanish compatriot Olazábal.

So when it came to the fateful meeting at Abu Dhabi's sumptuous Emirates Palace Hotel, all the indications suggested a discussion that would consider the merits of Lyle, Woosnam and Jiménez before a decision being taken to offer the role to Olazábal. The forty-two-year-old had been reluctant to discuss his candidacy because he was desperate to play in at least one more Ryder Cup, but as the meeting approached he did seem to be coming round to the idea that the time might be right for him. After saying that he would, of course, like to be playing in the 2010 match, he acknowledged the speculation linking him with the captaincy: 'I would love to be considered, I'm not denying that. I have never denied that. Captaining the Ryder Cup is something really special – it is a real privilege.' Olly had been a mainstay of European golf since turning professional in the mid-eighties. He was the Spanish apprentice to Seve's sorcerer and he and Ballesteros formed the most indomitable partnership in the history of the Ryder Cup. Olazábal confirmed his undoubted playing potential when he won the Masters in 1994, two years after rising to a career high of number two in the world rankings. But soon after that Augusta triumph his prospects could not have looked bleaker. He was struck down with rheumatoid polyarthritis. The condition, which took an age to diagnose, left him unable to walk and in severe and debilitating pain. He didn't play at all in 1996, having managed just seven events on the European Tour the previous year. Confirming astounding powers of recovery, he fought back to claim a second Masters Green Jacket in 1999 in one of the greatest sporting triumphs over adversity. Thereafter his career has been a constant battle dominated by his efforts to keep the effects of rheumatism at bay. He played his way into the 2006 Ryder Cup and it was the third time he'd been on the winning side in seven appearances. He is one of the best-loved figures in the European game, a genuine, sensitive and talented man with a huge passion for the Ryder Cup. He therefore ticked all the boxes.

In the build-up to the meeting pundits and press were, as you would expect, having their say. Derek Lawrenson, the experienced and respected golf correspondent of the *Daily Mail*, claimed there was 'no credible alternative to Olly'. Mark Reason, having just taken over the reins as correspondent for the *Daily Telegraph*, suggested a Lyle, Woosnam, Langer 'dream team', with the Scot being assisted by two record-breaking former skippers. In my reports for BBC Five Live I shared Lawrenson's view that the job would go the way of Olazábal, while Tom English wrote in *Scotland on Sunday*: 'If Sandy Lyle isn't appointed then the game of golf may deliver the greatest collective wince since Doug Sanders missed his tiddler at St Andrews nearly four decades ago.' Montgomerie's name didn't warrant a mention.

Not for the first time media speculation proved merely to be hot air. Supposedly informed comment and speculation proved to be, well, not very informed. Not that we should have chastised ourselves. No one had predicted Montgomerie would be appointed captain because no one saw it coming and not just in the sporting media. The same could be said of most of those who were in the meeting room, including Monty himself.

There was a discernible beginning-of-term feeling in Abu Dhabi that week. The European Tour's leading golfers were gathering for the first time en masse since the Christmas break. Some were coming from Thailand where they'd been playing in the Royal Trophy, others, like Masters champion Trevor Immelman, had travelled more than halfway round the world, having played in the American PGA Tour's opening event in Hawaii, and most were venturing out on Tour for the first time in 2009. Handshakes and smiles abounded on the range on the morning of Tuesday 13 January. Coaches and caddies stood with arms folded watching their charges, carefully checking the progress of winter swing changes.

Less relaxed were the committee members. As they tuned up their games on the range or perhaps headed out for nine holes' reconnaissance on the Abu Dhabi Golf Club course, their minds were also on that evening's meeting. Chairman Thomas Björn had arrived the previous day and, predictably, was giving away little. 'We are going to take our time. We don't

need to decide now; the time when we do is before the qualifying points start in September.' We would not have to wait
that long. Indeed, it was surely just a comment to deflect the
growing feeling of urgency for a decision.

Björn also had to face questions regarding his neutrality in
considering the candidacy of Ian Woosnam. The tall Dane is
a curious character. On the one hand he is a measured, articulate and intelligent ambassador while on the other he is a
passionate and emotional figure not afraid to speak out when
he feels he or his cause have been wronged. He was fined in
2006 for a furious outburst against Woosnam after the
Welshman's wild-card picks of Westwood and Darren Clarke.
Björn felt the captain had been guilty of bias against continental players in deciding to go with two UK golfers to
complete his team for the match at the K Club. He was also
very angry at being overlooked for a place in the team. He
branded Woosnam 'pathetic' and said his leadership ahead of
the match was 'the worst ever'. His comments to newspaper
reporters had been so unsettling the captain felt a need to
seek the backing of his players before deciding against quitting just ahead of the match. Björn was portrayed as the villain
of the piece and officialdom came down hard on him. Chief
Executive George O'Grady said the Tour would not tolerate
'personal and unacceptable remarks'. As well as being heavily
fined (the Tour don't publish punishments but it is thought
the amount was around £10,000) Björn made a humbling
apology. His resurrection from this position to that of being
Europe's Ryder Cup kingmaker spoke volumes for his diplomatic skills, not to mention the overall high regard he
commands among his golfing peers. 'Not my finest hour and
that will hang over me for ever,' Björn admitted ahead of the

Abu Dhabi meeting. 'But things have to move on. You get emotional at times and you regret what happened. I'm sure it's not at the forefront of Woosie's mind.'

The evening began with a meal. Sustenance was always going to be required because the participants knew it would be a long night. The Ryder Cup captaincy wasn't the only item on the agenda. Important discussions on the direction the Tour would be taking in the months and years ahead had to be aired and the committee needed to appraise developments at their Wentworth HQ. The credit crunch was starting to bite and this had implications for the Tour's schedule, player benefits and prize funds. The issue of who would succeed Nick Faldo as skipper was the headline-grabbing topic but the last item to be debated. They wanted to get the rest out of the way before taking on the subject that was dominating golf chatrooms, blogs and sports pages in newspapers. As the meeting progressed behind closed doors, an ever-growing group of golf writers waited outside in the hope of learning who would be offered the prestigious job.

We had no idea of the dramatic way in which the meeting had swung from the moment the captaincy discussion began and we remained oblivious when we were presented with the biggest clue after some three hours' standing guard. This was when the door swung open and out stepped a startled looking Colin Montgomerie. There are few golfers in the world more at home in the company of journalists. He is on first name terms with pretty much all of the main British correspondents and usually handles the media circus with aplomb. But at this precise moment the last people he expected or wanted to see were a bunch of jet-lagged golf reporters idling away time in the desperate hope of finding out who would be Europe's next

Ryder Cup captain. Yet there he was, the continent's next skipper, standing before us. It is just that we didn't know it. Monty took one wide-eyed look and blurted out, not altogether convincingly: 'I need to go to the toilet. Does anybody know the way?' He then headed at pace down one of the Emirates Palace's vast corridors in search of relief. This comfort break lasted fully twenty-five minutes, and the longer it went on the more we speculated on his peculiar demeanour as he emerged from the committee room. The best the specialist correspondents of the *Mail*, *Independent*, *Guardian*, *Times*, *Telegraph*, *Mirror* and BBC could muster was that he'd perhaps walked out in a huff after failing to win the argument on Sandy Lyle's behalf. 'Must be Olazábal, then,' we concluded.

Eventually Montgomerie returned – mobile phone clamped to his right ear, avoiding us in much the same way he tries to do after emerging from a recorder's hut following a disappointing round. Not that it seemed unusual for him to evade the press when such a sensitive subject is under discussion. The Tournament Committee prides itself on not making public its key decisions until it is good and ready and is able to do so in a proper manner. So the captaincy issue was shrouded in secrecy. But on this occasion they weren't able to keep a lid on what had been decided for as long as they would have wanted.

When it had become time to discuss the captaincy in the meeting, Thomas Björn made opening remarks and said it was his opinion that they should appoint the best man for the job. The person most qualified to win back the precious trophy for Europe. Sentimentality should not come into it. They shouldn't just appoint someone because it was their turn. Björn then asked whether everyone else was in agreement with this view and he received unanimous support. This effectively did for Lyle's chances. It was also agreed that an appointment needed to be made sooner rather than later. Olazábal's prevarication and stated desire that he would prefer to play rather than lead counted against him. It was known that Miguel Ángel Jiménez wasn't up for committing to language classes and Woosnam had done the job before. There was no suggestion that the unwritten one-off rule needed to be rescinded. So who should be skipper?

Before any real deliberation could begin, Henrik Stenson seized the initiative. The popular Swede, who had played in the two previous Ryder Cups and secured Europe's winning point on his debut at the K Club, announced to the meeting that 'the best man for the job is sitting in this room'. He then looked in Montgomerie's direction. Sources present say that there was a feeling that Monty would decline or at the very least demur, citing a desire to try to play at Celtic Manor or to wait for the 2014 match at Gleneagles. Instead, Stenson's assertion was met with an unexpected silence. Monty didn't appear averse to the idea; in fact it swiftly became clear that he was open to it. 'It was like a light going on in his head,' one eyewitness later recalled. Soon after this moment he was asked to leave the room so that his brand new candidature could be properly discussed by the rest of the committee. No wonder he looked rather taken aback as he emerged before waiting journalists.

Montgomerie has always contended that he didn't have the slightest inkling that he would come out of the meeting as the most likely man for the job, and there's no reason to dispute this. When he returned after that protracted 'toilet break' the decision was taken that all parties should have a week or so to mull over the captaincy issue. They considered announcing Monty as skipper that evening in Abu Dhabi, but decided that would be unfair on the other candidates. Also, the committee had taken such a dramatic and unexpected turn it was felt too impulsive to rubber-stamp the decision there and then.

As the meeting broke up after almost four hours, most committee members studiously avoided eye contact with the waiting reporters, but Stenson quipped on his way out: 'Expect something innovative.' That was the only clue that they had gone left field in their deliberations. We reporters had hoped for the proverbial white smoke, but, as the *Telegraph*'s Mark Reason noted, the only smoke to emerge was from Thomas Björn's post-meeting cigarette.

The next day it was the pro-am ahead of the Abu Dhabi Championship, a last chance to get ready for the first big tournament of the 2009 European Tour season. But the preoccupation was the captaincy. Something had come very close to being decided the previous night and those involved were trying to keep it out of the public domain. Of course, the decision – seemingly out of nowhere – had been to make Colin Montgomerie the leading contender to be the next captain. The Scot was giving nothing away and was happy to fuel the speculation that pointed towards a Spanish appointment.

'We've missed Olazábal since the K Club. The passion he brings to any Ryder Cup is evident, spurred on by his pal Seve,' he said. Monty went on to refer to Olazábal's inspiring intervention in the 2008 match at Valhalla when he was Nick Faldo's vice-captain. 'I heard that Olly was brilliant on the Saturday night last year. "Come on, we've done this in America before, we did it from 9-7 down, and we can do it again,"' Montgomerie said, recalling what he had heard of the Spaniard's words that brought tears to the eyes of the team ahead of the final day singles matches. Showing a leader's initiative, Olazábal had taken it upon himself to inspire the team after Faldo had offered just basic instructions on what was expected from them. Olly knew they needed to hear more. He told the players what he would be prepared to give to be one of them, to have the chance of overhauling a deficit to win the Ryder Cup for Europe. Crucially, Olazábal then told them that he was convinced they were the best twelve players to do the job. It was utterly inspirational; some players were openly crying with the emotion of his words; others were fighting hard to keep watering eyes in check.

With rumour and counter-rumour circulating at an increasingly feverish pace, it was becoming more and more difficult to know who to believe. It all changed on the Thursday evening of that week. Something about the day had suggested we were in for an unusual turn of events because a hailstorm, of all things, had delayed play on the first day of the Abu Dhabi Championship. Later the travelling press corps had been invited to dinner by a local public relations firm and it soon became apparent that a story was brewing that would eclipse even ice lying in a desert.

The story was of a significant shift in the Betfair exchange on who would be Europe's next Ryder Cup captain. Betfair is not a conventional bookmaker. It is an online conduit to enable punters to bet against each other. If you think a player is going to win an event you can back him with your money. If you think he will lose you can use the same company to lay the bet at your own price. Professional oddsmakers are not involved. In this case, from being a 50 to 1 outsider Colin Montgomerie's price had been dramatically cut to 2 to 1. It was a relatively small betting market and in reality it hadn't taken the staking of huge sums to prompt such a big shift, but the move suggested that the mood of the meeting had leaked. Betfair's Tony Calvin admitted to the *Guardian*'s Lawrence Donegan: 'Clearly someone has had a whisper that Mr Montgomerie was in the mix.' Conventional bookmakers were thrilled that someone as high profile yet unlikely as Monty was now the most likely candidate. 'We'll be dancing a highland jig and watching reruns of *Mrs Doubtfire* if Monty gets the gig,' said Ladbrokes, neatly tying together his Scottish heritage and one of his less favourite nicknames. Aware that the significant move had occurred in Abu Dhabi, the bookies were shutting down their markets on the captaincy and preparing to count the proceeds from not having to pay out on the long-time favourite Olazábal.

European Tour boss George O'Grady was less impressed at the turn of events. In a statement he said: 'No decision on the Ryder Cup captaincy has been taken. We have been made aware of movements in various odds in the betting markets. We invite any gaming company to contact the European Tour with any evidence of irregular betting activity. This will be fully investigated.' It was looked into, but details of the investigation were never published other than to say that the sums of money involved were 'minuscule'. O'Grady later said: 'We can't really believe anyone on the committee has actually used this information. The committee is appalled that someone, perhaps inadvertently, has leaked it.'

Naturally the most important reaction to this unexpected shift in the betting market would come from Colin Montgomerie but we would have to wait until he had completed his second round at the Abu Dhabi Championship. He had opened the tournament with an uninspiring level par 72 but his next round was far more encouraging, with no fewer than six birdies and only one dropped shot in a 67 that was one of the lowest scores of the day. But it wasn't his improving golf that we wanted to discuss. And it wasn't his carefully chosen words that convinced us he would become the next Ryder Cup skipper either. Nevertheless, we were left in little doubt after our exchanges with him in the midday sun outside the recorder's hut. His demeanour said it all.

'We are no further forward with the selection process than when we left the meeting on Tuesday, so I know as much as anyone else does' was his opening gambit. But then we heard him say this for the first time: 'Having played in eight Ryder Cups it doesn't really affect how I would help the European cause one way or another. I would like to help in any way, shape or form,' he said in his curious mix of Scottish lilt sprinkled with a Yorkshire twang that stems from a youth spent in the North of England. Then for the first time he referred to the possibility of him leading the side. 'It would be an honour to be selected . . . I will have to let you know if it has been offered. At this stage it has not.' But what about Sandy Lyle, the man Monty was backing for the job? Again he dealt with the enquiry with skilful tact but a discernible shift in position. 'It would be, as I've always said, a great shame if Sandy didn't get the captaincy.' It wasn't exactly the unequivocal backing he'd offered his compatriot prior to the meeting. Montgomerie spent around five minutes in what's known as a 'media huddle' after giving his initial thoughts to Sky's golf presenter David Livingstone. In the course of that interview Monty showed that his wit was as sharp as his golf game had been that day as Livingstone probed gently on the tumbling odds. Question: 'There seemed to be a mysterious twenty-minute bathroom break for you during the meeting; was that significant?' Answer, delivered with perfect comic timing: 'They are all significant.'

Radio microphones and Dictaphones were thrust under Monty's nose as he moved away from the Sky cameras and the captain-to-be continued to field questions. To my opener on whether the tumbling of the odds on him getting the job was a shock he said: 'I'm as surprised as you guys. I saw a lot of press around here and I was wondering why, because a 67 for me doesn't really suggest this number of press nowadays. I don't know why this should be. I don't know what's happened, we'll all find out on the Wednesday evening of Dubai.' He bobbed and weaved like a seasoned heavyweight to avoid being caught out. The *Telegraph*'s Mark Reason, as astute an inquisitor as there is on the golf beat, weighed in next: 'If the committee offered you the job on the condition that, should you play yourself on to the team, you would not take up the position, would you accept the job?' Montgomerie parried with charm: 'That's hypothetical,' he said. 'And therefore cannot be answered, but it is a very good question.' His tone throughout was light without belittling the significance of the story. There were lots of smiles and laughs, but with a core of substance running through them, recognising the need to avoid betraying confidences and a respect for the post for which he was now being considered. What is more, it was clear he was relishing the attention, just as he has done throughout his career. As he headed off towards the steps up to the huge, angular Abu Dhabi clubhouse (extraordinarily, it actually depicts a falcon with wings spread), Montgomerie looked over his shoulder and with a smile called back: 'Was that diplomatic enough, lads?' He knew and we knew and he knew that we knew. It was just that he was not at liberty to say it.

Monty was a genuine contender for the job. Olazábal still had a chance; Lyle, Woosnam and Jiménez were toast. Like the birds of prey that are emblematic of the Gulf region, Monty had appeared on the captaincy scene undetected. Now his talons were out; leading his continent in his favourite arena, the one where he has generated headlines since his playing debut in 1991, was the prey and it was now within his sights. There were just twelve days to wait.

2

29 SEPTEMBER 1991, OCEAN COURSE,
KIAWAH ISLAND, SOUTH CAROLINA

'I'd written him off'
– Bernard Gallacher, European Captain

He had wanted to be there. But not on this interminable journey to the tenth tee. And all because of those score-boards and that red number five that was screaming into his head, burning into his soul. His captain had written him off. He was close to taking the same view. This wasn't good, this was bad and he had to do something about it. He was being blown away. This wasn't the stuff of legend, yet this was the Ryder Cup and what an event it had become. He knew he couldn't give the homeboy an early lead; his skipper had told him so, but he couldn't do anything about it. This Calcavecchia was a machine; couldn't he feel the magnitude of this? The Americans were desperate to win and he hadn't a nerve in his body. It had been a strange week and it was going to get stranger. The scare on the plane, the Yanks lording it at the dinner, the car crash, the prank calls in the middle of the night. The skipper wanted the FBI involved in that one. What about the Yanks in their army caps? Didn't they know our boys were out there as well? It was nothing to do with golf anyway. But this was. The crowd were going mad; they thought they'd already got the trophy back. The rookie wasn't helping either – he was five down against Calcavecchia – an

Open champion, no less, and only nine holes to go. That was one in the bank for them. Unless, that is, the rookie got his act together. He hated to lose, hated it, and with a capital H. He always had and this wasn't the time to change. But for this match it was time to force a change; there was no other option. Where there was a will . . . and there was, it was welling up inside. At last, the tenth tee. What a time to stick a drive into the sandy wastes . . .

Colin Montgomerie's Ryder Cup debut was not the most promising and there wasn't much evidence in the overall standard of his golf to suggest that this biennial match between Europe and the United States would provide the core to his legacy. Monty was twenty-eight when he first played for Europe. It was 1991 and the match turned into one of the most famous – and infamous – clashes in the history of the Ryder Cup. It provided the event's most gripping finish, yet the ill feeling between the two teams and the intensity of the competition meant it was also dubbed 'the war on the shore'.

Everything about the contest, its setting and the nature of the matches, created as dramatic a background as could be for Montgomerie to make his entrance into the Ryder Cup fray. He was one of five newcomers in the European team; Paul Broadhurst, David Gilford, Steven Richardson and David Feherty were the other rookies. Of this fresh-faced quintet most was expected from the big, burly, curly-haired Scot. Montgomerie carried, as he has for much of his career, a few extra pounds around his waist but, more important, he bore an ever-expanding reputation for good golf.

The team travelled by Concorde to South Carolina and a brand new golfing location, the Ocean Course at Kiawah Island.

This was a relatively late change of venue because the match had originally been scheduled to be played at PGA West at La Quinta in California. European broadcasters had complained because the time difference from the American West Coast would have led to the match being screened too late at night for most of their viewers. The Ryder Cup was now big business. Europe had long since proved to be competitive under the previous captaincy of Tony Jacklin. They had ended America's twenty-eight-year domination of the Trophy with victory at the Belfry in 1985 and had shown it was no fluke by winning on American soil for the first time two years later, at Muirfield Village. Europe's unbeaten run continued back at the Belfry in 1989 when the match ended in a 14–14 draw, enough to retain the trophy. Now Jacklin had handed over the reins to Bernard Gallacher, who took a mixture of youth and world-beating experience to the US for the defence of the trophy.

America had never been more desperate to win. The ritual biennial beatings they used to dish out, non-contests that did little to stir the public imagination, were a thing of the past. There was no longer a divine right for the great Americans to hold the trophy and now they wanted it back with a passion.

On both sides of the Atlantic the Ryder Cup had become one of the most captivating sporting events of them all. The Europeans delighted in their new-found domination while the smarting US players and fans wanted to reassert the old order. It made for terrific sport and the television companies were starting to have to pay considerably more for the rights to show the match. Hence the European broadcasters, having invested heavily, had the clout to insist on the 1991 match being relocated to the East Coast where the time difference far better suited their schedules. Unravelling existing contracts with the original host course might have proved problematic, but Kiawah Island was owned by the Landmark Land Company, the same firm to whom the PGA West belonged. They therefore had a suitable replacement to hand, but this also meant staging the match at a barely completed venue and on a unique golf course.

The 7,301-yard layout was designed by Pete Dye, a controversial architect known for producing courses of brutal difficulty and, on occasion, questionable fairness. Dye is most famously responsible for the Stadium Course at TPC Sawgrass, the home of the prestigious Players' Championship, with its instantly recognisable island-green 17th hole. The fans love to gather there because it always delivers something to which they can react. Any player who misses the putting surface will see his ball disappear into the water. To the golfing purist this provides a potentially unjust punishment, far worse than the crime of only just missing a green, and with no chance of recovery. To the paying spectator it offers excitement, drama and value for money.

Dye had a similar philosophy when designing the Ocean Course on a barrier island jutting out into the Atlantic near Charleston in South Carolina. It was a course with no rough or bunkers, just sandy wastes that framed wide fairways and plateau greens. As at Sawgrass there are abundant alligator-populated water hazards and a memorable par three penultimate hole. He constructed a course that ran an awkward route partially in line with the sea, making it susceptible to fiendishly difficult crosswinds. By the end of the week those winds would breathe unexpected life into the fledgling but flagging Montgomerie Ryder Cup career.

First, though, the new boy had to endure the journey to the United States for what would be his initial taste of professional golf in America. Europe had done things in style ever since Jacklin had taken charge of the team. Only the best would do for his side and he was able to use the resources generated by the ever-expanding European Tour to make sure his players would always be made to feel special. For away matches Concorde was the only way to travel and for the Kiawah Island match it was no different. The plane was chartered and the first ten rows were set aside for the players and the captain, Gallacher, who cradled the famous trophy as he took his seat on board. The rest of the supersonic jet was taken up by officials and spectators who had paid handsomely for the right to fly with the team and its precious golden cargo. As a rookie, Monty was among those teammembers furthest back and he took the window seat next to his wife. He had first felt a sense of nervousness and anticipation when he saw the number of television camera crews that had gathered at Heathrow for Europe's send-off. Wearing his official team suit, Montgomerie commented to his then new wife Eimear: 'Bloody hell, we haven't even left the country yet.'

After the refuelling in New York, Gallacher asked the pilot if he could let his players catch a first glimpse of the course with a flypast over Kiawah Island. Spirits had been high on board. It was a confident Europe that boasted four of the top five players in the world: Nick Faldo, Severiano Ballesteros, José Maria Olazábal and the reigning Masters champion, and according to the rankings the best player on the planet, Ian Woosnam. Now, as the pilot tipped his wings one way and then the other, the players could see for the first time the course that over the next few days would bear witness to one of the greatest and most dramatic Ryder Cups ever to be played.

And they did not have to wait long for the drama to begin. Landing proved a less than comfortable experience for the debutant Montgomerie. Despite his total reliance on planes to enable him to do his job, he has always admitted to being a dreadfully nervous air passenger (this claim was once used in mitigation as he fought a driving ban) and what he witnessed ahead of touchdown did little for his state of mind. 'It became clear we were flying for longer than we should be,' he recalled. The reason was a problem with the landing gear. 'The next thing I knew one of the pilots was walking down the plane to around where I was sitting. He had a thing like a car jack in his hand. Then he actually lifted the carpet close to my feet to find a hole that led to the undercarriage. Then he used this jack thing to lower the wheels manually,' he said.

Relieved finally to be on the ground, the team were then astonished to see vast crowds gathered to witness the landing at the South Carolina air base. The European side had a certain celebrity, but the real star as far as the 30,000 or so who had gathered was the world's fastest passenger aircraft. It had never been seen in these parts before and drew huge numbers of sightseers who stood on car roofs and bonnets to catch a clear view of Concorde coming into land. They knew nothing of the drama unfolding on board before it had been able to find the runway.

When they had disembarked, each player was allotted his own chauffeur-driven stretch limo and they were accommodated in luxury beachside villas. At the course the clubhouse had not been finished so the team were given a static caravan-style trailer to use as their locker room. It was here that Monty's

Ryder Cup career made an inauspicious start. He espied a rack of golf shoes and recognised the pair of Stylos that he was using at the time. He tried them on and they felt a little tight, but he put this down to his feet probably still being a little swollen from the previous day's flight. No matter: it was time to hit the range and he headed out for his first practice session. Midway through, Montgomerie spotted the team's big beast and the one man in the side with a more imposing physical stature than himself. The great Nick Faldo was heading in his direction. Faldo had been the top player in the world earlier that year; he was a two-time Open and Masters champion and along with Seve Ballesteros the most important figure in the European team. He had a pair of golf spikes dangling from his fingers. 'Monty, what size shoes do you take?' he called over to the debutant. Montgomerie looked down at his identical yet strangely ill-fitting footwear and only then did it hit him. He was wearing Faldo's shoes. Talk about a rookie error. Montgomerie would later say that he felt 'about two feet tall' as he made his hasty apologies.

Not that Monty deserved an inferiority complex. He was an up-and-coming force in European golf and was enjoying the most successful season of his career to date. He had finished second behind Ballesteros in the qualifying table and just ahead of fellow rookie Steven Richardson. A mid-season purple patch had ensured Montgomerie would make his Ryder Cup debut at Kiawah. He was ninth at the Spanish Open in early May and in the next ten events he finished outside the top ten on only three occasions. By claiming the runner's-up spot at the Volvo PGA Championship and the Carroll's Irish Open he had ensured a healthy tally of qualifying points. Monty then made certain of his place in the team in style with victory at the Scandinavian Masters where he edged out Seve and Ian Woosnam to claim the title by a single shot. The win not only gave Montgomerie his spot in Bernard Gallacher's side, it emboldened him. Now he knew he could beat the best players in the world. He was ready to play for his continent in golf's most intimidating environment.

Monty could also draw on his experience of playing the US as an amateur when he was a member of the 1985 and 1987 Walker Cup teams. There was little indication then that these appearances for Great Britain and Ireland would prove the forerunners to a glorious Ryder Cup career but it was apparent that he could be set apart from most of the other players competing in those events. One of his team-mates and one of Britain's best-known amateurs, Peter McEvoy, recalled: 'He was so driven, so determined. Me and my peers were about ten years older and we could see him coming. It wasn't that he hit the ball better than anybody else but you could spot his determination. I can remember him telling me that he would hole a hundred short putts in a row before he could go to bed at night. I used to try to hole twenty and I don't think I ever achieved it.'

Now, as a pro and a Ryder Cupper, Monty played like one of the world's elite as the European team began practice to familiarise themselves with the Kiawah Island course. With five rookies in the team Gallacher had been keen to pair them up with his experienced men, those who under Jacklin had wrested the trophy out of American hands. 'I would put the likes of Monty and David Gilford with people like Seve and Olazábal and then I could get feedback on what they thought of the new guys,' Gallacher recalls. 'It would put the newcomers under a little bit of pressure in their practice, having to play with such good and experienced players, and it helped me as I tried to get a feel about them.'

Monty's report card after these practice rounds was stellar. Gallacher's trusted aides, the leading players in the world, were effusive in their praise. The new boy was straight, he was long, he was confident. 'We knew he was a good player, but we had no idea he was going to go on and win eight Orders of Merit. We didn't know just how good he was going to be,' Gallacher says. 'But I was always very impressed with his ball striking; he was a very straight hitter.' These qualities were borne out by feedback that could not have been more positive.

Gallacher is serious and astute as well as being a charming and generous man. He was forty-two at the time of the Kiawah match. He had played in eight Ryder Cups without ever finishing on the winning side. He was as keen as anybody to preserve Europe's unbeaten run and end his personal duck.

The build-up to the match had been a struggle in the face of unbridled American patriotism. Faldo summed up the feeling in the European camp when he said: 'The disappointing thing is that even though we have won on the last three occasions, the Americans won't recognise that we're number one.' The Europeans had been belittled at the gala dinner at the Charleston Convention Center on the Wednesday night when they had been made to walk around the outside of the ballroom before taking their seats. They then endured having to watch Dave Stockton's American side take centre stage when it was their turn to enter the room. The US players received a carefully choreographed heroes' reception.

A twenty-minute video depicting the great moments of the Ryder Cup concentrated solely on US successes. Never mind that they hadn't touched the trophy for eight years. 'We were made to feel like outsiders,' Montgomerie recalled. The then Executive Director of the European Tour, Ken Schofield, was outraged and indicated he was ready to walk out. It took all of Gallacher's persuasive powers to keep the Tour boss in the room and avoid a diplomatic incident.

Monty watched all this unfold with wide-eyed wonderment. There was more to come. He, along with other team members and wives, was the victim of prank alarm calls inspired by an overzealous local radio station. Charleston DJ Michael D launched a 'Wake Up the Enemy' campaign, urging listeners to call the Europeans' villas in the early hours of the morning. This was the final straw for Gallacher. 'If there are any more I'm going to call the FBI about it,' Gallacher said.

It was a relief when the skipper could finally concentrate on the golf and start making crucial decisions about who to send out in the opening set of matches. The Ryder Cup format requires four players to sit out each morning and afternoon sequence of matches on the opening two days. The Kiawah Island contest began with foursomes where players are paired together and have to take alternate shots. It is the most highly pressured form of the game because your partner pays for your mistakes. The nature of taking turns to hit shots means a player may go several holes without hitting a putt or chip; likewise, if his driving duties coincide with the shorter holes he might go half a round without using his driver or three wood. Suddenly that player might then be expected to nail a crucial drive just as the match is reaching its climax. Accordingly it is a format in which it can be very difficult to find any kind of natural rhythm. Foursomes play on the opening morning is no place for a rookie. Have a rest, guys, wander round and watch the old sweats who have been there and done it before. We'll rely on them; you newcomers soak up the atmosphere and ready yourselves for a more forgiving Ryder Cup entrance. Or so you might think.

Montgomerie's impressive play in practice and that of another newcomer, David Gilford, had persuaded Gallacher to depart from such conventional wisdom. This was all the more surprising given that both players plied their trade on the European Tour and had precious little experience of American golf in their professional careers. The skipper wasn't worried. Gallacher said: 'In a way I felt that was quite good. There was a hidden element and the Americans didn't know how good we were. They would get a shock when they saw how good Gilford was and how good Montgomerie is. Suddenly they see these guys on the first tee raring to go against them and psychologically that could be quite important.'

This wasn't the only reason Gallacher felt able to play his Monty card at the very first opportunity. 'To be honest with you, Monty and David Gilford were playing so well in practice, they forced themselves into the foursomes. They were such straight hitters and Seve came up to me and said: "Well, I don't see how you can leave them out", and I agreed,' Gallacher said.

Protocol dictates that both captains provide a list of four pairings for each sequence of matches. The pairs at the top of each list will play each other – America's second pairing play Europe's second pairing and so on. Montgomerie and Gilford were third on Gallacher's list for that opening morning of Friday 27 September 1991. Captains often try to second-guess their opposite number and attempt to engineer a match up that suits them best. They'll seek to counter the opposition's strongest pairings wherever possible, but of course luck can play its part as well. In this case fortune favoured the home side.

The European debutants could not have been handed a tougher contest. Fate played its part, however, because one of the US players, Steve Pate, had been injured in a car crash on the way to the gala dinner and Hale Irwin was drafted in after initially being told he would sit out the opening foursomes. This meant Irwin would team up with Lanny Wadkins. The European rookies were now facing American golf's two most steely competitors. They were players with a wealth of experience. They were the sort of characters who would relish eating a pair of new kids for breakfast, regardless of how well they had played in practice.

Montgomerie has always loved the spotlight and being the centre of attention. It gets his juices flowing. This was the Ryder Cup; he was making his debut against two of the meanest men ever to have swung a club in the US of A. He'd another newcomer at his side, the man they called 'Gilly', the man who hadn't missed a fairway in three days of warm-up play. This was what it was all about. This was the moment, the reward for becoming one of the most dominant players in all Europe. Except that it wasn't.

The crowds had largely dispersed. They were following the top match, a snarling, bad-tempered encounter in which the Spaniards Ballesteros and Olazábal were up against Paul Azinger and Chip Beck. If they weren't watching that clash they were with the American dreamboat Freddie Couples and his partner Ray Floyd who were taking on Bernhard Langer and Mark James. There weren't too many hanging round the first tee to witness the debut shots of the Monty/Gilly combo;

besides, the tee was more than 200 yards from the clubhouse and lacked the rarefied atmosphere you would expect at a Ryder Cup. It was unexpectedly anti-climactic and Montgomerie felt a lack of adrenaline. 'It was a strange feeling to be honest. It was low key, an awkward, quiet beginning to a very loud Ryder Cup record, I suppose,' Montgomerie told me.

Wadkins and Irwin, on the other hand, knew what it was all about. They were not reliant on inspiration from outside agencies. They could feed off twenty-six Ryder Cup wins and thirty-nine tournament victories between them. The Americans knew the importance of a fast start to put the rookies in their place. They birdied the first while Montgomerie and Gilford failed to make par. This set the tone. Monty holed a 16-footer for birdie at the second but it was matched by the Americans before Irwin put his approach very close to the hole at the third. That made it three birdies in a row for the home pair and they were two up after three, before going three up after five. As the wind freshened, Gilford's weakness around the green was exposed when Montgomerie put him into the sandy wastes on the sixth. Four down. Despite winning the seventh, the Europeans suffered another setback soon after and found themselves trailing by four at the turn. Wadkins and Irwin had played the front nine in just thirty-one shots, five under par and easily the best scoring of the opening morning. 'Some of Hale Irwin's shots were godlike,' Montgomerie observed. 'We played steady enough golf, but under that kind of fire there isn't much you can do.' With the benefit of hindsight the Scot feels it was probably wrong to have been sent out as a pair of rookies on the first morning. He said: 'Yes we were practicing well but in the Ryder Cup practicing doesn't really mean that much compared to what it is really like on that Friday morning.'

You could not ask to meet two more contrasting characters than Monty and Gilford and there was no chemistry between them. Montgomerie is larger than life in every respect, whether his mood is good or bad. He has a ready wit and is outwardly expressive. Gilford was always the quiet man of the tour. Perhaps silent is a more accurate description. His personality can be as introverted as his golf game can be precise. It is said that opposites attract: not on this occasion. They were five down after eleven. Just seven holes to go and the match was all but done. The Europeans did well to keep the contest alive until the 16th, but as the wind howled Monty's 12-foot putt to extend the match missed to the left. Irwin and Wadkins won the hole to go four up with just two to play and so the point went the way of Dave Stockton's American team. Monty and Gilford had played the sixteen holes in six over par, the worst scoring of the morning session.

'It didn't work out,' Gallacher conceded. 'Wadkins and Irwin came straight out of the traps, got early birdies and were never going to let go. Our boys could never get into the match. It's what can happen in foursomes play.' For Montgomerie it was played one, lost one and benched. 'I had other players who hadn't played. They should all get a chance,' the skipper said.

He wanted to be there, but with club in hand. He didn't want to be a cheerleader. He loved being a team member, the camaraderie, the spirit of all for one. That was why he'd so enjoyed cricket at school. You didn't get this week in, week out on tour where all you thought about was number one. Of course the other guys needed supporting; the team were down. Only the Spaniards had scored

– Seve and Ollie – the rest had spent the morning going the same way as him. The Yanks were 3–1 ahead, desperate to get back the trophy and on course to do it. The captain wanted the other guys to have a go – Sam, Feherty and Richardson. It was their go. They had to turn it around. Good luck to them, but he wished it was him. He was good enough; it was just that those Americans, Irwin and Wadkins, they'd seen it all before; they knew what to expect and didn't give him a chance. It hadn't worked with Gilford, the mix wasn't right. The mix, that's where he wanted to be, right in the middle of it. Not on the outside, looking in, watching the others. He needed to talk to the skipper . . .

Ever since 1927, when the St Albans-based seed merchant Samuel Ryder put up a 19-inch-tall gold trophy as the prize to formalise biennial clashes between the professional golfers of Great Britain and the United States, the matches had been played over a variety of formats. For the inaugural clash at Worcester Country Club in Massachusetts it was eight players a side. It began with four thirty-six-holes foursomes matches and concluded with eight singles. A total of twelve points was therefore up for grabs and the Americans enjoyed a thumping 9½-2½ win. This format remained in place until 1961 when two sessions of eighteen-holes foursomes play and two sequences of singles were introduced for the clash at Royal Lytham and St Annes. The idea was to make the matches more competitive because it was felt the British players would stand more chance over the shorter distance. When matches lasted thirty-six holes the better players are more likely to prevail.

The change made it a best of twenty-four points match and it expanded further two years later to become best of thirty-two points when better-ball fourball play was first introduced.

Now the Ryder Cup had become a three-day event for the first time. Another change came in 1977 when it was scaled back so that players didn't have to play two rounds in a day. The opening day consisted of five eighteen-holes foursomes, the second day five eighteen-holes fourball matches and the final day was made up of ten singles clashes. The idea didn't last. Indeed, this format was only used for that one match. Lytham was again the venue and the US were again the victors.

Two years later, at the Greenbrier at White Sulphur Springs in West Virginia, the organisers arrived at a new arrangement, one that has endured to produce the majority of the Ryder Cup's most memorable matches. For that 1979 contest the opening two days were split into morning and afternoon sessions. There were four fourballs before lunch and after it four foursomes. Eight players would be involved, leaving four others to sit on the sidelines on each of these sessions. Then, on the final day, all twelve pros on each side would play singles matches against each other. A total of twenty-eight points would be up for grabs and the first to 14½ would have an unassailable lead and win the trophy. This was the first time the Americans' opposition would be selected from the entire continent of Europe rather than just Great Britain or the combined forces of GB and Ireland. It was the birth of the modern era and of the Ryder Cup as we know it today.

On the first afternoon of the 1991 clash at Kiawah Island, Montgomerie found himself in the unlucky quartet made to sit out the session. He was one of the backroom boys. It was not his preferred role, but there was no disgrace because it is rare for rookies to play in every sequence of matches. Players usually have to grow into the role of being a trusted workhorse upon whom captains want to depend for an entire Ryder Cup.

44

This was the domain of Seve Ballesteros and José Maria Olazábal, a dashing Spanish combination which over the previous two Ryder Cups had forged a near unbeatable partnership. In eight contests in which they had partnered each other they had lost only once.

They were the natural pairing to send out first on the opening morning to try to grab the vital first point for Europe. But they needed to rally in that contentious clash with Paul Azinger and Chip Beck. Both partnerships accused the other of sharp practice. The ill feeling was a product of the high stakes the Ryder Cup now carried. America so wanted to win back the trophy, Europe were determined not to let go and something had to give. That first morning witnessed the demise of decorum and the intended spirit of the contest. Dear old Sam Ryder's sentiment, long ago expressed to BBC Radio, had been well and truly forgotten. He had said: 'I trust that the effect of this match will be to influence a cordial, friendly and peaceful feeling throughout the whole civilised world. I look upon the Royal and Ancient game as being a powerful force that influences the best things in humanity.'

Those words seemed to have been tossed away into the breakers crashing on to the South Carolina shore.

There was history. Ballesteros and Azinger had shared a bad-tempered clash at the Belfry two years earlier and now there was more to come. The Americans were upset early in this contest: 'Before the end of the second hole we were embroiled in another conflict over what I considered to be a controversial drop of their ball. We had another question over their lost ball on number four. It went like that all day long, just one bit of controversy after another,' Azinger recalled.

While the Americans were upset with the Spaniards, Seve

and Ollie were convinced their opponents were breaking rules by switching to different compression golf balls depending on the hole and who was hitting the drive. Three down at the turn, they confronted the home pair and called in a rules official. 'I can tell you we are not trying to cheat,' Azinger told Ballesteros.

'Oh no, breaking the rules and cheating are two different things,' came the Spaniard's reply. The Europeans were indeed correct in their suspicions, but because they had not raised the issue when the Americans had switched their ball on the seventh no penalty could be imposed.

But it proved a pyrrhic victory for the US pair because, although they weren't punished for the transgression, their opponents were galvanised by their sense of injustice. Ballesteros hit a huge drive at the par four tenth; Olazábal found the heart of the green and well inside the American ball. Azinger putted to four feet while Seve stroked his close enough for a grudgingly conceded par. Beck then missed for a half and the Europeans won a hole for the first time in the match. From then on it was one-way traffic, the Spanish matadors were inspired and the home pair had lost their way. 'Chip and I were shaken by all this commotion. Our game went downhill from there,' Azinger admitted.

Ballesteros and Olazábal won three of the next five holes to move ahead for the first time and were one up on the 17th tee, a 200-yard par three played all the way over water that then runs up the right side of the green. It is a Pete Dye special. It is a nerve-wracking hole at the best of times, but in matchplay the 17th so often proves pivotal. Olazábal willed his tee shot on to the front of the green and it ran twenty-five feet past the hole. Beck, meanwhile, left his American partner with

46

a long swirling putt that Azinger did well to leave within six feet. Then up stepped Seve. If ever there was a player with a sense of occasion it was this man, the most popular golfer ever to come out of Europe. Much of that popularity was down to his magical short game and his putter became a wand. He stroked home a downhill curling putt that bent from right to left and into the hole to seal a famous win.

It was Europe's first point on the board, but alas it didn't inspire the rest of their team-mates that morning. Montgomerie and Gilford were not alone in losing as the home side swept through the other three foursome clashes.

There was understandably no sense of surprise when Bernard Gallacher made changes for the afternoon fourballs but, equally as expected, the Ballesteros/Olazábal combination was kept intact. Believing that his opposite number, Dave Stockton, would reckon on the Spaniards being sent out first, Gallacher switched the order and put them out second, which was just where Stockton had decided to place Azinger and Beck in his order. A rematch, but it ended in the same result with Europe taking the point 2 and 1. 'I played the match of my life, making eight birdies,' Azinger said. 'And they still beat us. That loss was really heartbreaking.' For Ballesteros, who had commented 'the American team have eleven nice guys and Paul Azinger', it was the sweetest of days.

The debutant Montgomerie watched on. His friend from the West of Scotland Sam Torrance paired up with Irishman David Feherty (today a naturalised American after spending his post-playing career wowing his adopted nation with inspired, witty golf commentary) and they secured a half in the top match. Next came the expected point from Seve and Ollie, while Mark James, along with rookie Steven Richardson, added another in the following match. Only the much-vaunted team of Nick Faldo and Ian Woosnam failed for Europe and by the close of the first day the American lead was a slender 4½-3½.

It was a much rosier position for Europe than might have been expected after surveying the scoreboard at lunchtime. Monty had witnessed the fightback, but had wanted to be a part of it and resolved to speak to his captain at close of play.

'In the team room he said to me, "Can I speak to you?"' Gallacher revealed. 'I said of course, yes, and we went into a corner and he told me what he felt. He wanted another chance to play. I think having lost in the opening foursomes he didn't want me to write him off. And this is what I wanted to hear. It takes a lot for a rookie to do that and I admired him for it. He said to me: "It would be nice if I could play again and it would be nice if I could maybe have someone a bit more experienced with me." I reassured him that I did want to play him again; I just had to find a different partner. This was no offence to David Gilford, but we couldn't afford to throw two rookies to the wolves again. I felt Monty had something big to offer if I could get him another important player.'

Gallacher wasn't ready immediately to heed Montgomerie's request to play. Splitting up the faltering Nick Faldo/Ian Woosnam partnership, Gallacher asked Faldo who he would like to partner in the Saturday morning foursomes. The choice was Montgomerie or Gilford. 'Which one of them is playing better?' Faldo asked. 'Gilford,' the captain replied and so Monty was rested again. American fervour grew throughout that session as the home fans sensed the trophy was heading back their way after being the wrong side of the pond for too long. The US won each of the first three points, including a 7 and 6 mauling of Faldo and Gilford by Mark O'Meara and Paul

Azinger. Only the trusty duo of Ballesteros and Olazábal stemmed the tide with a 3 and 2 win over Fred Couples and Ray Floyd in the bottom match.

Europe were in trouble – big trouble. The Americans are always regarded as the stronger team when it comes down to the twelve singles matches on the final day and to allow them any kind of lead heading into Sunday would almost certainly mean defeat. Now there were only four fourball matches to be played before those concluding singles and Dave Stockton's side was ahead 7½-4½. 'I was quite dispirited walking along the range after the Saturday morning foursomes,' Tour Executive Director Ken Schofield remembered. 'I passed Colin Montgomerie and Bernhard Langer and they were quite the opposite in their attitude. Both said in their different ways we're going to go out and do to them what they've just done to us.'

Europe needed the afternoon of their lives; they had to shut up the US fans whose triumphalism was starting to stick in the craw of the opposition. These were buoyant times for the American nation which was basking in the success of the first Gulf War where they were kicking Saddam Hussein out of Kuwait. A couple of the American players were even wearing Desert Storm caps bearing the official Ryder Cup logo and the fans loved it. Chants of U-S-A, U-S-A were ringing out. 'You could see the American public hoisting their flags all over the course; they're cheering, they're booing and they're jeering,' Bernard Gallacher remembers.

But the captain's main preoccupation was who to send out for the crucial fourballs, the sequence of matches that would determine whether there would be any chance of holding on to the trophy on the final day of the match. It was time to turn to the rookies, to give them an old head to partner and see what could be done. Richardson got the call to team up again with James; Paul Broadhurst, the young midlander and baby of the team, was paired with the world number one, Woosnam; and Colin Stuart Montgomerie got his wish. He was back in action and this time he would have an experienced partner. He would tee off in the second match of the afternoon alongside the man with whom he shared the positive attitude witnessed by Schofield, the meticulous world-class German, Bernhard Langer.

A brisk wind swept across the course, the sun shone and the slick greens became more and more difficult to judge. The top match produced golf worthy of the best player in the world, but the man who headed the world rankings was being outplayed. Fortunately for Europe it was by Ian Woosnam's twenty-six-year-old partner Paul Broadhurst who had been held back until the second afternoon before hitting a ball in anger. Broadhurst was sensational on the back nine and inflicted yet more misery on Azinger who had been paired with Hale Irwin. The Europeans won 2 and 1.

Behind them followed Montgomerie and Langer. They faced Cory Pavin, the man who would lead the US against Monty at Celtic Manor, and Steve Pate, who was judged fit to play despite his car accident on the night of the gala dinner. Both Americans donned their beige Desert Storm caps in a bid to whip up the home crowds. 'I thought it was stupid,' Gallacher said. 'It wound up the galleries and they were becoming like a football crowd and they were booing our players and cheering theirs and every missed putt of ours. It was all provoked by the way they were dressed. Corey Pavin got carried away with the occasion.'

It was crass behaviour that lived with Pavin through to his

2010 captaincy. He was repeatedly asked about his controversial dress code nineteen years earlier. 'I just wanted to express support for our boys out in the desert, I make no apology for that,' he said in justification. Except that he did apologise soon after the Kiawah clash. 'Corey Pavin wrote me a letter and said, "I'm sorry about this, I realise this is not what the Ryder Cup is about,"' Gallacher revealed. 'I admired him for that letter.'

On the first tee at Kiawah Island back in 1991 Monty took one look at the opposition's headgear of choice and wondered to himself whether the US players were aware that British troops had been involved in the war effort as well. Langer pondered whether they also knew that US air bases in Germany had been strategically important in the campaign. Then they concentrated on the golf rather than the Gulf.

Putting the rookie Scot with the experienced German was an inspired move. Montgomerie loves reassurance; despite his immense talents he needs to be reminded frequently of how good he is and how valuable he is to the team. Defeated on the first morning and then benched for the next two sessions, his ego was fragile. So it felt good to Monty that he had been put with such a senior player – 'the best partner anyone could wish for'.

Langer recognised his role as the senior figure and on the way to the first tee the man who had won the 1985 Masters said he would hit first to take the pressure off Montgomerie. Moments later the then twenty-eight-year-old Scot was muttering a sarcastic 'Thanks very much, Bernhard' before pegging up his own ball. The usually ultra-reliable Langer had sent his drive out of bounds and the opening hole was all down to Monty. But he was up to the task and found the fairway, made par and secured an opening half. By the fourth, which was won by the Europeans, Pate was receiving treatment and clearly struggling from the effects of the car crash.

Not that it proved straightforward for the Monty/Langer combination. They were two up after seven but bogeyed the next two to leave the match all square at the turn. In the awkward conditions caused by the stiff wind, par was a good score even in the better-ball format where birdies are usually required to win holes and are sometimes not enough for a half. Langer's par at the tenth took the Europeans back in front and another German par at the 12th doubled the lead. Pavin hit a magnificent approach to the 13th that finished within inches of the hole, but under pressure Montgomerie was equal to the task, directing his to three feet to ensure a half that preserved Europe's advantage. Monty played the spoiler role again two holes later. Pate made a rare contribution, holing from off the green, and the Scot held his nerve to sink a downhill 20-footer for another half.

Players and fans could sense momentum swinging back Europe's way and these telling contributions from Montgomerie were going a long way to making sure it remained so. He and Langer were in touching distance of securing a vital point. Two up with two to play, they stood on the tee of the treacherous 17th and Monty struck a savage blow with a magnificent tee shot that defied the wind and water to finish on the back tier of the green. His ball was only 20 feet from the hole. Pavin's tee shot, hit with a one iron, could only find the front of the putting surface and he was miles from the pin. Montgomerie had two putts to close out victory and with sure judgement sent his ball to gimme range. Victory by 2 and 1, and the men in their military caps had been put firmly in their place.

More significantly from Europe's point of view, Montgomerie

and Langer had combined superbly to put a point on the board. The fightback was continuing. Monty was also one up in his personal rivalry with Pavin – not that either would be aware of its full significance for the best part of two decades.

'After that match we knew there was something special about Colin,' Gallacher said. 'Bernhard Langer was happy to play with him. They were a very good match and they have had a long friendship since 1991. Colin has always admired and looked up to Bernhard. He's a very nice guy and comforting to play with. I think Monty enjoyed playing with Langer who was a really top player at the time. Monty had only just come along but I think it was then that he realised that he was good enough to play at the very top. He realised that under pressure he was as good as Langer.'

Both players joined the European entourage to see whether their team-mates behind could maintain the momentum that was surging their way. They weren't disappointed as on that same 17th green Richardson and James flawlessly closed out a 3 and 1 win over Lanny Wadkins and Wayne Levi. So it was three out of three for Europe with the trusty Spanish duo still out on the course defending a 100 per cent record. They were involved in an epic duel with Payne Stewart and Fred Couples that went all the way to the final green. Couples had been the hero throughout but the match ended in an honourable half when, in the gathering gloom, Stewart saw well enough to hole from three feet to prevent a European whitewash.

Gallacher's side were back in it. They had taken three and a half points out of four in the afternoon to level the contest at eight points each. It would all be down to the concluding twelve Sunday singles matches. Montgomerie was relieved on two fronts: he was delighted to have broken his Ryder Cup duck and he was also pleased his name wasn't in his captain's envelope. For the singles he would be sent out third which was also good because, while he couldn't win the trophy in that position, he couldn't lose it either.

David Gilford was the unlucky man. Steve Pate's injury meant he couldn't play and the name of the player Bernard Gallacher had put in an envelope to cover such an eventuality became relevant. That player, Monty's partner from the first round, would miss out on playing his singles match. Protocol dictated that they would be awarded half a point each. 'The Americans pulled a bit of a flanker by pulling Steve Pate out of the singles,' Gallacher still contends. 'They got a guaranteed half point and didn't tell me until just before the opening singles. We were always a bit suspicious that they waited until then because it affected the draw. David Gilford was going to play Wayne Levi and he would have killed him. It made it difficult for me because I hadn't told David he was the name in the envelope and he was distraught to miss out on playing.'

The order in which a captain lines up his team may prove crucial. Gallacher sent out first one of his aces, Nick Faldo. Then it was a joker, David Feherty, a rookie, a wit and an unknown quantity. Next was Colin Montgomerie, of whom the captain had high hopes if he could get off to a decent start. Faldo was renewing acquaintanceship with Ray Floyd, whom he had beaten in a play-off to win the previous year's Masters at Augusta. Feherty faced Payne Stewart and Monty was up against the 1989 Open Champion, Mark Calcavecchia. The man from Nebraska wasn't having much of a year but was renowned for his fighting spirit and ability to get on a roll. Gallacher had a simple message for Monty before he teed off:

'Colin, the one thing you don't want to do against Mark Calcavecchia is let him get ahead. He's a gritty player and a great frontrunner so, whatever you do, try to stay with him.'

Monty could do nothing to fulfil his skipper's instructions. He played horribly over the first nine holes. 'I was doing everything that Bernard Gallacher told me not to do,' Montgomerie confessed. He took a hideous forty-two shots, six over par, and was five down. Calcavecchia was easing along. He'd opened with a birdie and picked up two more at the seventh and ninth. Europe weren't going to get anything out of this match; it was a banker for the home side. 'In all honesty, when I went five down, I was thinking that if I lost the next three holes, I would lose 8 and 7 to equal the heaviest defeat that anyone had ever had in Ryder Cup singles – I really wanted to avoid that so I knew then that I had to do something about it!' Montgomerie recalled in one of his Captain's Blogs for Europeantour.com.

Having just lost the ninth, Monty faced a long trek to the tenth tee. 'I was lucky there was a mile-and-a-half walk from the ninth green to the tenth tee. Not for me because I was in a bit of a state, but it went against him. He wanted to continue quickly and there was a twenty minute break.' Montgomerie also used the interval to have a long, hard conversation with himself and resolved not to let Calcavecchia walk all over him. 'During that time, I managed to get my head together,' Montgomerie said. But could he put it into practice?

Walking off the tenth tee the omens were not encouraging. The Scot had sprayed his drive into the sandy wastes that lined the fairway and finding the green in two looked unlikely. All he could do was find more sand. He was up against it and needed something to happen. It did. His third shot, some 40 yards from the pin, was bang on line. It crashed into the flag and disappeared for an unlikely birdie, his first of the round. Four down. Then another birdie followed at the 11th. Three down – this was better. But at the 14th Montgomerie hit the buffers again, raggedly surrendering the hole to fall four down with four to play. 'The end was nigh,' Monty accepted. 'I'd written him off,' said his captain.

Monty was being watched by his dad, James; Ken Schofield had given him an armband so that he could watch inside the ropes. And as Montgomerie Junior climbed to the 15th tee the Scot felt something in the air. He detected a subtle shift in the brisk left-to-right breeze. 'I didn't realise how he suffered in a left-to-right wind,' Montgomerie admitted. Calcavecchia went miles right with his tee shot, the conditions compounding the error, and he went on to make seven on this 468-yard par four. Not that Montgomerie covered himself in glory: he could only manage a six but it was enough to keep the match alive. The American found more trouble off the next tee; again he went right on the sweeping winds. 'The worst thing you can do to me is put me in a thirty-mph crosswind with my snap slice,' Calcavecchia admitted. 'I peeled one off into the ocean; I hit another one in the lake.' Par was enough for Monty at the 16th. He was now two down with two to play.

The news was relayed into Gallacher's earpiece and he knew this was the match at which he now needed to be present. His buggy sped to the penultimate test on this draining course. 'It was a tough hole, 220 yards across the water and a small target,' said Gallacher. 'I went to the seventeenth because I realised Calcavecchia was under the cosh and starting to feel it. The Americans hadn't won the Ryder Cup since 1983, so you could feel the pressure; it was palpable. So I just made sure Monty could see me. I didn't want to interfere.

'It was the most extraordinary thing. Monty went first and hit it in the water, in the reeds just to the right of the green. Well, "that's it" I thought. There was plenty of space to the left and Calcavecchia only had to hit it on to dry land. Just hit it anywhere left and he would win. He topped it. It almost didn't reach the water.' But it did.

To play their third shots, both players had to go to the ladies' tee which provided the drop zone. Monty's caddie Kevin Laffey had not planned for such an eventuality and couldn't be sure of the exact distance to the green. To pace out the yardage would have required the ability to walk on water. There was only one thing for it: caddie and player had to chance it. 'I guessed it was about 160 yards and I added ten because it was over water, water is cold and the ball doesn't tend to fly as far over water - weird but true. So I hit one more club and of course it was too big.'

They decided on a six iron and the shot settled at the back of the green. Now it was Calcavecchia's turn. 'By this time he was a basket case,' Gallacher observed, but the American also found the green; both were on in three strokes but some distance from the hole. Calcavecchia putted to inside three feet, tap-in range. Then Montgomerie's putt went stone dead. He was in for five and Calc had this tiddler for the match. Monty handed his glove and marker to his caddie; he was ready to shake hands, a beaten man. He'd considered conceding the putt, but thought such a move would not sit well with his senior team-mates, so he waited for his opponent to complete an apparent formality. 'If he's going to beat me let him hole the putt.' Calcavecchia putted to end this torturous contest with a short, fast, jabby action and the ball never touched the hole. It was an extraordinary miss for a professional golfer.

Monty had been ready to walk over and congratulate his opponent, but what was going to be a reluctant trudge turned instantly into a jaunty stride to the next tee.

The American had now lost three holes on the bounce, two of them to double bogeys. He seemed to Montgomerie to be eerily calm, but former captain Tony Jacklin, who was part of the European backroom, whispered into the Scot's ear: 'If you can stay standing you can win this hole.' Gallacher was keeping his distance. 'You don't want to say the wrong thing,' he said.

Monty hit a drive and then a two iron to the front portion of the 18th green. He was about 40 feet from the hole in two. Calcavecchia, struggling to put one foot in front of the other, somehow managed to get his second shot long enough to be through the green. He then pitched to around nine feet. As Montgomerie surveyed his birdie putt, Nick Faldo was watching in the BBC Television commentary booth. He'd just seen off Floyd on the same home green. Faldo said: 'It's uphill, over the ridge and there's a break. This has been a strong part of his game all season.' Monty stroked the putt, it climbed the ridge, began its descent to the hole, taking the break. 'Go, go, go . . . oh my God!' yelled Faldo into his microphone. The putt had been read to perfection. It stopped one revolution short of the hole. Calcavecchia was still alive, but only just. Monty was bent double in frustration.

This nine-footer could end the American's agony; he was mid-choke and he could end it right there and show his country that, actually, he was made for this kind of combat. But, no, Gallacher had been correct: he was 'a basket case'. Jacklin was right, too; Monty just needed to remain upright. The desolate Calcavecchia's putt, like the tiny one on the previous hole, never threatened to drop. 'A glorious end for Montgomerie. That was sensational,' commented Peter Alliss. The stunned Scot gave a half-hearted, rather understated double-fist pump before sharing a cursory handshake with his broken opponent.

'That result has served as a constant reminder to me that no game is ever over until the last putt drops,' Monty later said. He also pointed out: 'Sometimes it is good to look at the other guy and realise he's feeling awful too. It's easy to forget that if you are scared too.'

Calcavecchia would later accept that his failure to win from four up with four to play was the worst moment of his career. 'The bottom line is I missed a two-footer that I should have made, even after topping it into the water.' Speaking more than a decade on, he said: 'I still go back and look at the pictures of it. My face was kind of flushed. I was still kind of red about how upset I'd gotten about it.'

For Monty and Europe it was half a point but it felt like a whole lot more. 'I must admit it really helped me feel part of the team having won half a point for Europe while at the same time taking a half-point from the Americans. Thinking back on it, I was playing those holes down the stretch, not for me, but for the half-point gained for Europe,' Montgomerie recalled. 'On that Sunday, wherever you play, that point counts incredibly towards the end of the day to give the opportunity to the guys coming behind you to win the Ryder Cup. No one must ever forget that.'

Feherty had won; he beat Payne Stewart. Europe were now 11-9 ahead with just three more points required from nine matches to retain the Ryder Cup, three and half to win it outright.

Azinger and Pavin responded for Dave Stockton's team with narrow wins over José Maria Olazábal and Steven Richardson. But Europe had a rock in Seve Ballesteros. His

3 and 2 win over Wayne Levi gave the Spaniard four and half points out of a possible five. He had been brilliant, as was Paul Broadhurst in defeating Mark O'Meara on the penultimate green.

But the chants were still U-S-A, U-S-A. Chip Beck, Fred Couples and Lanny Wadkins claimed vital points to take the home side to within touching distance of regaining the trophy. It was swinging their way and coming down to the last match on the course, a tense dogfight between Hale Irwin and Bernhard Langer. America needed a half; Europe required Langer to win and make it 14-14, which would be enough for them to retain the trophy. The German had been two down with four to play, but bravely holed to win the 15th and halve the 16th. At the next – 'one of the most difficult short holes I have ever seen' was how Peter Alliss described that 17th – Langer showed astonishing nerve. He two-putted from off the green for a par that was enough to level the match with one hole to go.

It was all down to this: three days of intense, sometimes bitter and rancorous competition that had turned a golf match by the sea into 'the war on the shore' would be settled by the final match on the final hole. Langer found the fairway off the tee; Irwin did likewise despite a wayward drive that bounced out of the packed gallery lining the hole down the left. The American missed the green with his long approach, the German found the right fringe. Irwin's timid wedge shot finished 25 feet away. 'My disappointment after that pitch, no one on this team will ever know what it's like. I hope they never know,' Irwin later said. Langer then putted and nearly holed, but his ball had steam and ran on five or six feet.

The home player now had a 20-footer to win the Ryder Cup and end America's Ryder Cup drought, but amid the extraordinary tension of the moment it was always asking too much of him. Irwin left it two feet short and Langer conceded it for a bogey five. Now it was the turn of the man with the unique left hand below right split grip, a method that was his own invention to cure well-documented woes on the green. Europe has never been quite as united as it was that Sunday evening in trying to will Langer's ball into the hole. Montgomerie sat greenside behind the fingernail-chewing Spaniard Ballesteros. Their German team-mate had a six footer to win his match, to level the contest and ensure the famous trophy would return to Europe on Concorde.

Bernhard Langer: 'Probably the most important putt of my life.'

Seve Ballesteros: 'No one in the world can make that putt. It is too much pressure for anyone. Not even Jack Nicklaus in his prime will make that putt. Not even me!'

R and A Secretary Sir Michael Bonallack: 'The greatest pressure putt in the history of golf.'

Johnny Miller, NBC TV: 'The right kind of pressure finds diamonds. But it's hard to putt when you see three golf balls and don't know which one to putt at.'

Pete Coleman, Langer's caddie: 'People ask me how Bernhard stood up to all that pressure over the last three holes of the Ryder Cup. How about me? I not only had to stand up, I had to carry the bag as well.'

Mark Calcavecchia: 'This is probably the most pressure-packed event, world-famous golf event. It magnifies your weaknesses. When Bernhard was putting I was still kind of shaken up. Basically I knew when I lost those last four holes to Colin, that half-point – it was going to come down to that.'

Bernhard Langer: I saw two spike marks on my line. I talked to my caddie. He said: 'Hit it left centre and firm to avoid the spike marks.' That's what I tried to do. It did not go in.'

Hale Irwin: 'Imagine the shock and now the exultation of what happened. It was a 180-degree turnaround over the simple matter of a six-foot putt.'

Bernhard Langer: 'It's going to stick with me for a lifetime.'

Mark Calcavecchia: 'When he missed it Payne Stewart jumped up and gave me a big hug and said my half-point had won it for us. And that made me feel better at the time, but even though we won, I was still so freaked out that it all came down to that and it really didn't have to.'

Bernard Gallacher: 'Bernhard was inconsolable until Seve, Nick and I could get to him.'

Peter Alliss, BBC TV: 'I've been in golf all my life and my father before me, but I think this will stay in my memory: the sadness of Langer's putt, on the final hole, having played so well. The mistakes of Calcavecchia, the braveness of the players; it really has been an incredible event.'

Paul Azinger: 'I have not felt excitement like this in my whole life. The country's pride is back! We went over and thumped the Iraqis and now we have won this.'

Ken Schofield: 'In a strange way it was a wonderful start for Colin because it showed him that he really belonged in that environment.'

Bernard Gallacher: 'It was a hostile environment and we did all we could. I also think Colin Montgomerie realised what a very special event this is. I think Colin got the taste at Kiawah.'

Colin Montgomerie: 'It was a great Ryder Cup. I know they called it 'the war on the shore' but to me it was a fantastic rookie insight into what this competition is all about. This is where I fell in love with it. I noticed the senior members of the team and how they reacted. Woosie and Sam – there was a television in the corner of the team room that would never work again after showing the American celebrations. There was Langer and Seve hugging each other in tears, there was Faldo not knowing what way to turn because he was perplexed by the whole scene. I thought "hang on a minute, I want to be part of this and I want to grow with this team and gain from this experience."'

3

*'A new partnership and we haven't seen the last of
them'*   **– Peter Alliss, BBC TV**

*His right to be there was beyond question. What was more
he was a wanted man, wanted by the big beast, the guy
calling the shots. Faldo looked elsewhere at Kiawah, preferred
Gilly, but he knew who to choose now. This had the makings of
a dream team upon whom the skipper would count; it could be
a British version of Seve and Ollie. There wouldn't be any
watching now, no sitting out sessions; it was time to be a workhorse, the heartbeat of the team. Regaining the trophy was what
it was all about. It hadn't been with them on Concorde coming
home two years earlier and it didn't feel right. It was with the
other lot who were drenched in a delighted ocean of triumph.
They brought the Cup on the big bird for this match, flying back
to us at supersonic speed. Never been beaten at the Belfry, the
team had been waiting for this from the moment Bernhard's
putt failed to drop . . .*

Colin Montgomerie did not play his best golf at Kiawah Island,
yet he still managed to take his first shaky steps in building
his Ryder Cup legend. By somehow eking out that gloriously
ugly half against Mark Calcavecchia, from four down with

four to play, he helped stretch the contest to the very last match on the course. It was almost enough, but not quite. Monty had also begun his unbeaten record in Ryder Cup singles. That personal statistic carried negligible significance at the time, but grew in importance with each match that passed. Acquiring that 'can't lose on a Sunday' tag became one of the hallmarks of his career, yet it had been a topped tee shot and a missed two-footer away from never being stamped on Monty's CV.

This was of little concern heading into the next Ryder Cup in 1993. For the third home match in a row the duel would be played at the Belfry in the West Midlands, just to the east of Birmingham. European golf was sore from 'the war on the shore'. The agonising defeat had hit hard and might have broken a lesser man than Bernhard Langer, who had, remarkably, returned to the European Tour and won a play-off with Australia's Rodger Davis to land the German Masters one week after his putt had failed to drop on the home green of the Ocean Course. Two years on he topped the qualifying points table for this Ryder Cup.

Concorde had felt empty on the way home without the beloved trophy. America partied hard from the moment they had secured their win and threw their victorious captain, Dave Stockton, into the Atlantic in celebration. But they had been roundly criticised for their overzealous patriotism, the Desert Storm caps and their jingoistic approach to the contest. This wasn't what the Ryder Cup should be about, but it is what it had become. Such was the compelling nature of the competition.

In 1985, two years after losing in America by a single point, Europe had ended their losing streak with a thumping and much celebrated win at the Belfry. In the matches that followed Europe had won by two points at Muirfield Village, shared a home draw and then suffered that narrowest of defeats at Kiawah Island in 1991. A total of eighty-four points had been up for grabs in those three matches and on aggregate Europe were ahead 42½-41½. It was the perfect statistic to illustrate how delicate was the balance of golfing power between Europe and the United States. However, all that really counted was who held the trophy and it now lay in American hands.

For the 1993 clash Bernard Gallacher had been reappointed captain. He had spoken for all of his team at Kiawah Island in the immediate aftermath of that defeat when he said he couldn't wait for the opportunity to win back the trophy. The Ryder Cup had grown into such a big event that it was sold out long before the first tee-shot was struck, and was as eagerly anticipated a sporting event as any that year. Players had competed harder than ever on Tour to secure their place in the European team.

Gallacher used two of his three wild-card picks to select Severiano Ballesteros and José Maria Olazábal, neither of whom had won a tournament that year. They were joined by fellow Kiawah survivors Langer, Montgomerie, Faldo, Mark James, Sam Torrance and Ian Woosnam. The rest of the team was made up by four newcomers: local man Peter Baker, Italy's Costantino Rocca, Englishman Barry Lane and Gallacher's third pick, Joakim Haeggman, the Swede who had finished one place out of the automatic qualifying spots.

Montgomerie knew that he would be asked to play a pivotal role. He had just turned thirty and was established as one of the most consistent forces on the European Tour. He finished third behind Langer and Faldo in the qualifying table and the previous year had almost won the US Open at Pebble Beach. Famously, Jack Nicklaus congratulated him live on American television 'for winning our national championship' because on a windswept day Monty had set a target the great man could not envisage being matched by anyone still out on the course. Nicklaus was wrong. Ultimately, Montgomerie had to settle for third place behind an inspired Tom Kite. His perform-ance in California was, nonetheless, a sign that it surely would not be long before the Scot would be joining the likes of Faldo, Sandy Lyle and Ian Woosnam as a modern-day British winner of one of the big four titles in the game.

But in 1993 he did not threaten to win any of the four majors and uncharacteristically missed the cut at the Open and US PGA. His best results were in European Tour events. He finished in a share of second place at the prestigious PGA Champi-onship at Wentworth and won the Dutch Open to herald a midsummer run of four top tens that ensured he was in his best form of the year at just the right time to take on the Americans.

It was during this encouraging run that Monty took delivery of a mystery parcel. It contained a box of golf balls from the manufacturer Bridgestone. This was the firm that supplied Nick Faldo with his balls; Montgomerie was a Titleist man in those days. Faldo had tipped off his team-mate that a package was in the post and the message was clear. He wanted to team up with Monty in the Ryder Cup foursomes where partners take alternate shots playing the same ball. Furthermore, it would be Faldo's ball and Monty had better become accus-tomed to its playing characteristics. This was of no concern to Montgomerie, who could barely tell the difference between the Bridgestone and the ball he regularly used. And who was he to object, anyway? Faldo was now regarded as Britain's greatest golfer, having won a third Open and fifth major with his victory at the 1992 Championship. He was the top player in the world, competing in his ninth consecutive Ryder Cup and was a figure of such substance that he could pick and choose his partners. For Monty it would be an honour to play with him.

'Faldo requested Colin,' confirmed Bernard Gallacher. 'They looked a good, strong combination. Monty was happy to play with the world number one and I was happy if they wanted to play together. I wasn't going to resist it. I asked Nick if there was anybody else he wanted to play with, any of the younger guys, and he said no, he wanted to play with Monty.'

Faldo recognised that Montgomerie was the most reliable bet, the most dependable team-mate available. 'He admired him and admired his game,' said Gallacher. 'Nick could see Colin was a lovely straight hitter and would give Faldo the opportunity to express himself. He would be able to attack more because he knows Monty is down the fairway, on the green. Everyone wanted Monty; he had the perfect game in foursomes and the perfect game in fourballs because he doesn't hit wild shots and you know what you are going to get. Faldo wanted Colin Montgomerie because he could see that Monty was a very special player and he would complement his game.'

This suited the skipper because he knew that Nick Faldo's mood as well as his golf would be crucial to his team's chances. 'I wanted a happy Faldo and most of all I wanted points. Monty could help give me both,' Gallacher added. 'I always thought that Nick was nursing Colin along and he [Colin] was very happy to be submissive to Faldo, despite the fact that everyone in our team felt that Colin, in striking the ball, was every bit as good as Nick. Colin was happy to play Nick's game and Nick was "I'm the guy, I'm in charge, I'm the best player – you do what I say" and Colin went along with this.'

Their partnership began before they had even arrived at the course. Monty was always regarded as a superbly accurate driver from the tee box and he also has a passion for driving cars. He would far rather take on a three-hour drive home after a round than spend a night in a hotel. Playing regular Tour events at the Belfry, he would commute from his Surrey home, a round trip of more than two hundred miles. He had adopted a similar habit when playing the Wales Open at Celtic Manor, happy to put up with the Severn Bridge tolls for the chance to spend time at the wheel of one of his luxury cars listening to his digital radio.

At the start of Ryder Cup week in 1993 Montgomerie was driving north on the M40 motorway towards the Belfry. A huge car enthusiast with a ready eye for the best motors on the road, he spied a top-of-the-range Mercedes in his rear-view mirror. It then pulled alongside. Faldo was driving; he wound down his window and shouted for directions to the course. 'Follow me,' Monty yelled back and appropriately they arrived at the Belfry in convoy. They would be inseparable for the rest of the week.

During the first day of practice Monty and Faldo played twenty-seven holes together which meant they spent more time in each other's company than any of the other prospective European combinations. They played eighteen holes in the morning and tagged on nine holes of foursomes after lunch. Their enthusiasm to be put together was more than apparent and sent a clear message to Europe's skipper. 'Faldo's his own man and I don't know whether he really respects any other golfer, but for some reason he did have a certain amount of respect for Monty,' recalled Montgomerie's caddie Alastair McLean. 'I don't know why he cottoned on to Monty. Faldo was a fitness freak and, at the time, Monty was a food freak,' McLean told Norman DaBell in his book *How We Won the Ryder Cup*.

Their approaches to life were undoubtedly different, but they shared a common trait: a hatred of losing. That week Montgomerie and Faldo practised together and ate in each other's company. It helped that their caddies and wives were friends, too. Captain Gallacher saw Montgomerie as the conduit to bring Faldo, with his loner's instincts, into the rest of the group. 'Colin always wanted to be part of the team. He enjoyed the locker room; he enjoyed people supporting him inside the ropes whereas Nick would have been happy to play with nobody there. It was like a major to Nick; you always felt he didn't want to join in the team room. He was there to do a job and that's it.'

The American team was captained by Tom Watson. As a five time Open champion he was and remains a hugely popular figure in Britain. He was the ideal man to heal the wounds after the acrimony of the previous match. 'I have to reduce this "war on the shore" mentality we created in the last couple of Ryder Cups. This isn't war,' Watson said.

It might not have been war, but he was still answerable to his country's Commander-in-Chief, although this posed its own problems because Watson was forced to play the role of diplomat before his team had even left the United States. Several of his players objected to taking up an invitation to a rallying meeting at the White House with President Bill Clinton. 'Where I grew up you were better off telling people you were a garbage man than a Democrat,' commented reigning US Open champion Lee Janzen. 'I don't want to shake hands with no draft dodger,' said the ever politically correct Paul Azinger. Watson countered by saying that whatever Clinton's politics he was America's 'First Golfer' and that the team would honour the invitation. 'Mr Clinton told me my job was to bring back the Cup. They were the last words he said to me.'

So Watson had his presidential orders and he knew what to expect over the three days of competition. 'We're going over there to try like hell to kick their butts and they are going to try like hell to kick ours. That's as it should be, but when it's over, we should be able to go off together, lift a glass and toast one another. That's what the Ryder Cup is about,' he said.

But the portents were not good as even the pre-match gala dinner could not pass without a degree of acrimony. The custom at such functions ahead of previous matches was that players would sign each other's menu cards to create a souvenir of the occasion. This often led to other guests queuing for autographs, something the Americans were keen to avoid. Unaware of this, Sam Torrance asked Watson to sign his menu and the US skipper refused, leaving the Scot 'too angry to talk about it'. Watson was swift to apologise and said he was happy to sign menus at a more convenient time. Gallacher backed his opposite number: 'It was a small incident that shouldn't have been blown up.'

Both captains were determined to make the match cordial and one way and another snuffed out all controversy in the remainder of the build-up. They could do nothing about the weather, though. On the morning of Friday 24 September 1993 the West Midlands were shrouded in autumnal fog, forcing a delay to the start of the match. For Montgomerie and his partner Nick Faldo it meant an exaggerated period of hanging around. Not only did they have to wait for the fog to burn off, they were also going to have to let the first three foursomes matches tee off before they could start. This indicated their importance to the team because Gallacher was sending them out in a crucial position in the draw. There is only ever a single point at stake, but the final one in a session usually determines the tone. That single point can enhance and confirm a team's positive momentum or stem the tide if it has been with the opposition.

The British 'dream team' was up against a tough pairing in fifty-one-year-old Ray Floyd and Fred Couples. It was reasonable to assume that the European pair could not have been better prepared, having practised together all week. It would have been wrong to do so, though.

Throughout foursomes practice the two men had worked on Faldo teeing off on the even numbered holes. That remained the plan until just twenty minutes before tee-off when Faldo exerted his seniority because of a sudden loss of confidence. The man who spent ninety-seven weeks as the world number one had been hitting a controlled fade, moving the ball through the air on a left-to-right path. It suited him to hit the tee shots on the even numbered holes. Accordingly, Montgomerie had been preparing himself to hit off the odd numbers. More immediately, given the intimidating nature of the Ryder Cup and the fact that this was his home debut, he had been concentrating on the nerve-wracking task of hitting off the first tee. But that morning Faldo lost belief in his ability to execute that fade and unilaterally decided that he would switch the batting order. He, not Monty, would take the opening stroke. This left the Scot to contemplate driving on holes to which he had devoted no thought for foursomes play. 'Monty just shrugged in that Monty way of his,' Faldo later recalled.

Bernard Gallacher has his own theory as to why Montgomerie appeared nonchalant at this unexpected turn of events. 'Colin was happy to go along with whatever Nick said. I think Colin was playing a game, because it was taking the pressure off him,' the captain said.

Despite feeling the need to change the order in which they hit, Faldo was still fired up for this Ryder Cup and Montgomerie felt the same. The fact that they were up against Floyd in the opening foursomes heightened the feeling because he and Faldo had an enduring rivalry. It was against Floyd that Faldo had won his play-off in the 1990 Masters and the Englishman had also edged their singles contest at Kiawah Island.

Faldo's drive off the first set up a safe par and it was enough for the European combination to claim the opening hole. Floyd and Couples hit back to level by taking the third with a birdie. Montgomerie's immaculate pitch to the fourth set up a European birdie that put the home pair back in front, then at the short eighth Monty chipped in to extend the advantage.

That week much was made of the famous short par four tenth, regarded as a perfect matchplay hole where players could gamble on trying to hit the green with their tee shot. The target was some 275 yards away, tucked behind water with tall, mature trees standing guard to the front right. Three down at the turn after failing to par the ninth, Floyd, playing his eighth and last Ryder Cup, struck a mighty three wood that finished just five feet from the hole. Couples stepped up to hole for an eagle to cut the arrears.

Monty and Faldo had been combining beautifully and were

still in control but at the 13th they bogeyed to let in the Americans and give the visiting pair genuine hope. Furthermore, with Europe struggling elsewhere, this clash was, as expected, taking on extra significance. So it was time to reassert European authority; time to step on the gas. At the par three 14th Montgomerie sent his tee shot to 12 feet. A pumped-up Faldo drained the putt, the ball urged into the hole by the throaty roars of packed galleries who had recognised the significance of this match. Back to three up. Then at the par five 15th Monty holed from eight feet for an unmatched birdie – four up with three to play. It was all over. After that brief mid-back nine scare it was a case of job done and the precious point belonged to Europe, their partnership thoroughly vindicated.

Two years earlier the foursomes had been the weak link for Bernard Gallacher's team at Kiawah Island. It was in those sessions that Europe had lost the match, not so much Bernhard Langer's missed six-footer on the final green of the closing singles. This time in the alternate-shot format they had fared much better, even though the usually dependable Spanish combo of Ballesteros and Olazábal had lost to Tom Kite and Davis Love III. The point secured by Faldo and Montgomerie levelled the sequence at two points each and it was the first time since 1987 that Europe had not been behind after the opening session. 'The competition was so intense you could have written a novel about it,' the American skipper Watson reflected.

Commentating on BBC Television, a thoroughly impressed Peter Alliss said of Montgomerie and Faldo: 'A new partnership and we haven't seen the last of them.' He was correct because, as expected, they were sent out again for the afternoon fourballs, this time third in the order. As in the morning they faced Fred Couples, but the languid American was this time partnered by the feisty Paul Azinger, who a month earlier had won the US PGA. Azinger was another of Faldo's great rivals, the man he had beaten to land his first major, the 1987 Open at Muirfield.

With the added frisson of this personal rivalry it turned into the best match of the opening two days and it wasn't completed until the next morning. Montgomerie and Couples were largely bit-part players as Faldo and Azinger went toe to toe. Both pairs reached the turn in a better-ball thirty-one shots – five under par. The highlight on the front nine was Faldo's chip in for birdie at the seventh. Montgomerie wasn't at his best but his combativeness was beyond question. Perhaps it was best summed up by what happened at the tenth, where his attempt to find the putting surface from the tee ended in a flower bed that adorned the front of the green. With his second shot Monty took a furious smash at the ball to try to propel it towards the pin. Petals, leaves, roots and earth were jettisoned all around as his ball flew over the green. It cleared spectators and headed out of sight. Still the Scot thought he could contribute and it took Faldo to convince him that a birdie to match the one that Azinger had just slotted was out of the question. He waved his junior partner to the next tee to indicate that not only Monty's ball but the hole had gone. The European pair had to accept that they were now behind for the third time in what was turning into a thrilling contest.

Faldo brilliantly won the 13th to level, pitching and then putting an awkward left-to-right ten-footer for birdie. Azinger responded with three straight birdies. Faldo matched the first of them by chipping in for the second time in the contest and a hole later, at the par five 15th, the Europeans made another birdie to maintain parity.

The early morning fog meant play was a long way behind schedule and dusk was fast approaching as Azinger's birdie at the 16th put the US one up with two to play. 'I was a bit annoyed,' Bernard Gallacher admitted. 'Darkness was coming in as we came up the sixteenth and I didn't like this. No one could see and I thought it was giving our side a disadvantage because I thought we were the better team and it could have turned into a lottery. So after Azinger had holed across the green to go one up I said to Colin to pack it in now. I couldn't see how you could make a birdie up seventeen when you couldn't see where you were going.'

Faldo had raced to the penultimate tee and against the captain's wishes the match continued. 'Colin said to me that Nick wanted to carry on because he thinks we have got them on the run!' recalled Gallacher. How falling one down with two to play is putting the opposition on the run is anyone's guess but somehow Faldo was proved correct. It seemed he acquired a prophetic kind of infra-red vision. His immaculate third shot to the par five set up a vital birdie. 'I knew where the pin was, I knew the yardage and I hit the shot as quickly as I could,' Faldo said. In the gathering gloom Azinger and Couples were unable to find the hole with their birdie putts and the match was levelled. However, there was no question of it continuing that Friday evening.

All the other afternoon fourballs had been completed and Europe led 4-3. As long as Faldo and Montgomerie could avoid losing the final hole on the resumption they would preserve their team's precious advantage. The match resumed at eight o'clock the next morning. The Belfry's famous closing hole is treacherous. Players have to drive over water to a fairway that swings left. The more of the corner you try to cut the more likely you are to see your ball making an unwanted splash. The second shot is also over water that guards the front of a three-tiered green. Montgomerie's drive was straight and true but ran through the short grass and finished with an awkward lie in the semi-rough. Faldo cut the corner and found the fairway. Couples' ball was wet and he was out of the hole. Azinger ripped a drive that finished 20 yards closer to the green than Faldo's ball. 'It was probably the best drive I've hit, under the circumstances,' the reigning US PGA champion said.

Monty's five-iron second shot never stood a chance and plunged into the lake. Faldo found the green but on the wrong tier, some 50 feet from the hole, while Azinger's eight iron superbly settled on the correct level to leave an 18-foot birdie putt.

The green was wet with overnight dew and Faldo's long-range birdie chance pulled up ten feet short. Now Azinger had a putt for the match, but his brave attempt veered right of the hole at the last moment leaving the Englishman with a chance for a half. Monty was out of the hole but still had a role to play. Faldo wanted his opinion on reading the line. The Scot felt the ball would break from the right lip; Faldo said he thought it was a straight putt. Monty couldn't be sure his partner would heed his advice as caddie Fanny Sunesson lined up her man. Once struck, the putt never looked like missing and soon after it dropped Montgomerie asked his partner which line he had chosen. 'I'll never tell you,' he replied.

'Well, that's typical Faldo. He wouldn't want to give him any credit for anything,' said Gallacher when he learned of this conversation. Not that the skipper cared in the slightest.

'Whatever you say about Faldo, he produced the goods.' He most certainly had in this epic halved battle. Both pairs had knocked it round in a better-ball 63. Faldo had made seven birdies, Azinger six, Couples three and Montgomerie two. Europe were 4½-3½ ahead with the whole of the second-day schedule still to go.

Naturally, Gallacher kept his British combination together and sent them out first to take on Corey Pavin and Lanny Wadkins and there was none of the hanging around of the previous morning. From departing the 18th green there was time for a quick bacon sandwich, a couple of practice putts and then it was on to the first tee. Monty and Faldo were clad in distinctive red sweaters rather than the salmon pink being worn by the rest of the Europeans that day. The official team cashmere jumpers were too long in the sleeve for Faldo and earlier in the week he'd dispatched his partner to buy new ones from the pro shop. But it wasn't their garb that was making them stand out. They were unbeaten and had already accrued a haul of one and a half points from a possible two. Buoyed by Faldo's putt at the last, they were on a roll and Pavin and Wadkins merely provided the next obstacle to be flattened. 'They didn't stand a chance,' said Monty.

That early morning putt had set the agenda. Faldo and Montgomerie were buzzing, keen to put to the sword the arch competitor Pavin and Wadkins, a wily old pro who knew how to get under the skin of the opposition. 'When Lanny is on his game, it's like having a cobra in the basket with the lid off,' Watson had warned. But the British pair were an impregnable force, completely in tune with each other all the way round. They sealed their victory with a piece of brilliance from Montgomerie on the 16th green where he demonstrated one of his less-vaunted attributes as a golfer. Players, fans, caddies, coaches and captains will always speak of Monty's competitiveness and the accuracy of his ball striking. 'Fairways and greens, fairways and greens' as Faldo and Gallacher had identified, but Monty also possesses a wonderful imagination and the ability to think through and execute shots that others just can't see. The 16th green at the Belfry has two tiers. The upper section forms the right side of the green, the lower part is to the left. Montgomerie was faced with a birdie putt from the higher level with the hole cut at the bottom of the slope. But it wasn't just a delicate downhiller. Monty identified that there was around 15 feet of break; he would have to aim way to the left of the hole because borrowing anything less would mean that, no matter how slowly he hit the putt, his ball would take too much slope and charge past the hole.

The Scot judged it to perfection, the ball settling next to the cup for a par that was enough to give Europe victory by 3 and 2. It also gave Monty another win against Pavin, the man he would face as captain at Celtic Manor.

Momentum is everything in a Ryder Cup and Montgomerie and Faldo had ensured that it was firmly with the home side on that Saturday morning. Only the rookie pairing of Barry Lane and Peter Baker were beaten as Europe took the session 3-1 to move ahead 7½-4½. 'An American official, whom I knew very well, before lunch on that Saturday was conceding the match to me,' Ken Schofield remembered. 'And not frivolously. He said to me, "Ken, you guys are better than us this time."'

There was one sequence of fourballs and the twelve singles left to be played. Understandably, Monty and Faldo, who had become the bedrock of Europe's challenge to regain the trophy, were sent out at the top of the order. This time they were hot favourites because Tom Watson felt the need to blood two players he had yet to use in Chip Beck and the rookie John Cook. Surely they were lambs to the slaughter given the form of the imperious Faldo and his willing Scottish apprentice?

Montgomerie was feeling uneasy, though. By his own admission he is 'ridiculously superstitious' and he didn't like the fact that his partner had changed from white to blue golf shoes for the afternoon. Faldo was more concerned that his feet were damp.

Cook was the man Faldo had beaten to claim his third Open title in 1992. What was it about this Ryder Cup? It kept lining up Americans seeking revenge on Faldo for personal losses. Maybe one day Montgomerie would find himself in the same position because it seemed pretty clear that it would not be too long before he would have a major title or two to his name.

As it turned out, Cook was able to succeed where Ray Floyd and Paul Azinger had failed and managed to gain a measure of solace from beating the man who had deprived him of a major championship. It was nothing to do with Faldo's choice of shoes; Europe's top pair simply ran out of steam in a tight fourball clash. 'Faldo and Montgomerie probably thought they drew an easy match,' Cook observed. The Englishman broke the deadlock to give the home duo the lead with a five iron to within inches of the hole for a birdie at the sixth, but Cook quickly levelled and Monty missed from short range for a half at the eighth to give the Americans a lead they would never surrender.

Faldo's previously assured putting began to desert him and Montgomerie was struggling to make an impact. Cook and Beck continued to dovetail nicely and when both Europeans failed to take decent birdie chances to level the match at the 16th they were one down with two to play. Their unbeaten run was on the line as the home players both lipped out for hole-winning birdies on the 17th. At the last Faldo fired in a superb second shot, but couldn't make it count from 12 feet. Montgomerie had tugged his approach left and then overhit a desperate pitch that he knew had to drop to provide any chance of a half. Cook was sitting pretty and had two putts for the match. It was handshake time. The Americans had won two up and clinched a point that Tom Watson would later identify as the most important of the entire three days. Watson was quizzed about his pairing by Ken Schofield, the week after the match, at the German Masters. The Scottish Tour boss wanted to know how the American captain had decided upon the unlikely heroic combination. Schofield said: 'Tom gave me that Huckleberry Finn smile of his, looked at me and then looked around before admitting it had been his last throw of the dice. He'd just stuck them out and he obviously felt whoever came up against Monty and Faldo were probably going to lose. There was no question their win was the turning point.'

Europe were under pressure. Resources were stretched on the Saturday afternoon and they really could have done without Montgomerie and Faldo losing. Seve Ballesteros, troubled with back pain, had been struggling throughout the match. 'Seve couldn't hit a cow's arse with a banjo' was how his caddie Billy Foster put it and the great Spaniard asked to be rested for the second fourball sequence. This meant his trusty amigo Olazábal was given a new partner in Joakim Haeggman. Bern-hard Langer had struggled with a neck problem and Costan-tino Rocca came into the fray. Then there was Sam Torrance, who had been nursing a toe injury and hadn't played since the opening morning.

Only a stunning putting display from Peter Baker in partnership with Ian Woosnam thwarted a Saturday afternoon American whitewash. The visitors claimed three out of the four points on offer and were now just a solitary point behind with the twelve singles to go. That figure soon became eleven because Torrance was not fit to play. Bernard Gallacher had alerted Tom Watson the night before and the US skipper was spared an awkward decision by Lanny Wadkins. As a wild-card pick and not someone who had qualified for the team, Wadkins felt it only right that he should volunteer to be the man to drop out. So when Torrance was officially withdrawn he and Wadkins were each awarded half a point.

Gallacher sent out former Masters champion Woosnam first, rookie Barry Lane second and Monty third, the same position in the draw that Monty had occupied at Kiawah Island. 'My view was that Monty was a strong player and we should put him out near the front and try to get the momentum going,' Gallacher said.

The captain's main worry was Ballesteros. 'Seve put a bit of a cloud over the dressing room that week. The way he was playing and feeling and he was usually the top guy,' Gallacher recalled. 'If ever there was a point in big-time golf where Seve's decline started it was that Ryder Cup because he just didn't want to play. He didn't know where he was going. People were working on the practice ground with him and the dilemma was that he could do it on the range, but then on the course it was like a different Seve.' The Spaniard was sent out fourth from last, in the fervent hope that his match with Jim Gallagher Junior would not prove vital. Europe also had the insurance policy of having José Maria Olazábal, Langer and Faldo to bring up the rear.

But for those giants of the European game to have an impact it was crucial that the likes of Montgomerie made a contribution. Certainly the ragged play of his singles debut in South Carolina would be of no use against the man he faced, the reigning US Open champion Lee Janzen. It turned into a tremendous battle. Both players were nervous on the first tee, but Monty coped better with pars on the first two holes which proved good enough for him to open a two-hole lead. It was only then that the American started to relax into the match and to pressure his opponent. Montgomerie was up to the task, but Janzen whittled away and managed to level the contest with four holes to go.

It was at the long 15th that Monty struck the key blow, with one of the finest shots of his Ryder Cup career. Having been comfortably outdriven, the Scotsman knew he had to find the green in two to have any chance of matching his longer opponent. Montgomerie smashed a mammoth two iron, threading it through the bunkers that guarded the front of the green and his ball finished 45 feet from the flag. Janzen responded like the major champion he is by sending his approach to within 20 feet. Advantage Janzen, with only three holes left after this one.

As Monty settled over his putt he knew there was a danger of three-putting. Avoiding taking more than two putts was an absolute priority, at least make his opponent have to putt for the hole. He took a deep breath and sent the ball on its long journey holewards. The line was perfect and the ball disappeared for a stunning eagle three. It was a killer blow from the ropes. A hole that Janzen was the clear favourite to win and seemed certain not to lose had been ripped from his grasp. His 20-footer was now for a mere half. 'All I could think as I was standing over my putt was if you miss you are going to hear an unbelievable roar,' Janzen said.

The crowd responded as he had expected. The American had missed and the decibel level went through the roof. Montgomerie was back in front.

The match might have been all over at the 17th but Monty failed to hole out for a birdie from short range and so it went to the last. The Belfry's closing hole had not been a happy place for him; the right-to-left dogleg didn't suit the left-to-right fade that is his natural shot. He really would have much rather holed that putt on the 17th to avoid having to stand on the closing tee. Montgomerie hit a three-wood drive that safely found the fairway 190 yards from the flag. For his second shot he wanted to hit a five iron, but his caddie Alastair McLean had noted that adrenaline was kicking in and that at the short 14th his six iron had travelled the same distance they were now facing. Monty always held McLean in the highest regard and went with the caddie's advice. His approach shot was the perfect length, the ball finishing a foot or so to the right of the green.

Montgomerie was first to putt and came up two feet short. To his astonishment Janzen conceded him a par four. 'There's no way I would have given anybody that putt, not in this situation,' the grateful Monty whispered to McLean. The caddie couldn't believe it either, knowing there was a little break to be negotiated as well. Janzen was lining up a downhill 16-footer that needed to go in to snatch a half. The US Open champion missed and gave Montgomerie his first full singles point in a Ryder Cup. 'He was a gentleman,' the Scot told reporters afterwards when asked about his opponent's surprise concession.

Monty's win meant that Europe were still ahead by the slenderest of margins. 'It was a big deal for me as he was the reigning US Open champion having won the tournament three months previously at Baltusrol, so to claim his scalp gave the team a big boost,' he recalled.

Woosnam had halved with Fred Couples in the top match and Barry Lane had fallen to Chip Beck on the final green. Each of the first five matches went to the closing hole, with Peter Baker and Joakim Haeggman following Montgomerie's success by stretching Europe's lead to three points with narrow wins.

But out on the course the holders were demonstrating their huge appetite for retaining the trophy. The leaderboards were turning red, an indication that the US were ahead in the matches that remained. One by one, Tom Watson's team turned those positions of superiority into points. Payne Stewart beat Mark James, Seve fell to Jim Gallagher Jnr ('I never thought a Gallagher would beat a Ballesteros,' quipped a rueful European skipper), Costantino Rocca to Davis Love and the ailing Bernhard Langer stood no chance against Tom Kite. When Ray Floyd, the oldest man ever to play in the Ryder Cup, took an unassailable lead against José Maria Olazábal with two holes to go, it was all over. There was nothing Faldo in the anchor match against Azinger could do to influence the result.

Europe had been chased down. America had won at the Belfry for the first time in three events. The trophy headed back Stateside. The spirit of the Ryder Cup had been restored, a triumph of diplomacy for both captains given the acrimonious atmosphere of the previous match. The real triumph belonged to Watson's team, however. They had fought back magnificently against an often inspired Europe. The injuries to Ballesteros, Langer and Torrance took a heavy toll, but America deserved their win. Watson had obeyed his President's orders.

Montgomerie is convinced the withdrawal of Torrance had a big bearing on the eventual outcome. 'To this day I still wonder what might have happened if Sam had been fit and had played where he should have done in the singles order,' he said. 'Would the outcome have still been the same or, if Sam had played and won, would it have shifted the momentum to our side?'

But for Monty it was a much improved contribution compared with his debut. A haul of three and a half points is always impressive, even if he had been carried by Faldo's brilliance in the Friday afternoon fourballs. 'I have to be honest and say that I learned an awful lot from Nick that week as he was world number one at the time and we became a pretty formidable pairing,' Montgomerie said. 'I learned an awful lot about how to play Ryder Cup golf. I learned a lot about myself. It was a great experience playing with Nick. I was thrilled with my three and half points out of five and that was the start of me playing all five matches in Ryder Cups, the start of a record 32 matches in a row – a record of which I'm very proud.' But the Saturday afternoon defeat proved so important to the outcome. 'I believe the heart of our victory was Cook and Beck winning their fourball,' Watson said. That result against Europe's leading pair had given America the belief that they could complete their comeback in the Sunday singles.

There was some consolation for Monty. Spending the week

in close proximity to Britain's greatest golfer was hugely beneficial. It did wonders for his standing and self-esteem to be
mentioned in the same breath as Faldo. It reinforced Montgomerie's desire to become his continent's dominant player.
Eventually to be thought of in the same way as his partner
that week, that was a burning ambition.

But it was now two Ryder Cups played and two defeats, a
bottom line to be abhorred. He was a *winner* and that's why
one day his continent would call for him to be its leader.

4

'I believe my Ryder Cup record will be my legacy to the game and, yes, a victory as captain would complete that' — **Colin Montgomerie**

Once it became clear that Colin Montgomerie was a candidate for the job of Ryder Cup captain it triggered a wave of optimism throughout the European game. His playing credentials were outstanding, his stature within the European game made him a natural leader and his communications skills seemed perfectly suited to the job. But Montgomerie is a complex character; controversy is never far away. It therefore wasn't a shock to find him at the centre of media scrutiny and creating both positive and negative headlines from the moment Captain Colin became a possibility.

The meeting to decide who would lead Europe was set for Wednesday 28 January 2009 in the clubhouse at the Emirates Golf Club, the home of that week's Dubai Desert Classic. Two names were considered: Montgomerie and José Maria Olazábal. Five days before the meeting the Spaniard's long-time manager Sergio Gómez left no one in any doubt that his man did want the job. 'His chances of making the team are not what he wanted or expected so he made up his mind he would accept the captaincy if it is offered,' he said. Gómez also admitted: 'Even if he is made Ryder Cup captain his heart will be bleeding because he still wants to be a player.' Montgomerie, meanwhile, was continuing the mantra of happy to serve 'in any way, shape or form' and saying that he would be as happy to do the job in America as in Europe. This struck a chord with something that he had said way back in 2005 when he was first asked about the prospect of leading the team in 2014. 'While Gleneagles would be super, I would take the captaincy if it was in Timbuktu.' No one should ever doubt Montgomerie's passion for the Ryder Cup, but now he sensed the chance to lead the team sooner than he had anticipated.

What is more, he had the important backing of Europe's pre-eminent golfer of the era, Padraig Harrington. In 2008 the Irishman had won back-to-back majors with his defence of the Open Championship at Royal Birkdale and then at the US PGA at Oakland Hills. No European had won the PGA since the American-based Scot Tommy Armour in 1930, when the tournament was a matchplay event, so it was an historic win for Harrington in Detroit. He was the only man from Europe to win the final major of the golfing year in modern times. Now, as a three-time winner at golf's top table, he could consider himself on a par with such huge contemporary figures as Phil Mickelson, Vijay Singh and Ernie Els. Harrington carries plenty of clout in the European game and he was unequivocal in endorsing Montgomerie. 'I believe he is the best man for the job,' he said of the player he'd partnered in the opening matches on the first days of the 2004 and 2006 Ryder Cups.

As players, officials and a larger-than-usual pack of reporters arrived at the Emirates Golf Club ahead of the meeting, there was almost a feeling that the decision had already been made. The discussion seemed likely to be nothing more than the rubber-stamping of Monty for the job. The first rumour was that a banner had been spotted in the clubhouse reading 'Congratulations Colin Montgomerie'. But talking on the range the influential former Tournament Committee chairman Jamie Spence was at pains to stress Montgomerie's appointment was not a foregone conclusion. He said: 'It's not a done deal yet, there's still a lot of talking to be done.' He was categorical that no decision had been made and the opinions of every committee member had still to be aired.

Players were fine-tuning their games on the range and one by one the committee members headed off towards the clubhouse. Darren Clarke was last to leave, having been blasting drivers to the final moment before he needed to jog off to the meeting room. He hadn't been in Abu Dhabi for the initial meeting and had never been particularly close to Montgomerie. Clarke is one of the Tour's big beasts and is no doubt a future captain, having been at the heart of four European wins in five Ryder Cup appearances. He carried sufficient influence to have been able to swing the meeting if he was of a mind so to do. The odds still favoured the Scot, though.

And as it turned out, the decision to appoint Montgomerie was not excessively drawn out. One hour ten minutes to be precise. The meeting thrashed out the credentials of both potential captains. The feeling was that Montgomerie was better suited to a home match and that Olazábal, who has played much of his golf on the American PGA Tour, would be a more appropriate appointment for leading Europe on US fairways.

There had been considerable speculation that the committee would make a double announcement to take in the next two contests, in the way that they had for Ian Woosnam in 2004 and then Nick Faldo two years later, but it didn't pan out that way. Unlike Monty, Olazábal wasn't at the meeting in Dubai and in a phone call with Thomas Björn he turned down for the moment the chance to captain Europe at Medinah, near Chicago, in 2012. Björn had explained to the Spaniard why they had plumped for Monty to lead at Celtic Manor. Olazábal's manager Sergio Gómez later confirmed that the 2012 job had been offered and had been turned down for the moment. 'Who thinks that far ahead? He said to them, "Come back to me in 2011." I believe he thought, through the whole process, that he would become healthy again and could make it as a player,' added Gómez. 'Then he said to me that he made up his mind one week too late, so he has regrets about that and he is disappointed.'

That hesitation when Olazábal had been initially sounded out by Björn had been the crucial moment that let Montgomerie into the picture.

As in Abu Dhabi, the Scot had been asked to leave the meeting room while his candidacy was discussed. On his return, the Tour Chief Executive George O'Grady put it to Montgomerie that he had unanimous support and they wanted him to win back the Ryder Cup for Europe in 2010. 'I will leave no stone unturned' was the new skipper's response. Within an hour of the decision finally being made he was beaming and was undoubtedly the happiest and most excited man in his sport as he addressed a media conference that was transmitted live around the world on television and on the internet as well as back to Britain, broadcast on Radio Five Live.

Clad in Europe's colours of navy blue blazer and yellow tie and flanked by committee chairman Thomas Björn, O'Grady and Ryder Cup director Richard Hills, Montgomerie addressed the assembled international media: 'This is obviously one of the most proud moments that I can think of, and I'm very, very proud and honoured to be selected. Not just honoured, but it's a huge responsibility as well. Having lost the last Ryder Cup at Valhalla, I promise you that I will be doing everything I can to claim back the Ryder Cup in Wales in 2010.'

As he was speaking, advertisements were being placed on the European Tour website for corporate hospitality packages for the match at Celtic Manor. Yes, his primary aim was to win back the famous old trophy, but his eloquence and ability to handle media, sponsors and the corporate quarter made him the ideal Captain Credit Crunch as well. Not that he would be drawn on such a premise. 'All I can say is that the Ryder Cup is a very financially rewarding exercise for the European Tour as a whole, and we aim to claim it back.' That was the theme. Winning, winning, winning; Montgomerie couldn't countenance anything less and in essence nothing else mattered. It was that attitude that has run like the lettering in a stick of rock throughout his Ryder Cup career. 'We feel something is missing on the table here, and the last three captains have had the privilege of sitting here with the Ryder Cup in front of them. We don't this evening and it's my job to make that come true for our following captain in 2012.' With such a view he was firmly in tune with those who had chosen him to do the job.

'It became very obvious in the discussions in Abu Dhabi that we wanted the right man for 2010,' Thomas Björn explained. 'As that meeting progressed, Monty's name came more and more into the frame. And I can say that the whole committee unanimously thought that the man sitting to the right of me is the right man to win the Ryder Cup and the

right man to lead those men into battle.' Some observers had
pointed out that there was no past captain in the committee
that took the decision, but the chairman predictably saw no
problem with this. 'Ten of us have played in the Ryder Cup
and we also talked to other leading players like Lee Westwood,
Sergio García and Padraig Harrington. They were all for
Monty.' It became apparent that age was also an important
factor in the decision-making process. Montgomerie would
be forty-seven when the match was due to be played, four
years younger than Nick Faldo had been at Valhalla. There
was a feeling inside and outside the committee that the last
skipper had been out of touch with his team because he was
the wrong side of fifty. Monty knew that he would be in exactly
the same position if he waited until 2014 to lead Europe at
Gleneagles. 'It just seems that the time is right for me to take
the helm,' he said.

This age issue is an interesting one and threatens to carry
more significance than it deserves. Faldo was undoubtedly out
of touch with some of his players in the 2008 match, but that
was down to questionable man management. This failing
would have surfaced at whatever stage of his life he had led
the team. Faldo made some poor decisions at Valhalla, his
treatment of Lee Westwood being a prime example. The
Nottinghamshire golfer had been unbeaten in the previous
two Ryder Cups and was on his way to equalling Arnold
Palmer's record of going twelve matches without defeat. Westwood had never been benched representing his continent, yet
Faldo saw fit to drop him on the second morning in Kentucky.
That is a captain's prerogative but to inform Westwood that
he was being left out midway through the afternoon fourballs,
as he was striving to equal Palmer's record, was hardly great

timing. It also showed scant regard for the Englishman's pride in playing every sequence of matches since his Ryder Cup debut in 1997. You don't suddenly start making such seemingly crass mistakes because you have turned fifty, but the age factor gave the committee a good and diplomatic reason to look towards Monty for 2010. It provided the man himself with good cause, too. Committee member Paul McGinley had taken the opportunity to stress to the Scot that now was the time. 'Paul made a number of very persuasive points in the captaincy meeting which helped clear everyone's thinking,' admitted Montgomerie. This was backed up by Tour Chief Executive George O'Grady, who said: 'I think the committee have taken a view that they want a captain in tune with the players.' He felt sure they had been attracted by Montgomerie's passion for the Ryder Cup and added: 'I think they do, generally speaking, want a captain more of the same age as some of the players still playing.'

Combining this thinking with a loss of playing form Montgomerie had suffered in the previous year, it was easy to see why he had realised that 2010 was the right time for him to take on the leadership role. 'Yes, there will be a part of me that will regret not captaining the team in Scotland, but it was the same for Ian Woosnam who did the job in Ireland in 2006, rather than wait for it to be played in Wales. I am sure he would not swap his experience for anything and hopefully I will feel the same when the 2010 match is over,' Montgomerie told reporters after the formal press conference had been concluded. 'I have to say that team golf has defined me and my career. I have won Ryder Cups, World Cups, Dunhill Cups and Seve Trophies and loved every minute of it. I believe my Ryder Cup record will be my legacy to the game and, yes, a victory as captain would complete that,' Montgomerie added. 'It's hard to see why being part of a team seems to have brought the very best out of me. But I do love the camaraderie, the atmosphere of the team room and the whole feel of participating in such a huge event alongside your golfing peers. It is that passion that I will hope to transmit to players as their captain.'

The atmosphere could not have been more euphoric. He had been unanimously appointed and it was impossible to find a dissenting voice outside the committee room either. Westwood summed it up neatly when he said: 'Seeing Monty there on the first tee in Newport as captain will make me feel like we're already one up. He's good in the team room, he pulls everyone together. He's very vocal around the table and he will lead like he's done when he's been a player.' Paul Casey, who climbed into the world's top three in 2009, said: 'I experienced Captain Monty before in the Seve Trophy.' This is the biennial match played in non-Ryder Cup years between a Great Britain and Ireland team and a side representing continental Europe. Casey pointed out that it's not the same pressure-packed environment of the more illustrious Europe versus USA clashes, but added: 'I think it has given people an indication as to what he would be like and he was excellent. He looked after the players brilliantly and the communication was superb. The passion you see Monty put into the Ryder Cup, he comes alive,' Casey added. 'I think you are going to see that in how he approaches his captaincy. I think he's going to be fantastic. I want to get back on that team and be part of the side that brings the cup back, not only for Europe but for Colin.'

Another significant figure to welcome the appointment was the exciting youngster Rory McIlroy who had just blazed round the Emirates course in a stunning 64 shots in the opening round of the Dubai Desert Classic. It was a round that had playing partner Mark O'Meara, the long-time friend of Tiger Woods, raving about the quality of McIlroy's golf. O'Meara went as far as to say that the Northern Ireland youngster, who was only nineteen at the time, appeared a better prospect than Woods had done at the same age. Indeed, that round paved the way for McIlroy's first Tour win and he was already regarded as a dead cert for Monty's Ryder Cup team. 'He's never lost a singles,' McIlroy observed of the new captain. 'To win one Order of Merit in your career is a great achievement, to win seven on the bounce and eight overall is a massive achievement. I've got to know him over the past couple of years and he's been very friendly to me and he makes me feel very comfortable out here. I think he will be quite an inspirational character, to be honest. I think the team missed him last time. He'll be able to get the players up for it; he will be a very good captain. The good thing about Monty is he's still playing on Tour so he knows the guys and that will be critical when he comes to select his wild-cards as well. He'll do things right. He knows what the Ryder Cup is about. He would hate to lose, obviously. He's been so used to winning it. It would be great to get on that team.'

It seemed Monty was incapable of doing any wrong. Immediately bookmakers adjusted their prices to make Europe odds on to win back the trophy. Even Ian Poulter, the colourful Englishman with whom Montgomerie had traded insults in the run-up to the naming of the 2008 side, was delighted. 'We've had our little ding-dongs, but he's such a great person and as captain you would perform for him. He'll have great respect from everyone and you'd expect him to get the best out of you.' Oliver Wilson, a debutant under Faldo, added: 'Anyone who makes his team will know him really well. Everybody's going to be comfortable with him. Faldo and Montgomerie have two very different personalities. Monty is going to be more communicative with the players. Everyone will know him better than Faldo and they may be more comfortable with him because he is younger.' Darren Clarke weighed in with this observation: 'He's been the Ryder Cup talisman for many years. He'll be very player-oriented; he'll take a keen interest in how the players are doing.'

So the golfing world was united in its praise for the new captain and even the press tent was in agreement. The *Guardian*'s Lawrence Donegan, a correspondent never afraid to dish out criticism and rail against the golfing establishment, had been won over. He wrote: 'Tiger Woods aside, a case could be made for saying that no one sells the sport better than Montgomerie – certainly no one embodies the Ryder Cup and the concept of team golf more than he does.' In America, where the captain has never been short of critics, there was also support for the appointment. 'Montgomerie is the correct choice,' commentator Brian Hewitt told the Golf Channel. 'You may not like the stuffy Scot because of the ill-tempered manner in which he handles his bad days. Fact is, Montgomerie doesn't have a whole lot of friends on the other side of the pond either – until, that is, it comes to the Ryder Cup, an event that biennially transforms him from a goof to a god in the eyes of Europe.' Hewitt's comments illustrated America's take on Monty's apparent split personality. On Tour the Scot can be a solitary figure, aloof from the other players who he regards as rivals and opponents. In the team environment however, Montgomerie seemed to be everyone's friend, playing his most effective golf that in Ryder Cup terms helped him acquire his legendary status.

'He's obviously going to be a great captain,' said Phil Mickelson. 'He knows what it takes to win. He's been on many winning teams and he's tough,' added the man beaten by Monty and Padraig Harrington in the tone-setting opening fourball clash at Oakland Hills in 2004 when Mickelson's partner was Tiger Woods. It was the emphatic downing of a supposed 'dream team' and it set Europe on their way to a record-breaking victory.

There was mischief afoot in the United States' reaction as well. Perhaps it was best summed up by internet pundit Jay Busbee from the golf blog Devil Ball. 'Nothin' but love for ya, Colin,' he said. 'Mainly because we can't wait for you to have a volcanic meltdown when things don't go your way. While Monty has been one of Europe's surest golfers and probably pound for pound the best never to win a major – he's also got the kind of temper that, let's be honest, is awesome to watch so long as you're not the target.' American golf fans have been intrigued by Montgomerie's temperament throughout his career. He's been a soft target, rarely able to conceal his feelings and has proved well worth winding up by beer-fuelled followers. They have often provoked a reaction: Monty once told a bunch of US hecklers that the only thing worse than losing was having to spend time in their country. But such weakness has never surfaced in the Ryder Cup. He is somewhat like John McEnroe was when he faced Björn Borg. Those were the matches that mattered most to the self-styled 'super-brat' of tennis and there was no room for histrionics in those contests; likewise for Montgomerie in the Ryder Cup, often despite vicious provocation from US galleries. Brian Hewitt was right to tell Golf Channel viewers of the way Monty is transformed when he plays team golf.

Back home the enthusiasm for his appointment was reflected in a poll carried out by the London *Evening Standard* that gave the new skipper a 64 per cent approval rating. It had been a heady start to the year for the Scot, who just a fortnight earlier had been seen as a rank outsider to land the most prestigious job in European golf. It appeared he could do no wrong; indeed, as he played his first round in the Dubai Desert Classic he was standing over an awkward putt from the fringe of a green and said to himself: 'You can hole this, you can hole this – you're the Ryder Cup captain.' The putt duly rolled in and playing companion Ross Fisher quipped: 'Well done, captain.'

It was not the first or last time that Monty would have a little chat with himself in the process of playing a shot. The media know him as 'the best talker' in the game for his ability to steal headlines with interesting and insightful quotes, but he also likes to listen to himself, especially when he is looking for inspiration or, on occasion, reassurance when the pressure is on.

Yet within two days of his appointment he had gone from Captain Fantastic to Captain Cock-up. Those much vaunted communications skills of his were supposed to give him a parachute to save him from plunging into awkward territory, but amid the euphoria of his coronation he forgot to pull the ripcord. As a result he hurtled into the first controversy of his tenure almost before it had begun. Inevitably Montgomerie had been asked about the man he beat to the job, José Maria Olazábal in the news conference that immediately followed his appointment. No one was surprised to hear the captain say how much he wanted the Spaniard to be on board. 'I think it's quite obvious that José Maria will be part of my team at Celtic Manor,' Monty announced.

He was being presumptuous.

The next morning ahead of the first round of the Dubai Desert Classic both men embraced warmly outside the clubhouse, Montgomerie saying, 'We need to talk.' They have known each other since their first meeting in the 1984 British Amateur Final which was won by the Spaniard. 'I'm of a great understanding and respect for him,' Monty had said. Unfortunately he didn't understand him sufficiently well to realise that effectively appointing him as a vice-captain without approaching him first would not sit well with Olly. The new skipper had also failed to take account of the fact that this was a very important week for Olazábal, regardless of the captaincy issue. He was at last sufficiently recovered to start playing golf again, having made only two tournament appearances since May the previous year. It was a stressful time for the Spaniard, particularly as fatigue is one of the side effects of the drugs he was taking to control his rheumatic condition. Embarking on 72 holes of golf in such circumstances was heading into worryingly uncharted territory. Reporters seeking his reaction to Montgomerie's appointment were told that he would not make any comment until his first competitive round in three months had been negotiated. When Olazábal did speak he was prickly to say the least. One of the game's gentlemen but not one to be taken for granted, he was asked about Montgomerie's assertion that he would be part of the back-up team at Celtic Manor. 'That's news to me,' Olazábal said. 'When I got to the clubhouse I congratulated him and he said that we need to talk.' Asked whether he assumed it was the vice-captaincy that Monty would want to discuss the Spaniard said: 'I am not going to guess anything.'

'He said he would like to invite you if you didn't make the team?' queried one reporter.

'He didn't say that to me.'

'He said he already had.'

'Well, you know more than me. That is why you are the press.'

Clearly the thought that the new skipper had chosen to discuss this issue with the media before talking it through with Olazábal had riled the man who acted as Faldo's vice-captain in 2008. 'Would anyone like to find out they've been given a post through the newspapers?' the Spaniard's manager, Sergio Gómez, said later. 'I don't know if Monty was trying to cheer José up, but there is a correct way of doing these things.' Montgomerie's response was to say that the dialogue between him and his prospective number two would continue, but already he was encountering his first negative headlines as captain. The *Sun* said: 'Olly's Mad with Monty'. But he wasn't nearly as mad as the captain was later in the year when the second and far more damaging controversy of his reign struck just before the Open Championship at Turnberry on Montgomerie's native Ayrshire coast.

5

*'Monty played a large part in that discussion
and this was at a time when we had big powerful
figures like Seve, Langer, Faldo and Woosie in
the team'*
— **Ken Schofield, Executive Director, European Tour**

He was there to be shot at — a target for the opposition and a big target at that. Not so much waistline but because no one at Oak Hill was playing better golf than him. He'd become a leader. Week in, week out he would lead tournaments and win his share. This week he was a different kind of leader, the sort that sets the example and inspires his team-mates, shows them the way. No wonder Faldo wanted him again: anyone would like him alongside. Tee to green, there was no one better on the planet and the Americans knew it. So did Europe: they were counting on him. No trophy on the journey across the pond and that hurt. Over in America they were convinced the Cup lived in these parts; the late eighties were a blip. Now normal service had been resumed; effectively, Europe turned up to lose. That was how the Yanks seemed to view it. They might have been in for a shock, though. Trouble was, Seve was out of sorts and there was no Olly. Faldo seemed a bit distracted and this bloke who had identified himself as the European team's leader could not have been more nervous . . .

Rain was forecast. It was destined to be a day more suited to the Scottish glens than upstate New York, but there was no mistaking the location: this was the United States of America. The chanting crowds made it abundantly clear and so did the golf course at the Oak Hill Country Club, situated close to Rochester, NY. The layout could not have been more American either. A muscular course, just a few paces short of 7,000 yards with only two par fives, overall a par 70 with ten of the par fours measuring more than 400 yards. It was a major test and little wonder that Oak Hill had previously staged three US Opens and the 1980 US PGA Championship. The setup was typically American, too, with the home skipper Lanny Wadkins insisting on narrow strips of fairway lined by thick, clumpy rough. This was the home of the 1995 Ryder Cup, where Wadkins' team were trying to make it three wins in a row. For Colin Montgomerie, if that happened it would mean his career in the biennial matches beginning with an unpalatable hat-trick of defeats.

Wadkins, the man who had volunteered to miss out on the singles when Sam Torrance was injured for Europe at the Belfry in 1993, had been appointed successor to Tom Watson. Europe had stuck with Bernard Gallacher for the third match running. Again he boarded Concorde in the desperate hope that the trophy would be with him for the return journey a week later. The Edinburgh man had tried and failed to emulate the successes of Tony Jacklin in the previous two contests and this would be his last chance of glory. Gallacher took a very experienced team. There were only two newcomers, Sweden's Per-Ulrik Johansson and, from Ireland, Philip Walton. Apart from José Maria Olazábal all of Europe's big guns were there. The Spaniard had by now fallen victim to the rheumatic condition that would blight much of his career. Olazábal's compatriot Seve Ballesteros qualified fifth on the money list and Gallacher's two wild-card picks were Nick Faldo, who had played most of his golf in the US that year, and Ian Woosnam, who had just missed out on automatic qualification.

Even though he had not broken his duck in majors, Montgomerie was playing the golf of his life in 1995. His defeat in a play-off to Steve Elkington in the US PGA a month before the Ryder Cup was one of an astonishing eleven top-four finishes that season. Monty won the German Open and the Lancôme Trophy and was banking sizeable cheques every time he teed it up. By the time the Ryder Cup came round he was well on his way to winning a third successive Order of Merit. He was first in the Ryder Cup qualifying table and had grown to believe he was better than almost anyone else he was put up against. This wasn't outright arrogance; it was just the core confidence that lay at the heart of his sustained success, in effect his fifteenth club.

On the eve of the Oak Hill contest commentators openly speculated that, despite what the rankings stated, Montgomerie was the best golfer in the world. Monty was the last person to argue, such was his self-belief. The official stats had Greg Norman as world number one ahead of Nick Price and Ernie Els – a trio of southern hemisphere stars geographically ineligible for the Ryder Cup. Faldo was fourth in the rankings, Bernhard Langer fifth, with Montgomerie sixth. The highest ranked American was Corey Pavin, one place behind Monty.

Before handing them in, captain Gallacher had thought long and hard about his pairings. The default combination of Seve Ballesteros and José Maria Olazábal was no longer an option and his most dependable duo appeared to be the Montgomerie/Faldo team. They had combined well at the Belfry and had become the natural choice to form the bedrock of Europe's challenge. The skipper needed Europe to make a fast start and decided to open with his strongest hand. Monty and Faldo were to lead off in the top match. Convention dictates that the visiting team hits first on the opening tee. It was foursomes and Montgomerie was given the duty of driving on the odd holes. He would hit the opening drive of the 1995 Ryder Cup.

'Faldo would want that because Monty is such a straight hitter,' Gallacher observed.

Although his stellar form at the time meant that confidence was coursing through his veins, Montgomerie still found this an intimidating prospect. The Ryder Cup can have this frightening effect on the most seasoned of golfers. With threatening clouds overhead and buoyant home support more than evident, finding the narrow ribbon of fairway on the 440-yard first hole at Oak Hill was going to be some task. Indeed, in Montgomerie's nerve-wracked mind that was not the main priority. His sole objective was to make sure the club head simply made contact with the ball, the sort of ambition that is more suited to an absolute beginner rather than the best player in the world. Such was his level of concern that he argued with his caddie on the first tee. Alastair McLean wanted him to hit a three wood while Monty wanted to use a driver, reasoning that the bigger head on that club would make it less likely he would miss the ball. In the end McLean's soothing manner won the day and the three wood was used, and to good effect as a solid, straight drive found the short grass a decent distance down the hole.

The all-British pair were up against Pavin and a thirty-six-year-old rookie, Tom Lehman, the newcomer who would hit first for the Americans in what proved a classic encounter. 'I was so calm it was unbelievable,' Lehman said. 'I felt I should be here and I should hit this shot.' The late-bloomer from Minnesota, who went on to win his only major at the Open at Royal Lytham the following year, was bold. He went with his driver and smashed it 290 yards down the fairway, careering past Monty's drive, which suddenly looked rather puny in comparison.

From the word go the momentum was with the American pair and Europe's top combination were rattled. Pavin hit a beautiful approach to seven feet and Lehman knocked it in for a birdie that put them one up.

Faldo was edgy. It later transpired that his marriage was on the verge of collapse and at times he seemed distracted, a sharp contrast to the focused figure who had performed so well for Europe two years earlier. This state became apparent as the rain began at the second where Faldo sent an uncontrolled chip across the green before chastising Lehman for holing out from short range after his putt to win the hole had been conceded. 'When I say it's good, it's good,' Faldo barked. This didn't play well with the feisty Lehman. 'I wasn't going to put up with any of that crap, especially after he stretches his arms out as if to say, "Put the ball in your pocket, you idiot!" I was hot,' he said. Montgomerie was determined to avoid any spats and to concentrate on his golf.

If Lehman was 'hot' so was his golf. At the 202-yard third he put his tee shot to within seven feet of the pin and his partner rolled in another birdie to make the home side three up after three and then it became four up after five.

Faldo and Montgomerie were clearly not producing what was required by their team. It was time for Monty to make an impact and he did with a 12-foot birdie putt at the sixth that was greeted with a huge pat on the back from his illustrious team-mate. Lehman then found the creek at the next and at the eighth a par was enough to give Europe their third hole in a row. This was better.

After halving the next four holes the players arrived at the mammoth par five 13th where Montgomerie defied the driving rain to power a three wood on to the green. Faldo capitalised with a monstrous putt, read to perfection, which dropped for a hole-winning eagle. Four down after five had become all square with five to go.

Stung, the diminutive Pavin, with his Charlie Chaplin walk, stood tall at the next. Monty's opposite number at Celtic Manor fired home a 25-footer that put the home side ahead. Lehman drove into the crowd at the next and Europe made no such mistake to draw level again. It was quintessential Ryder Cup foursomes: errors were being punished and moments of inspiration were being rewarded. The 16th and 17th holes resulted in tense halves, leaving the players all square on the closing tee.

Oak Hill, meanwhile, had become Soak Hill. The rain was saturating, squeegees were required to make the greens playable and yet nothing could detract from the tension of this top match. Faldo and Pavin both found rough from the tee. Montgomerie did all he could with Europe's second shot but that was merely to hack out into the fairway. Lehman was faced with a 186-yard shot off a downhill lie out of soggy rough. The rookie referred to his senior partner for advice and Pavin told him to go with his best club and commit totally to the shot. Lehman's five iron found the front of the green while the ragged Faldo hit a wedge into a greenside bunker. With Europe unable to make par from there, the Americans needed just two putts from 40 feet to close out the match. Appropriately, given the standard of his play in his first Ryder Cup match, Lehman stroked home the tap-in to secure a point that felt like a whole lot more.

Europe's 'dream team' had been downed. This illustrious pair, who had been expected to secure a significant haul of points and set the tone for their team, departed the soggy scene empty-handed. 'It was a nice script,' said Pavin after taking the congratulations of his captain Lanny Wadkins.

It is one of the curiosities of the Ryder Cup that points are often collected in unexpected quarters. While Monty and Faldo had failed to give Europe the start they wanted, Sam Torrance and Costantino Rocca quickly made up for the disappointment. Torrance had a poor record in foursomes and had not won in this format in twelve years. Rocca had never experienced alternate-shot golf. Statistically speaking they should have stood no chance, but their ebullient personalities gelled and they beat Fred Couples and Jay Haas 3 and 2. The other European rookie, Per-Ulrik Johansson, teamed up with Bernhard Langer to edge home on the final green against reigning Masters champion Ben Crenshaw and Curtis Strange in the bottom match. With Davis Love and Jeff Maggert comfortably beating Howard Clark and Mark James, it was honours even at two-two after the first session.

Despite their defeat there was still no cause to question the wisdom of keeping Montgomerie and Faldo together for the afternoon fourballs. Still Europe's top pairing, they had pushed Pavin and Lehman all the way. Now they were being sent out third against Couples and Love who had expected to be put together because they had formed a deadly combination in winning three World Cups for the USA.

Two years earlier at the Belfry, Faldo had effectively carried Monty in the fourballs; this time saw a complete role reversal. While there was not much wrong with the Englishman's game tee to green, he was hopeless with his putter. Faldo described Montgomerie's contribution in keeping them in the match as 'magnificent' but ultimately the Scot could do little to stem the American tide.

As expected, Couples and Love proved the perfect combination and they quickly took control of the match, moving four up after six holes. Montgomerie was a constant source of support to his struggling partner, and it was his determined golf that kept Europe in with a chance of gaining something from this clash. He birdied the 12th and the 14th to cut the arrears in half, Faldo having missed from six feet to win the 13th. Had that one dropped, the outcome might have been different, but Couples and Love had plenty to spare in closing out a 3 and 2 victory. For Monty and Faldo it was a miserable played two, lost two. Their mood was not improved by what was happening elsewhere because their team-mates, too, were struggling.

The unlikely pairing of the exuberant Seve Ballesteros and the team's quiet man, David Gilford, provided Europe's only success on that first afternoon. The defeat of Montgomerie and Faldo was one of three losses for Bernard Gallacher's side as the US took a useful 5–3 lead by close of play.

It was easy to spot what made the difference on the scoreboard: the defeats suffered by the players on whom the European captain was most depending. The American writer Rick Reilly summed it up in *Sports Illustrated*: 'The Americans took to a rainy Friday and jumped into a 5–3 lead, mostly by beating Europe's King and Kong, Faldo and Montgomerie.'

Faldo is convinced that it was Monty's desire to chivvy along the disgruntled British number one that persuaded Bernard Gallacher to keep them together the following morning. The skipper felt 'lightning had struck twice' to cause their defeats and it couldn't and wouldn't happen again. His top pair were due a win and his team desperately needed it.

To reiterate his faith in them, Gallacher sent Faldo and Monty out first for the foursomes on a pleasant morning with an autumnal chill. Europe knew that they had to dominate the session and much was riding on the team's leading pair. Montgomerie and Faldo were up against Curtis Strange and Jay Haas. Strange had been a controversial wild-card pick, short of form but with great memories of Oak Hill, having won the US Open there in 1989. On paper the experienced Americans made a formidable pairing. They had played together twice in the Walker Cup, the amateur equivalent of the Ryder Cup, and had successfully combined in the 1983 Ryder Cup. They were, as the Americans would say, three for three.

Montgomerie set the perfect example for Europe with a superb drive down the first, while Strange put his drive under an overhanging tree in deep rough. The home pair hacked their way down the hole, which was easily won by Europe with a regulation par. There was nothing 'regulation' about the birdie that doubled the lead at the long par five fourth. Having found trouble from the tee, Faldo was left with a third shot fully 200 yards from the green. He struck a magnificent three iron, carrying a dangerous bunker to find the putting surface and set up a previously far from likely birdie. Monty made no mistake and they went two up.

Despite losing the sixth, the European pair went to the turn with a three-hole advantage. The standard of golf had not been from the top drawer but Monty and Faldo were doing what was required. 'The key hole was the thirteenth,' Faldo recalled. 'A ridiculously treacherous green, so I asked Monty to give me a straight uphill birdie putt with his approach shot. That's exactly what I got, it was perfect.' The win there restored Europe's three-hole lead. Haas missed from six feet to win the 15th and Strange's long-range putt missed for par a hole later to end the match. Monty and Faldo were at last on the scoreboard.

The US pair had been left to rue some sloppy golf, while their opponents were relieved finally to be making a contribution. They had played fifty holes together and, despite some decent play from Monty, they were a disappointing collective four over par. They had played a key role that morning, though, by putting blue on the board throughout the session, having been ahead from the opening hole. This percolated down to the other Europeans out on the course and they took the session 3-1, the highlight being Rocca's hole in one at the sixth as he and partner Torrance trounced Love and Maggert 6 and 5. By the end of the session the overall score had been levelled at 6-6. It was just the morning Gallacher needed to keep alive hope of an away victory. Had it gone the other way America would have been nigh on out of sight.

Europe felt they had to maintain the momentum because, with Seve Ballesteros hopelessly out of form, they were going to require an advantage to take into the final-day singles if at all possible. This prompted Gallacher to make a big call and signal the end of the road for the Montgomerie/Faldo partnership. 'I could see Nick wasn't happy about it, but I felt that if I split them up we would get two points out of them. At the moment we were only getting one,' Gallacher explained.

'There's a history of great Ryder Cup partnerships having only one cycle or two at the most,' noted former Tour Executive Director Ken Schofield. 'We saw it with Faldo and Ian Woosnam; they had to be split at Kiawah after a wonderful partnership in eighty-seven and eighty-nine.' Montgomerie was put alongside his fellow Scot Torrance, a combination both players had indicated to the skipper they wanted. 'Colin and Sam were friends and had played a lot together because they were both playing well that season and had been last match out together at tournaments many times.'

'We thought no one could beat us,' Torrance later said. First out in the afternoon the Scots were up against Fred Couples and Brad Faxon. It wasn't until the sixth hole that the deadlock was broken when the American pair nudged ahead.

Faxon was renowned as the best putter in the game and had won his place on the team by holing from 15 feet for a final round 63 at the US PGA. It gave him a top-five finish and enough qualifying points to make it into Wadkins' side. His magic on the greens was evident in this match and he made sure the Americans stayed ahead in a tight affair. But it was Couples who struck the decisive blow when Europe seemed certain to win the 13th after a superb Torrance pitch to within inches of the hole. Couples went one better, dramatically chipping in for an unexpected half that stopped their opponents in their tracks. The shot was greeted by deafening roars from the American fans, Couples jumping up and down to milk the moment, high-fiving with his partner. 'It was a thrill I'll never forget,' said the ever-popular Couples. 'I figured I might as well let the people realise it.'

Walking to the next tee, Torrance strode up to Couples and whispered in his ear, 'F*** you'. It's not often that those words are used as a term of affection, but they were typical of the laconic wit of the man from Largs. When Couples later repeated this exchange to team-mates some were appalled, but the American quickly put them right. He was good mates with Torrance and knew the spirit of the remark because it had had a humorous origin. On the eve of the match, Couples had made an unscheduled late-night visit to the European team room with some photographs he wanted signing. He had crawled in, unnoticed, on hands and knees before leaping up to shock a group of the European wives. Their screams were heard down the corridor by Torrance as he was desperately trying to get some sleep ahead of the big day. The Scot hauled himself from his bed to find out what was going on. Discovering that it was down to Couples' high jinks prompted plenty of pre-match banter with the Californian, much to the bemusement of American players and fans on the range the next morning.

But this was Saturday afternoon and the European mood wasn't so good. Faxon collected his fourth birdie of the round at the 16th and Monty couldn't match it. Game, set and match: it was all over. The point had gone and the momentum had swung the way of the home team. Montgomerie had a sorry return of just one point from a possible four. What is more, Faldo, in partnership with Bernhard Langer, went down as well. Gallacher was left to rue splitting the pairing he had identified as his top partnership. 'I felt such a twit,' he admitted. 'But I still don't consider my thinking to be so bad. Monty and Sam lost because Couples holed his wedge from off the green on a hole we were going to win.'

That afternoon America opened a commanding 9-7 lead to take into the final day singles. Corey Pavin's sensational chip-in from the back of the last green, where the ball rattled the back of the cup, popped up and disappeared, secured the full point against Faldo and Langer. It was a hammer blow, a shot that is remembered down the years and the kind of competitive deed that ultimately identified him as captaincy material. At the time it just sent the Americans into a state of delirium. Gallacher could only watch on. Knowing this was his last time as captain, never having tasted victory as a player or on the previous two occasions he had led his continent, he knew it was not a time to give in, no matter how bleak the scoreboard was looking. 'When Pavin chipped in and the Americans went into their two-point lead, Lanny Wadkins started to cheer and charge round the green as if they had won. I said to my wife, "Well, they can have their thing tonight. We'll be cheering tomorrow night because we are going to win this."'

Best player in the world? It didn't feel like it, not when you looked at the scoreboard, just one point from four: an unexpectedly poor return. He was playing okay but the opposition had been hot, inspired. Couples had produced a hammer blow holing off the green. And Faldo had struggled; needed to be encouraged, cajoled along. Talk about a role reversal. He felt able to do it, it was his place because he was that good these days. And Nick appreciated it. Sam had been brilliant all year; together they should have been too strong. They weren't, though, were they? The skipper still thought they could win this. That unbeaten record in singles would have to stay intact, though. The pressure was on. The Masters champion to be beaten. A great putter, a great competitor but Crenshaw had not yet won a point. It needed to stay that way.

Europe were determined to show that America had suffered

a case of premature celebration. Bernard Gallacher sought help as he agonised over the order in which to send out his players for the concluding twelve singles matches. 'On the Saturday evening after Pavin had chipped in I was in the locker room and witnessed Colin Montgomerie's influence,' Ken Schofield revealed. 'Monty and Sam Torrance were with Bernard and they were already thinking about tomorrow. The view of them, all three of them Scots, was that it would be the middle eight games that would decide it. The decision was to play what they collectively thought was the best eight players between three and ten in the order. Monty played a large part in that discussion and this was at a time when we had big, powerful figures like Seve, Langer, Faldo and Woosie in the team.'

Mark James and Howard Clark, two less celebrated stalwarts of the European cause, had been rested on the Saturday afternoon. Gallacher didn't want them expending emotional energy supporting those who were playing. He wanted them out on the course practising, readying themselves for the Sunday action. 'You will have a big role to play tomorrow,' he told them. He also knew that Monty and Faldo would have to come good. There was a two-point deficit to overhaul in the format that is traditionally America's strongest suit.

While the scoreboard showed Europe behind by two, the reality was that they trailed by three. Seve Ballesteros had completely lost his game. The Spanish legend had no idea where the ball was going off the tee. It was inconceivable that he could win a match all on his own. So, in working out his strategy, Gallacher's main worry was where to place Seve in his batting order. 'We had to put Seve somewhere and we knew that he would lose,' Gallacher recalled. The captain didn't want to hand an easy point to one of the weaker US players. 'We decided to put him out first because we knew Lanny would put a big gun up front.'

And so Europe packed their talent into the middle of the order. This is the section where the Ryder Cup would be lost for the third match running if they didn't perform. Equally, success in this portion of the draw could pave the way for the trophy to head back across the Atlantic. Clark, James, Woosnam, Rocca and Gilford followed Ballesteros. Sent out seventh in the order, Montgomerie began the heavyweight section, followed by Faldo, Torrance and Langer with Philip Walton and Per-Ulrik Johansson the last to tee off. 'I wanted strength in the middle of our draw and Colin led off that section. He had a big role to play,' Gallacher said.

Monty felt he had been rather tucked away in not a particularly high-profile part of the order, but he was under no illusions about what was expected of him. Nor did he want for determination to see through the job. The hurt of the last two defeats could still be felt and he wasn't alone in recognising it. That's why the captain's inspirational speech the previous evening, when they were still reeling from Pavin's chip-in, had struck such a chord. Faldo had been particularly impressed and the feeling spread through the team that they could do something very special on the final day. Only once before had a visiting team won the Ryder Cup on American soil.

It helped enormously that Ballesteros' short game was as good as ever. Without seeing a fairway all day, he managed to prevent his opponent Tom Lehman, from running away with the first point. Seve took him all the way to the 15th before succumbing to a 4 and 3 defeat. Clark and James were performing even greater heroics. James was always in control as he wrapped up victory over Jeff Maggert on the 15th green, while Clark's touch with the short stick held up over some nerve-twitching short putts to beat Peter Jacobsen on the final green. Ian Woosnam halved with Fred Couples but Costantino Rocca couldn't sustain his brilliant form of the week and he fell to Davis Love.

While these matches were being completed, Montgomerie was stuck in a tense dogfight with Ben Crenshaw, the man who had won the Masters for the second time earlier that year. Known as 'Gentle Ben', the Texan was in truth anything but. A fierce competitor, he was determined to improve on the two defeats he had suffered earlier in the match. Montgomerie could not stand to lose either. Crenshaw's game was based around his ability on the greens and, with the putting surfaces now thoroughly drained of the rain that had fallen on the Friday, they were fast and treacherous. This might have played into the American's hands, but they weren't proving as steady as usual when gripping his putter.

The golf in this match had been nothing to write home about, but it was exciting enough. A bit like one of those typical England versus Scotland rugby internationals, the quality of play was not of the highest but it was tense and tight and no one could guess who was going to win. It was all square after thirteen, but the match swung unexpectedly at the next. Montgomerie had pushed his drive into the thick rough and did well to find the green, but he was miles from the hole. Crenshaw had played the par four in textbook style and was looking at a 12-foot birdie putt. He seemed ready to pounce. Monty's birdie attempt required binoculars to read: there must have been nearly ten feet of break to negotiate. Monty took it upon himself to decide on the line, leaving his caddie Alistair McLean to watch and hope. The player's priority was to make sure he only took two putts, to ensure that Crenshaw had to hole his putt for the win. It was a typical lag putt, aimed to leave it within the circumference of a dustbin lid from the hole. The ball set off on its long-haul journey, caught the break and started to track towards the hole. McLean, Crenshaw and Monty watched in utter disbelief as it found the centre of the hole. Birdie! It was a moment to match those outrageous blows struck for the Americans by Couples and Pavin the previous day, a vicious haymaker no one saw coming, an echo of what he'd done to Lee Janzen at the Belfry two years earlier. Crenshaw was on the canvas; his putt for a half was always going to miss after that.

One up with four to play, Montgomerie strode confidently to the next tee ready for the kill. He hit a fine five iron to the short 15th to make sure of a steady par and then at the 16th his approach to four feet set up a hole-winning birdie that put him two up with two to play.

It meant that he could not be beaten. The record was intact, but the imperative was to land a full point for his continent and to do it as quickly as possible. The 17th offered a difficult challenge from the tee and it was vital he found the fairway. He wrestled with the option of a safe ploy. Should he take a two iron or three wood?

What the hell? It was time to be bold and, adrenaline coursing through his veins, he reached for the big stick and drew his driver from his bag.

Up ahead, Gilford was heading up the 18th one up on Brad Faxon. Behind, Faldo was keeping pace with Curtis Strange, Torrance was ahead against Loren Roberts and Philip Walton was making good progress against Jay Haas. This Ryder Cup was going to the wire and Europe needed a full point from

Montgomerie. Driver in hand, he smashed an imperious tee shot down that treacherous 17th. It was an absolutely monstrous hit under the circumstances and into a position from which it would be very difficult to lose the hole. Crenshaw would need to do something special to take it to the last. No chance. Monty knocked his approach to six feet and then holed for a fourth successive three to win two up. A precious point for Europe, and another followed almost simultaneously. Gilford had found all sorts of trouble up ahead and did well to bogey the last, but Faxon's par putt slipped by. Between them, Gilford and Montgomerie had levelled the match at 11½-11½.

Monty might have felt tucked away, but he had delivered a crucial point, one that his skipper treasured. 'I just went up to Colin and said that was a terrific win,' Gallacher said. 'That inspired our players. It was worth more than the single point that went on the board.'

Behind, Torrance finished off Loren Roberts on the 17th green, but the brilliant Pavin had taken out Langer 3 and 2. It was too close to call and there was enormous pressure on Faldo and Strange. Ultimately, Faldo's nerve held as he famously wedged to four feet at the last and then holed out for a winning par. Despite his indifferent form earlier in the week, it became one of the defining moments of his career, up alongside his major wins, because it put Europe within touching distance of the Cup. Faldo was instantly swamped by a giant Italian bear hug from Rocca. Monty was next on the scene with a hearty pat on the back for his old mucker. Europe sensed the moment was becoming their own.

All eyes were now on Philip Walton, who was three up with three to play against Jay Haas. All Europe needed was for him to turn the advantage into one whole point. Haas rallied, Walton wobbled and Monty fretted as he watched on. As the American won the 17th to take it to the last, Gallacher shepherded his team with a 'Come on boys, let's go'. Walton needed all the help he could get.

Fortunately for Europe, it came from Haas as he drove into the trees. He had no chance of making the green in two, but Walton's approach came up short on to the thick, grassy slope at the front of the putting surface. Needing to win the hole, Haas pitched on in three; it was dead in line with the flag and Walton feared his opponent might have holed out for the second time in the match as it disappeared from view. The Irishman was relieved to see it eventually reappear running to the back of the green. Using a tip on how to chip from thick rough given by Ian Woosnam, Walton knocked his third shot on to the green, barely clearing the top of the bank. Safely on, he knew and Europe knew that the Cup was almost back in their hands. Realistically, Haas had to hole from the back of the green and his attempt ran five feet past. Walton, with his broom-handle putter, had two blows to win the Ryder Cup for Europe. His captain, his team, their wives and his wife all watched on, barely daring to breathe. Walton knocked his 12-foot par putt towards the hole and up it rolled to tap in range. It didn't drop, but it was good enough.

Gallacher sprinted on to the green, leaping into the air, both arms aloft, fists clenched, and then embraced the quiet Irishman who was now the toast of Europe. Monty remembers the sound of spring-back plastic seats in the stands clanking with defeat as American fans made for the exits. Europe didn't care. For only the second time the U-S-A had been beaten at home. The trophy would be coming home on Concorde.

Fifteen years on, Montgomerie recalled: 'To win in America from that position was a fantastic effort from everybody concerned. I think we pulled it all together for Bernard Gallacher, really. We all pulled it out of the hat and I don't know, to this day, how we did it.' Gallacher himself can't look back on the climax of the 1995 Ryder Cup without his eyes filling with tears. The night of his life? 'It was,' he said. 'It was a release, really; you didn't feel you wanted to get drunk; there was no need. The players didn't have that much of a party. We were up early the next day, we had a bit of a singsong in the team room, but really we were all shattered.

'The rumour was that Bill Clinton was flying up to present the trophy and quickly backtracked when they realised America had lost, which I really enjoyed. I don't know how true that was but it is what I was told,' Gallacher added.

It was the most satisfying of victories. There were heroes in every quarter for Europe. Walton and Faldo at the end, but, as Montgomerie has always contended, key roles had been played by Howard Clark and Mark James for their early wins.

His captain doesn't disagree but also points out the significance of that middle section, the part of the draw that Monty and Torrance said would determine whether Europe could complete an unlikely triumph. Montgomerie had produced four threes in a row, three of them birdies, just at the moment his team needed them most. An inspired monster of a putt, superb approach play, brave driving and a secure touch on the greens – it was golf worthy of the best player in the world. As Gallacher says: 'Colin Montgomerie played an inspirational role. That was an important victory, beating the Masters champion in America. That started it for us.'

6

*'It is not an easy tee shot, but I'm proud to say I
hit one of my best ever drives'*
– Colin Montgomerie

He was top dog again and this time the trophy was with him. Back where it belonged, in European hands. It had been hard-won in the opposition's backyard and now it was his team who were the home side. They were well acquainted with the surroundings, yet it was unfamiliar territory. This wasn't the Belfry – not England or Scotland. This was new ground for the Ryder Cup: Spain. No question who was the centre of attention: the skipper, the legend, the man who had made European golf sexy. This week would be all about one man: Seve. It would be the tried-and-tested guys whom he would depend upon. The skipper was full of enthusiasm but he had better not interfere too much; this stalwart knew what he was doing, thank you very much. The skipper wouldn't be able to resist, though, but he would be forgiven just as long as Europe hung on to the trophy.

As Bernard Gallacher raised the Ryder Cup at the presentation ceremony at Oak Hill in 1995 so thoughts turned to Europe's defence of the trophy. It would take place at Valderrama on the Costa del Sol and would be the first match to be played in continental Europe. There were no prizes for guessing who would lead Europe, because there was only one candidate: Severiano Ballesteros. His game had deserted him so he would be no use to the side as a player, but it was inconceivable that a Ryder Cup could be staged in Spain without Seve playing a leading role. No one had done more to popularise the game in the boom years of the eighties and nineties in Europe. His dashing good looks, electric smile, swashbuckling style and combative attitude connected with fans all over the world and in particular in Britain where he won three Open Championships. As Colin Montgomerie would say on more than one occasion, Seve was Europe's version of the great Arnold Palmer.

'He is the most charismatic figure the European Tour has ever had,' Montgomerie told the *Observer* in 2003. 'He has an aura around him that very few people in the world have. The only other person I have met with the same effect on people was Sean Connery. The thing about Seve is that he can walk into a room and you know he's there even though you can't see him.'

Monty's regard for Ballesteros and his effect on the game could not be higher. The two players have enjoyed a long and fruitful friendship, as Seve indicates in his foreword for this book. They also shared a healthy rivalry from the moment the Spaniard pipped the Scot in a play-off for the 1991 Volvo PGA Championship at Wentworth. That was the year they became Ryder Cup team-mates for the first time. In the early nineties they were often contesting titles as Monty began to muscle in on the territory occupied by Ballesteros, Nick Faldo, Ian Woosnam, José Maria Olazábal and Bernhard Langer at the top of the European game.

No one disputed Ballesteros' right to succeed Gallacher as captain. He had unanimous support. The Spaniard's sheer enthusiasm for the role during the match became its defining characteristic. It sometimes led to unwanted interference from the skipper. Monty was one of those on the receiving end. It was as though Seve wanted to hit every shot and influence every development. Sometimes it was a hindrance, but no one doubted his motivation and it ultimately served as an inspiration to the European team. 'Being captain in his native Spain, he desperately did not want to be on the losing side and as a result he was everywhere that week,' Montgomerie told his Captain's Blog at Europeantour.com. 'We joked there must be ten Seves on the course because whenever you were about to get ready to hit a shot he seemed to be there. I think he was the only captain in living memory to have put his golf buggy through a 10,000-mile service at the end of the week!'

It was appropriate that the Ryder Cup should be taken to continental Europe for the first time in 1997. Of the twelve players Ballesteros led only five were from the British Isles, the smallest contingent in the history of the match. Europe showed six changes from the team that had won back the trophy in New York State two years earlier. Mark James, Howard Clark, Philip Walton, David Gilford and Sam Torrance made way for an influx of new blood. There was an abundance of untried talent that had forced its way into the team: the likes of Darren Clarke, Lee Westwood, Thomas Björn and the captain's pick, Jesper Parnevik. The return of José Maria Olazábal and a debut for Ignacio Garrido boosted the Spanish contingent in the absence of Ballesteros as a player while the Swede Per-Ulrik Johansson and Italy's Costantino Rocca retained their places. So did Ian Woosnam, Bernhard Langer and, of course, Colin

Montgomerie, who again topped the qualifying points table after thoroughly dominating the European Tour season. Nick Faldo was the other wild-card selection for what would be his record eleventh, and last, Ryder Cup.

The assembly of the European team was not without controversy because another Spaniard, Miguel Ángel Martín, had claimed the last qualifying place but suffered a wrist injury that required surgery. Ballesteros insisted that his compatriot needed to prove his fitness to be able to play, especially as he was keeping Olazábal out of the side. It was clear who Seve would prefer in his line-up; he effectively wanted a third wild card to ensure Olly played. Martín was reluctant to comply with the fitness test request and the row rumbled on in the build-up to the match. It was resolved when the European Tour did a deal with Martín that accorded him full status as a member of the side to include exemptions to play in certain big tournaments. Only then did the injured Martín agree to go quietly and allow Olazábal, who happened to be the next highest ranked qualifier, to return to the team.

Montgomerie had also caused his own controversy in the build up to the match. He had given a routine interview to a group of Scottish newspaper reporters in which he was asked to give his thoughts on each of the players in the American team. 'He gave pen pictures on all the American players, just two lines on each,' recalls John Huggan, one of the journalists present and a former Scottish amateur team-mate of Montgomerie. 'When it came to Brad Faxon, Monty said words to the effect of: "He's going through a terrible divorce, he won't be himself", that kind of thing. When he said it, I thought to myself I wouldn't use it, and initially it didn't appear in my paper, the *Glasgow Herald*. But some of the other journalists decided to report his comments and it all kicked off from there. Once it appeared I then had to write about it,' said Huggan, who is a close friend of Faxon. It was, as Huggan readily agrees, a classic story from which the tabloids could make plenty of headlines – a player calling into question an opponent's ability in the face of personal difficulties.

Naturally, the story flew across the Atlantic. It didn't show Montgomerie in the best light and didn't impress the Americans. The comment would ultimately drip with irony because the Scot found himself in exactly the same position as Faxon seven years later.

Perhaps Montgomerie's guard was down as he was talking to Scottish reporters with whom he would regularly meet and enjoy a good rapport. Monty also probably felt a need to make his observations about Faxon because Europe were being forced to talk up their chances. Despite holding the trophy, they were considered serious underdogs for the 1997 match. Europe's big guns were seen as being past their best, there were too many newcomers and the Martín affair had been unsettling. By contrast, the American team, which was captained by Tom Kite, could boast nine of the world's top sixteen players. Europe had two. In America, *Golfweek* went as far as to say: 'To think Europe will win this Ryder Cup is to think Clinton gets a third term.' The Americans had the reigning Open Champion, Justin Leonard, the recent winner of the US PGA, Davis Love, and the youngster who had begun the major year by winning the Masters. His name was Tiger Woods.

Montgomerie wasn't the only one in the European contingent who felt obliged to talk up their chances of retaining the trophy. Nick Faldo, who had won his sixth and final major title when he won the Masters the previous year, was compelled to explain what he believed was the key statistic from the previous dozen years of Ryder Cup action. He pointed out: 'Since 1985 the European team has a better record in the Ryder Cup than the American team.' Such posturing is in stark contrast to the way captains and players have regarded more recent matches, where the 'phoney war' has been all about which team can successfully argue the case for being considered underdogs. Montgomerie ended that sequence in early 2010 when he pronounced his European team to be firm favourites to regain the trophy at Celtic Manor. 'With so many of my players near the top of the world rankings how can we be considered anything other than favourites?' he said.

This bullish attitude was evident thirteen years earlier when Seve Ballesteros was captain. The Spaniard had no problem in talking up his team. Europe felt aggrieved that so few observers were giving them any chance of beating a mighty American side that counted the young phenomenon Tiger Woods in their number. 'This is the first time Tiger Woods plays in the Ryder Cup,' Ballesteros was quick to say. 'I think any of my golfers can play against Tiger Woods and beat Tiger Woods.' Colin Montgomerie would not have to wait long to find out if his captain was right.

With so many newcomers in their team, Europe were counting on Montgomerie as never before. His crucial singles win over Ben Crenshaw at Oak Hill maintained his growing reputation as one of Europe's most important players and helped counterbalance his disappointing return of just one point in partnership with Faldo and Sam Torrance. In 1997 he was undoubtedly Europe's number one player, even though he had missed out on another major opportunity when he lost the US Open to Ernie Els by a single shot at the Congressional Country Club in Washington. Monty had been in tears as he departed, having missed from around five feet for a par at the 17th to drop out of a share of the lead with the South African. It was made all the more disappointing because Els had beaten Monty in a play-off for the same title in 1994 and the Scot had now been runner-up in a major on three occasions since finishing third on his US Open debut five years earlier. There was no need to press any panic buttons, but Els had established himself as the pre-eminent golfer of the time, despite Montgomerie's evident ability to have claimed that mantle. Majors were coming and going with Monty constantly arriving among the favourites and departing alongside the also-rans.

The week before his US Open near-miss, Montgomerie won the European Grand Prix at Slaley Hall in Northumberland. He fired a final-round 65 to win by five shots and then drove from the North East of England back to London in a journey that lasted eight hours rather than the four he had expected. He was barely home in time to catch his flight to Washington the next day. This was typical Monty: never mind that it was a major the following week. He was on a relentless march, collecting titles on the European Tour and taking his chances with the biggest events on the calendar, rather than targeting them for extra preparation. Later in his career he would acknowledge the error of his ways and he was left to rue being hit by jet-lag-induced dizziness during a bad-tempered, rain-interrupted, second round 76 that had followed a pace-setting 65 at the Congressional. 'That second round is where I lost that US Open. I might have done things differently with hindsight,' he later admitted.

Even so, he backed up his European Grand Prix win with

that runner's-up finish in the US Open and then returned to Europe to win the Irish Open. Also that year he won the unofficial Accenture World Championship matchplay event, his one tournament victory on American soil, and claimed the individual title at the World Cup. Montgomerie had started 1997 as the third best player in the world and was ranked number five at the time of the Ryder Cup behind only the number one Greg Norman, Nick Price, Els and the man who had rocketed to number two in the world, Tiger Woods.

Woods had burst to the fore with his stunning win at the Masters five months earlier and Montgomerie had the closest of views of the then twenty-one-year-old's extraordinary talents. Rounds of 72 and 67 had provided the Scot with his best Augusta start and he found himself three shots behind Woods in second place at the halfway stage. It was enough to put him in the final pairing with the eventual champion. Monty confessed to feeling very nervous in Woods' presence as they stood on the first tee. He was worried about not being able to match Tiger's prodigious driving and felt in awe of the golfer who was now capturing the imagination of the sporting public. Both players made par fours at the first, the distance of Monty's opening drive assisted by an energising bounce off the back of a fairway bunker that propelled his ball beyond that of his playing partner. It was the only time there was any sense of parity in a dramatic third round. Woods brought the famous Augusta National to its knees with a scintillating 65, a round that first gave thought to the notion that courses would need to be 'Tiger-proofed' in future. Montgomerie was blown away as he slipped out of contention with a miserable 74. He knew he was witnessing history being made and had been 'mesmerised' by Woods' performance.

Only one thing was more startling than Woods' golf that day and it was that Monty agreed to go to the Augusta interview room after such a disappointing round. 'Of course he will win,' a shattered Montgomerie told the assembled reporters. 'What is more he will win by more than nine shots.' Monty was proved correct as the young American swept to a record-breaking twelve-shot victory while the Scot's hopes of being the best of the rest disappeared with a shell-shocked final-round 81.

At Valderrama there was the chance of a measure of revenge for Montgomerie. His long-standing partnership with Nick Faldo was at an end and instead he was reunited with the German with whom he had teamed up on his debut, Bernhard Langer. Like the Monty/Faldo combination this was another pairing that brought together two of Europe's biggest names. Ballesteros knew their value and sent them out in the strategically important final match of the morning fourballs – the European skipper having preferred to start the Ryder Cup with the better-ball format rather than foursomes. Naturally Tom Kite wanted his own heavyweight duo for such a contest and so Montgomerie and Langer found themselves up against that man Tiger Woods, who partnered his great friend and Tour mentor Mark O'Meara.

Play was delayed by a severe storm that swept through southern Spain and would have left any other course unplayable for the rest of the day. It was only the exceptional drainage system installed at Valderrama that made play at all possible.

Montgomerie was eager to get going. He had found the practice days rather tiresome, having never been one for spending hours on the range in the week of a tournament.

For Monty the purpose of a practice round is to learn the course, but this was a layout he knew better than the back of his golf glove because it was a regular stop on the European Tour. He couldn't escape, though. Practice rounds are an intrinsic part of Ryder Cup week. Tickets are sold and those who pay to attend do so in expectation of seeing all the players. This is where Tiger Woods has often been allowed to disappoint spectators because captains indulge his desire to complete his preparations in solitude before the gates have been opened.

Monty played most of his practice rounds with Langer as it seemed more than likely that he would be paired with the meticulous German. Their partnership was living proof that opposites can attract because Montgomerie is a player who gets on with the game at speed while Langer will leave no divot unturned in his exhaustive preparation for every shot. Monty was unconcerned and believed that Langer's slower pace of play might help his own game by giving him more time to think through his shots properly.

Not that this was evident in the opening clash against O'Meara and Woods. The European pair failed to find their best form and the great Tiger Woods also seemed overawed. By contrast, his partner O'Meara was like a man possessed and he was the difference between the two teams. There was no question of the Europeans being intimidated or inhibited by the prospect of taking on the young Masters champion: they relished the opportunity. It was just that they could do nothing in the face of the fine golf being played by Woods' partner once the youngster had put the Americans ahead. Woods played the par five fourth like a veteran rather than a young tyro. He forwent his driver off the tee, laid up with a nine iron, flicked a sand wedge on to the green and holed from inside 20 feet for a winning birdie. It was the kind of precision golf that Valderrama has always demanded, with its narrow fairways, claustrophobic overhanging cork trees and tiny greens.

Despite all those unwanted practice rounds Monty had lost the feel for where to position the ball in his stance and his hooked tee shot into the gallery on the first set the tone for a miserable morning for the Scot. After falling behind at the fourth, neither of the European players managed to par the sixth and Woods and O'Meara carried their two-hole advantage to the turn. Woods then birdied the tenth from seven feet to increase the advantage. It was a rare flicker from Tiger who was thankful for the steady and efficient play of his partner. Europe won their only hole at the 13th when both Americans slipped up, but O'Meara immediately atoned with an immaculate birdie at the 14th. Then he holed from just off the 16th green with a sweetly judged right-to-left putt that he knew all the way was going to drop. It wrapped up a 3 and 2 win that ultimately meant the opening session was shared two points apiece.

In the other three matches the golf was scintillating. José Maria Olazábal in tandem with Costantino Rocca edged home against Davis Love and Phil Mickelson in the top match, and Fred Couples and Brad Faxon were taken all the way to the last before beating the new combination of Nick Faldo and Lee Westwood. Then, in the third match, the Swedish combination of Per-Ulrik Johansson and Jesper Parnevik won another tight contest against Tom Lehman and Jim Furyk. The extrovert Parnevik, who wore his cap with an upturned peak that became his trademark, brilliantly birdied the last two holes to hold off the Americans. Less had been expected of the

Swedes: they were hardly Europe's headline act, yet they were round in a better-ball 65 that firmly put the much-vaunted Montgomerie/Langer combination in the shade.

Ballesteros still believed in the partnership, though. Monty is a doughnut to Langer's Ryvita, but the strength of this duo didn't so much lie in their diversity as in their mutual respect. That had been born when they paired up for the first time at Kiawah Island and stayed with them throughout their careers. The Spanish captain knew he wanted to keep them together even though Montgomerie had been hitting it all over the place. Ballesteros spoke to both players and Langer reassured the skipper by saying the course was set up perfectly for them in foursomes and so they were given another chance. Again they were up against Woods and O'Meara and the younger of the two Americans was delighted. 'Perfect,' he said when he heard the draw, but it better suited the Europeans because it gave them an immediate opportunity to avenge the morning defeat – just so long as Monty could get his act together.

Montgomerie skipped lunch on the Friday and instead he went straight to the range to link up with his coach, Bill Ferguson, to fix his long game. The way he had sprayed the ball around in the morning fourballs was completely out of character and the man who normally uses the practice facilities for nothing more than a quick tune-up and pre-round gossip knew some serious cramming was required. Montgomerie has always been a very pragmatic golfer, wary of too much theory getting in the way of what he knows works for him. Other players concentrate on the technical side of the game; Montgomerie is very much a feel player who uses the same length of swing for every shot. For example, if he wants the ball to fly lower into the wind he will swing more softly because this will impart less backspin on the ball. 'That's what makes it fly higher, so less backspin means a lower ball flight,' he reasons. That interval on Friday was all about finding the fix that would enable him to return to the form that had yet again made him Europe's top player that year. It was perhaps the most important practice time spent by anyone on either side in the 1997 Ryder Cup.

Montgomerie was a new man in the afternoon while Tiger Woods, the youngest player in the match, struggled with the alternate shot format. Monty now had confidence in his setup and swing and it helped further that half of his shots were being played by the ultra-reliable Bernhard Langer. They quickly moved ahead and were two up after three holes. The American pair bogeyed the second and the Europeans beat par for the first time all day when they birdied the third. Woods' extra distance paid off at the long fourth to cut the arrears but the European duo found themselves two up again after eight. Then, on the ninth, Montgomerie's recovery of form was confirmed with a stunning long iron approach that set up a birdie that put them further ahead. Langer had switched putters at the interval – 'I always travel with two' – and the switch was paying dividends. Woods never changes his putting blade (not until he experimented at the 2010 Open anyway), but must have felt tempted after missing from inside six feet at the 14th to fall four down with four to play. Throughout the match the twenty-one-year-old seemed to be trying too hard; his efforts proved counter-productive and one spectator's t-shirt which read 'Tiger – not the full Monty' was being proved correct.

Langer sensed the moment to finish off the match one hole later. The greens were still soft and receptive after all the early morning rain and he launched a tee shot of supreme accuracy on the 200-yard par three that landed like a dart into a board no more than four feet from the hole. Woods could not match such precision and O'Meara's long-range birdie attempt missed, leaving Monty with two putts for the match. He needed just one, curling the birdie attempt into the centre of the cup.

It was a thumping win – 5 and 3 – and heralded a fine afternoon for Seve Ballesteros's team. No one was more relieved than the skipper. He said: 'When Colin and Langer lost in the morning 3 and 2, I'm sure that 90 per cent of people wondered why has Seve put those two players back out in the afternoon? They won 5 and 3 so I was lucky. But if they lost I would have been a terrible captain.' These comments came as he awaited a resumption in play. The previous afternoon's session still needed to be completed the following morning.

Once the golf resumed the young Lee Westwood was faced with a match winning ten-footer on the 16th green. Ballesteros's decision to pair the English debutant with his legendary compatriot Nick Faldo was a masterstroke. Westwood revelled in showing off his talents to a partner of such repute. The rookie from Nottinghamshire calmly rolled in the putt to give threefold benefit. It gave Faldo a record twenty-fourth Ryder Cup point, and Europe the lead as well as a significant sense of momentum off the back of Monty and Langer's victory the previous evening. In the bottom match two more rookies, Ignacio Garrido and Jesper Parnevik, held their nerve to claim an important half with Phil Mickelson and Tom Lehman, ensuring the underdog Europeans stayed ahead. They led by a single point 4½-3½ at the completion of the first two sessions.

Ballesteros decided to split the Monty/Langer combination to blood the debutant Darren Clarke alongside the Scot. They had practised together earlier in the week and Clarke had finished second to Montgomerie in the qualifying table. The man from Northern Ireland was determined to make a point. Clarke was particularly upset that he had not been used on the opening day, given that he had qualified for the team in such an elevated position. But one overwhelming factor outstripped such feelings of slight and frustration – an inevitable and huge desire to beat the USA and keep the Cup.

Montgomerie was thrilled to effectively be put in charge of a newcomer. He relished such an avuncular role, the feeling that he was the 'captain of this partnership'. It was fourball play so there was room for Clarke to grow into the match, but they were up against the top American pairing of Fred Couples and Davis Love III and it was the lead game where Europe had the chance of sustaining the momentum that seemed to be with them.

It proved to be an outstanding contest, although Montgomerie was stunned by the antics of his partner's caddie as early as the third hole. Clarke had made his par three for a guaranteed half, but the Scot was still to play from a greenside bunker. If he could hole it Europe would win the hole. 'Monty sculled it flying across the green,' recalled Clarke's bagman, Billy Foster. 'It shot past the hole towards me and I stuck my hand out, took a great catch and yelled "HOWZAT!" You should have seen the look on Monty's face.'

The Americans were one up at the turn thanks to a stunning piece of work by Couples at the short par four eighth. He had around 75 yards to the flag and struck a beautifully judged wedge that landed on the soft green some ten feet past the pin before spinning back towards the hole, eventually dropping for a spectacular hole-winning eagle. Couples then birdied the tenth to double the American lead, but this simply spurred the Europeans back into action. Clarke birdied the long eleventh and then Montgomerie hit a superb tee shot at the par three 12th and rammed home the birdie chance to level the contest.

The key to successful fourball play is to dovetail, to make sure you are in when your partner is out. The Americans call it ham and egging it – you don't have to be at your best all the time, just when your partner is in trouble. This was something the European pair were incapable of achieving at the 13th. Monty rattled around the cork trees to leave duties to Clarke, who missed for par from six feet and they were one down again. The match was turning into a thriller. Clarke hit his approach at the next to inches and it was all square again. The 16th was halved in spectacular birdies as Couples matched Monty and both pairs went to the 17th knowing this controversial par five designed by Europe's skipper would prove pivotal.

The hole measured 511 yards, the fairway was undulating, there was a patch of short rough across the middle of it beyond driving distance. Water stretched down the left of the hole and then swept round the front of the green that sloped from back to front. Bunkers guarded the back of the green which was less than a cricket pitch in depth. The hole called for power, accuracy and good fortune. It didn't require interference from the skipper, even if he had designed it; at least, that was the view of this European pair. Ballesteros could not help himself, though. He knew the importance of this match. Couples and Love were America's super-pairing, the momentum was with Europe and it could not be allowed to falter, especially on this hole – *his* hole. Seve arrived to direct operations, much to the annoyance of the senior partner in this pairing. 'Sometimes he's better just staying in his buggy,' Montgomerie would later say.

Both Clarke and Monty drove into the rough and that should have made up their minds to play the percentages and lay up short of the water. But Ballesteros thought Clarke could smash one on to the green and encouraged the rookie to take it on. It was a conversation that Montgomerie felt he, not his captain, should have been having with his junior partner. He had been helping him all the way round, lining up putts and doing as Langer had done for him on his debut. On this occasion his advice to Clarke would have been diametrically opposed to the counsel the Ulsterman was receiving from his enthusiastic captain. Clarke was persuaded to go for the green even though Monty and his experienced caddie Alastair McLean could see it was a silly decision. The inevitable splash followed.

Montgomerie and Couples laid up short of the water while, as the only man on the fairway, Love was able to power his second shot just beyond the back of the green. The pin was cut at the front, tantalisingly close to the pond.

As Montgomerie began to weigh up his third shot, Ballesteros became involved again. He instructed Clarke to take his penalty drop further back than he would usually and close to Monty's ball. That way he could play first and show his partner how the ball would react on the green. Clarke played a fine shot to 12 feet. Couples now insisted that Clarke should mark his ball, but the Europeans weren't sure that he was able to do so from 80 yards away in the rough. The players deferred to their captains on this issue and Ballesteros insisted this wasn't allowed. His opposite number, Tom Kite, disagreed and the chief referee John Paramor was called to settle the dispute. All this was going on as Monty was trying to prepare for a vital wedge shot over water to a narrow strip of green. The referee sided with the US, leaving a disgruntled Ballesteros and four very nervous golfers as Clarke went off to mark his ball.

Monty was particularly worried. He had left himself 58 yards to the pin, a dreaded 'in-between' distance that was neither one thing nor another. It wasn't a full-lob wedge, nor was it a half-lob wedge. Certainly the only thing that was full was the banking around the green – it was packed with spectators as thousands gathered to witness this crucial hole. Seve came over to Monty. 'Are you okay?' he enquired.

Monty wanted none of it, telling his skipper he was 'as nervous as hell' and to leave him alone. He finally settled over the shot. As his lob wedge came through at contact there was a large splash from the sodden fairway. The ball cleared the water and then the pin before landing, hopping forward, stopping and then trickling back past its own pitch mark down the slope towards the hole. A brilliant pitch just became better and better. Montgomerie's nerve stayed with him despite the most intense pressure and scrutiny imaginable. Couples hadn't put his pitch from the rough close and Love struggled with his chip from the back of the green. Suddenly the lead partner for Europe, the continent's number one, had a birdie putt of around eight feet for the hole. It was downhill, with a vicious break. Sometimes he would ask his caddie McLean to help with the reading of putts, but on fast downhillers their policy was to leave it to the player. He was the one who could *feel* the putt and instinctively calculate how much borrow to allow for and how hard to hit the ball. Confidence coursing through his veins, relishing the role of senior partner, determined to show his captain he could do this on his own, Europe's number one judged it to perfection. One up with one to play, a guaranteed half at the very least and every chance of a full point for Europe. Amid deafening roars Monty touched knuckles with Clarke and shook hands with his captain as he marched to the final tee.

Like the closing hole at the Belfry, the last at Valderrama did not set up well for Montgomerie and the left-to-right flight path of his shots. The hole swings in the opposite direction and the prime position for an approach shot is the left half of the fairway, which is particularly hard to find for someone who fades their drive. Monty tugged his tee shot into the left rough, while Clarke hit a belter down the middle. Both players then found the green, the Scotsman with a sensational blind approach having been blocked out by the cork trees. Love and Couples, who by now had won four World Cups for their country, were reeling. Couples was bunkered and Love was in light rough just off the putting surface. Montgomerie's putt for the match shaved the hole and to have any chance Love then had to hole from off the green. He failed and Europe had won another point and the father figure Montgomerie was the hero.

Immediately afterwards Monty was asked about the role of his captain, particularly on that crucial 17th hole. Grinning and thrilled with the win, the Scotsman hardly provided a ringing endorsement of his leader. He said: 'He sometimes gets a bit too intense. You know you're going along okay until he arrives and the whole thing then buzzes and shuffles around. You wish he would just relax a bit, especially on the seventeenth. There are many ways to play the hole, yes, but there is only one way to play it at the time.'

But they were still desperate to win the Ryder Cup for

Ballesteros. It was this imperative that drove on the team as the momentum they had gained at the end of the first day turned into a full-blown Saturday surge. Montgomerie and Clarke's win was one of three that went the way of the Europeans. Only Mickelson and Lehman managed to garner anything for the visiting team from the fourballs and that was a mere half-point in the bottom match against the Spaniards José Maria Olazábal and Ignacio Garrido. Europe went into the afternoon foursomes with a commanding 8-4 lead and Tom Kite's team, the pre-match favourites, were wobbling badly.

Ballesteros wanted to capitalise on the advantage and offer the opposition no respite. Naturally he turned to Montgomerie and reunited his number one with the trusty Bernhard Langer. Monty was delighted to serve, but couldn't quite believe he had been sent out first again for the afternoon session. He only became aware when Langer intercepted him as he departed the 18th after his fourball victory to say that they were an item once again. 'When are we off?' Monty asked. 'Ten minutes ago,' came the reply. There followed a frantic rush, a quick change and lunch on the run as Montgomerie bounded to the first tee wondering why on earth he had been given such a rapid turn-around. They were up against Jim Furyk and Lee Janzen, who was without his regular caddie, the Englishman Dave Musgrove, who thought to help America would be a conflict of interest.

Despite losing the first to a birdie, the European pair were soon in front of what proved another tight contest. Montgomerie's imperious approach to the back of the ninth green set up a birdie that put the Europeans two up at the turn. On the inward half fortune fluctuated one way and then the other before the home pair found themselves two up with two to play. The Americans hit back at the 17th where Janzen knocked in his birdie putt that had him confidently pointing his index finger and mouthing 'one more, one more', as he headed for the final tee.

Given the morning weather delays this was going to be the only match that would finish that evening and taking a full point to bed was of the utmost importance.

Beneath reddening skies and in gathering gloom, Montgomerie and Janzen both failed to find the fairway from the tee. For the Americans Furyk chased their second shot up to the front of the green, while Langer had no chance of locating the putting surface with Europe's second shot. 'I remember saying to Bernhard on the way to the ball, "Just focus and play your own game because Seve is bound to be there" and, sure enough, when we walked down to the ball, Seve was there, with his hands on his knees, peering down to study the ball. Where he had come from I just don't know, but that was the way it was all week,' Monty said. 'The ball was dead, absolutely dead.' Ballesteros was trying to imagine an elaborate shot that only he in his prime could contemplate and Langer was having nothing to do with it. 'As Seve was pacing up and down the fairway, Bernhard had already chipped out. Believe me, it was the fastest shot he ever played in his life!' Montgomerie recalled.

The Scot was left with a nine-iron third which he struck with deadly accuracy to draw a huge roar from the crowd as it settled five feet from the hole. Now it was time for Janzen to putt from fully 50 feet away. He struck it well, too well, and the ball charged towards the hole. A crouching Tiger Woods could be heard imploring the ball to slow down: 'Sit, sit, sit, sit,' he whispered urgently. Janzen's ball didn't heed the call: it charged on to the back of the green ten feet past the hole.

Furyk's desperate return went five feet long and with Europe having two putts from the same distance for the half they needed Janzen had no alternative but to offer a congratulatory handshake.

Montgomerie now had three from a possible four points, an astonishingly improbable haul given how poorly he had played on the opening morning. More important, Europe were in an incredibly strong position, leading 9-4 as darkness fell with the Saturday schedule still not completed. To win back the trophy America would have to score ten and a half points from the fifteen that were left to be played for in the match. 'In other words they were slightly more dead than Franco,' Rick Reilly told readers of *Sports Illustrated*.

The remaining three foursome matches resumed on the Sunday morning. Scott Hoch and Jeff Maggert secured victory as the Nick Faldo/Lee Westwood team lost its touch on the greens but it was Europe's only defeat. Parnevik and Garrido halved with Woods and Justin Leonard and Olazábal and Rocca trounced Couples and Love 5 and 4. Europe had claimed six points out of eight from the second sequence of fourballs and foursomes. They would need just four points from the closing twelve singles to win the Cup for the second match running and a mere three and a half to retain the trophy.

It seemed that from Europe's point of view little could go wrong. The hard work had been done and Montgomerie, who would be sent out late in the order, appeared to be nothing more than an insurance policy. The thought that it could come down to him seemed remote to say the least.

Rather than go with his big guns first to try to kill off the opposition early, Seve Ballesteros chose to pack the back end of his batting order with his better players. This strategy was the outcome of a sleepless night as he consulted with vice-captains Miguel Ángel Jiménez and Mark James. He lay awake plotting his Seve strategy to retain the precious trophy. From a position of taking a five-point lead into the singles anything less than winning the match outright would be deemed a failure. The Americans were shell-shocked and enlisted the help of former President George Bush Senior to provide a pep talk. Brad Faxon had told television viewers in the eighty-five countries receiving pictures of the event that the game was all but up, that it was very hard to envisage any way back for his team. Tom Lehman had no truck with such a defeatist attitude. 'I think those guys can be had. I like our chances,' he said.

Fred Couples gave them the perfect start. For the third time he had been drawn to face Ian Woosnam and thrashed the diminutive Welshman 8 and 7. But Per-Ulrik Johansson condemned Davis Love to another defeat, the US PGA champion's fourth in four matches. Next in the order was Costantino Rocca, who had been desperate for a crack at Tiger Woods and who had said beforehand he felt it was his destiny to meet the Masters champion. Rocca had been in the final pair with Woods in the last round at Augusta and marked his record-breaking scorecard. Mind you, as Ballesteros had pointed out: 'Everyone wants Tiger.' It was the Italian who got his wish to take on the mighty American and he gained a measure of revenge for the dusting he received at the hands of Woods the previous April. Three up with three to play the forty-year old Italian came up with a low, skimming one iron from under the cork trees to set up a par that was enough to close out a famous victory. 'It's called golf, you can't always win. I gave it all I had today,' Woods said. 'It just wasn't enough. I've hit the ball well this week, but I just couldn't get the putter to roll and build any momentum that way. Consequently I will have a disappointing record.' It read played 5, won 1, lost 3, halved 1. Europe, meanwhile, were now just two points from outright victory with nine matches still on the course.

Then the fightback began. Justin Leonard halved with Thomas Björn in a match of the highest quality. Europe were within a single point of retaining the trophy but Ballesteros was starting to fret. From where would that point come? Clarke, Parnevik and Olazábal all lost and further down the order Garrido in the last match out had already perished 7 and 6 against Lehman, whose optimistic prophecy was starting to look less and less outlandish. Faldo in the penultimate match was struggling against Furyk and Westwood was down against Maggert.

Europe were going to have to lean on their dependable duo – Bernhard Langer and Colin Montgomerie. The German was sent out eighth and was up against Brad Faxon. Monty was tenth in the order facing the rookie Scott Hoch. As the late-afternoon rain started to fall Langer closed out victory on the 17th green to ensure that the trophy would indeed remain in European hands. But that would be rendered a hollow achievement if the match was not won outright. The glory would be all America's for a stunning final-day fightback to earn a draw.

The rain was hammering down now and there was just one match left on the course, Montgomerie's absorbing clash with Scott Hoch. 'We spent four hours of hell together, really,' Montgomerie recalled. He had been two down early on and by the turn was trailing by one hole. 'At the tenth I was happy because it looked like we might get a walk in the park,' Montgomerie said. 'But it didn't turn out that way. My caddie and I became aware around the twelfth or thirteenth hole that it might come down to us. It was quite a nerve-wracking experience.' Monty crucially halved at the 14th without having to do anything spectacular. A par was enough.

It was still all square when a massive roar echoed across the course as they stood on the 16th tee. A steward erroneously told Hoch it was because Europe had reached the magic figure of 14½ points. 'The official said he heard it over his earphones. I momentarily let my guard down and hit it in the right rough,' Hoch said. The match was, in fact, still alive and Hoch's mistake handed Montgomerie the lead for the first time with only two holes to go.

There was now much more on this than Monty's unbeaten record in singles play, but that provided some crutch upon which to lean at such an important moment. In the soaking conditions both players laid up short of the water on Seve's 17th before Hoch hit a hole-winning pitch to within inches of the hole.

It was all square going to the last. Europe needed just a half from Monty to win the Ryder Cup for the second year running. Caddies and other members of the European entourage had aborted their celebrations as vice-captain Mark James instructed them to head back on to the course to offer Monty as much support as possible. Hoch had the honour and pulled his drive into the left rough. Sensing the moment has always been the Scotsman's greatest Ryder Cup asset and he seized it with a magnificent drive that split the narrow fairway. 'The tension was incredible as we stood on the final tee,' Montgomerie recalled. 'It is not an easy tee shot, but I'm proud to say I hit one of my best ever drives, a shot later voted European Tour Shot of the Year.'

Roars of delight seemed to echo across the mountains of Andalusia, but there was relatively little applause because spectators were clinging on to their brollies in the teeming rain. As the players left the tee it was as though they were being followed by a relentless wave of umbrellas from the trailing galleries. 'In the circumstances that was one of the greatest drives we've ever seen because on that eighteenth at Valderrama anything can happen,' remembered Ken Schofield.

Hoch tried to find the green from the saturated rough but it was never a realistic prospect. Montgomerie's wonderful trusty three wood from the tee set up a routine nine iron that found the heart of the green. The game was all but up. Hoch pitched on for three and Montgomerie had a guaranteed two putts to win the Ryder Cup. He was also desperately keen to win his match as well.

The birdie putt trundled up towards the hole to prompt a roar the equal of a cup final winning goal. Montgomerie had made par and could not be beaten, Europe had triumphed and if Hoch missed from 13 feet Monty would win his match and claim a stellar haul of four points out of five. The rain poured down and forward stepped captain Seve Ballesteros, picking up Hoch's marker to concede the putt and give the American a half. This act of sportsmanship from Europe's captain denied Montgomerie a full point. What did it matter? Europe had won by 14½ points to 13½. Monty was the hero. He was mobbed as the green became a swarm of soaking, jubilant humanity as the vanquished Americans trudged away. It was a sweet, sweet moment for Monty, arms aloft in the centre of it all. Except it could have been even sweeter had he been allowed to complete a personal victory.

When competitive juices flow as readily as they do through

Montgomerie it is hard to close the lock gates. It is even harder to accept them being shut by someone else, even when that person is your captain. His singles record, that began so unpromisingly at Kiawah Island in 1991 where he somehow gained a half from Mark Calcavecchia's implosion, was now an increasing source of pride. It was starting to become one of the defining aspects of his career. But, ultimately, Monty had steered Europe to the all-important destination of 14½ points. That is what truly mattered most and he knew it. Nowadays he is pretty magnanimous about Ballesteros' concession. Montgomerie said: 'After having four hours of battling around, of course I wanted to win that match. But at least he never gave it to him for a win, at least it was only for a half and that was fine by me.'

Monty was a hero and his popularity among the home fans had never been higher. His standing as a Ryder Cup fighter soared further and his deeds in that team environment helped his growing reputation in a game famed for its sense of fair-play to climb to an even more elevated position.

He was where he wanted to be, the position he would occupy for so much of his career: centre of attention. Often he would crave such scrutiny, but there were occasions when he would not.

7

25 MARCH 2005, THE ENJOY JAKARTA
STANDARD CHARTER INDONESIAN OPEN,
14TH HOLE, CENGKARENG GOLF CLUB, JAKARTA

'If the spot where the ball is to be placed is impossible to determine, it must be estimated and the ball placed on the estimated spot' – **Rules of Golf**

*H*e didn't want to be there. He didn't want to be in Indonesia, in Jakarta, on this golf course, on this hole, on this bunker face where he couldn't stand without nearly falling over. He didn't want to be under that cloud. The dirty, big, black one that was about to explode. He wouldn't have needed to be there if he'd finished first the previous week. The tournament in China he'd won in 2002; if he'd won it again he wouldn't need to be in Indonesia, Jakarta, on the 14th hole looking at this horrible little shot with a massive black cloud hanging over him. Stubborn things those clouds, hard to shift. But he hadn't won last week, missed the play-off by two shots. Not good enough. Needed better to get back to where he belonged. The elite, the top fifty, that's where he should have been. Then he wouldn't have been in Jakarta. He would have been back with the big boys. The TPC, the Players' Championship, the 'fifth' major, Sawgrass, Florida, that's where he would have been. Not Jakarta, Indonesia. But needs must and the Masters was just round the corner; climb four more spots in the rankings and he'd be there, Augusta,

Georgia in April. Only place to be for the elite. One more push and he could be out of the wilderness. A win would do the job. Work to be done, though. Three under, it wasn't good enough, might not even make the cut. He needed a 62 today and he was still only level par and he'd got this horrible little shot . . .

The klaxon sounded. The electrical storm everyone knew was coming was too close for golf to continue safely. Colin Montgomerie knew this and his mood was not good. He was in need of birdies to make sure he would be around for the weekend action, to survive the cut, to give him the chance of forging an unlikely victory. Such a win would be one of the most valuable of his career. Not the most prestigious, by any stretch of the imagination, but still of serious value because it would provide enough ranking points for him to climb back into the world top fifty. Once that status has been achieved, golfers are able to dine at the game's top table. Eligibility follows for all of the biggest tournaments. Montgomerie had started 2005 as the world's eighty-third best player and would end it celebrating an eighth Order of Merit. He was in the process of restoring his career in the wake of his marriage break-up the previous year. Monty had put together an impressive string of results and he'd been performing under pressure. His main objective was to earn the right to an invitation to the Masters, the first major of the year. The Scot had made thirteen consecutive appearances at the glorious Augusta National and he naturally wanted to keep that run intact. A week earlier he had finished sixth at the TCL Classic in China. Had he won that event the job would have already been done; indeed, he would have been back in the top fifty in time to be playing in America at the prestigious Players' Championship instead of slogging it out in sweaty Indonesia.

The Enjoy Jakarta Standard Charter Indonesian Open was the event that was left for the downstairs brigade. A tournament jointly sanctioned by the European and Asian Tours, it was for rank-and-file players not the high-flyers, who were in Florida competing at the rival PGA Tour's lucrative flagship event. Missing out on the tournament dubbed golf's unofficial 'fifth major' was a blow to Montgomerie's pride, but could be easily rationalised given his marriage split. He was through the worst and putting back together his career. His golf remained solid, a better reflection of his undoubted talents, and he was steadily climbing the rankings. His only enemy was impatience because he needed the ranking to match his ability in time for the start of the major season and the clock was ticking.

On the 14th hole of his second round in Indonesia Montgomerie's immediate prospects looked as bleak as the weather. He was unaware of the consequences of what would happen at that hole, the damage that would be done to his otherwise glorious career. The fallout would rumble through the game with an endurance that no clap of thunder could match. The clouds would periodically clear, but they would return and darken his reputation far longer than he would have wanted or could have anticipated.

The hole in question is guarded by a deep bunker to the front left of the green. The storm was imminent and a poor pulled approach shot had resulted in Montgomerie's ball charging towards the hazard. It came to rest in clinging rough on the sharp down-slope just short of the pale white sand. He was agitated; the day hadn't been going as he'd hoped. The night before, Monty had told guests at a golf clinic that he needed rounds of 62, 61 and 61 to get the win he so desperately wanted.

Sixty-two was not on the agenda now. The leaderboard showed Montgomerie level par for the thirteen holes completed, three under for the tournament. He was a dropped shot away from missing the halfway cut and suffering a fruitless week for prize money and, more significantly, world ranking points.

When Montgomerie arrived at his ball he surveyed what was going to be a nasty little chip. It was clear the ball would be above his feet and assuming an effective stance was proving very tricky. Where he would ideally have wanted to stand to make the shot there was only thin air; below lay the sand of the bunker. Taking a stance *in* the bunker was an option but not an attractive one because he would have to hold so far down the club that his hands would be on the graphite section of the shaft rather than on the rubber grip. Monty is a quick player, not one to faff about over shots. But like all pros he recognises the need for due diligence and continued to probe the area trying to find somewhere he could stand to be able to execute the shot. As he gently prodded the grass on the edge of the bunker with his right foot, testing whether it could provide a stable platform for his stance, the hooter sounded. This is the universal signal to players that it is unsafe to continue playing because electrical storms are nearby. They must cease play immediately and the accepted protocol is for them to mark their ball with a couple of tees, put it in their pocket and leave the course. Here a flustered Montgomerie made a key error of judgement.

At the sound of the klaxon he clearly decided the problems of the shot he faced could wait until tomorrow. It might not be so difficult to fathom in fresher morning air after a decent night's sleep. He looked up, sprinted up the slope of the bunker, marched across the green, and slammed his wedge into his golf bag. He had not taken the trouble to mark his ball. By not so doing he had broken no rules, but he was in breach of the accepted code of practice for pro golfers in such circumstances. Golf balls can disappear during weather interruptions, especially those that last until the next morning as this one most certainly would. If a ball becomes the property of an enterprising souvenir hunter then it becomes difficult for it to be replaced in precisely the correct spot. Better to leave a couple of tees in the ground to mark the correct location and take the ball with you.

That afternoon Montgomerie's problems on the 14th hole were being shown live on television and another player in the field, Denmark's Søren Kjeldsen, was watching. He was intrigued by how this celebrated figure, the highest ranked player in the field, would extricate himself from this awkward spot. He would have to wait until the following morning to find out.

Upon the resumption Montgomerie returned to the hole to find that his ball had disappeared and no doubt had become the prized memento of an Indonesian golf fan. The culprit could have had no idea of the impact of this act of petty theft. Rule Six, which deals with 'Player's Responsibilities' in the pocket-sized two-hundred-page book that governs the game of golf deals with how they should continue in such circumstances. More precisely, Rule 6–8d states: *Play must be resumed from where it was discontinued, even if a resumption occurs on a subsequent day.* The rule goes on to deal with the circumstance Monty was now facing. *If the player's ball or ball marker is moved (including by wind or water) while play is discontinued, a ball or ball marker must be placed on the spot from which the original ball or ball marker was moved.* So the onus was on Montgomerie to replace his ball on the precise spot where it had lain the previous evening when he had marched with haste from the course. The rule has a further note: *If the spot where the ball is to be placed is impossible to determine, it must be estimated and the ball placed on the estimated spot.* **Penalty for breach of rule 6–8d, Stroke Play Two Strokes.**

The scene that greeted Montgomerie on his return was somewhat different from the one he had left the night before. The course had been bombarded by heavy rain and hailstones. The lush, thick grass that had been standing proud the previous evening had been flattened, and of course Montgomerie's ball was gone. Now he had to estimate the spot where the ball should be replaced and did this in consultation with the two other players in his group, Indian Arjun Atwal and Thongchai Jaidee, of Thailand. Neither player had had much of a view of Monty's predicament the previous afternoon because they were on the green, but they were happy to go along with the Scot's judgement.

Søren Kjeldsen was again watching the television and the coverage of the tournament was back on the 14th green for Monty's chip. Unlike the previous evening he could make a stance that didn't involve standing in the bunker and the top half of the ball was visible. The better lie could be explained by the rough being flattened by the rain, but the positioning of his feet suggested he'd replaced the ball in the wrong spot. The margin was perhaps a little more than the width of a scorecard, but the ball was now in a more advantageous place. Monty played a delightful shot and saved par. Kjeldsen wasn't impressed.

Thereafter that Saturday morning Montgomerie went on to birdie the 16th and 17th holes and, although he bogeyed the last, his 69 was good enough to make the cut. He then fired a third-round 66 before coming agonisingly close to becoming the first man to shoot 59 on the European Tour in the final round. He left a ten-foot birdie putt on the last green just short in a stunning 60 that included a record nine birdies in a row. He finished 18 under par to share fourth place with Frankie Minoza of the Philippines, and took home €34,708 and a useful collection of world ranking points but not enough to claim a place at the Masters. 'I'm trying my hardest to get back to where I feel I should be. I'm trying to get back as many world ranking points as possible,' Monty said. 'This is my eighth tournament in a row where I've not finished outside the top ten [he was actually eleventh in the Heineken Classic, but never mind; his point remained valid]. It's the best golf I have ever played, even back to the mid-nineties.'

Kjeldsen, meanwhile, had contacted the tournament director to express his concerns over where Montgomerie had replaced his ball on the resumption of the second round. José Maria Zamora reviewed television footage and decided there was no need to take any action.

This didn't stop rumblings of discontent in the locker room in the weeks that followed. Breaches of the rules are not tolerated in the professional game; it is the core of the game's code of conduct. Despite his having consulted his playing partners and being cleared by the referee, the concerns that had been raised meant Montgomerie's actions needed to be examined further. When he viewed split-picture footage that confirmed he'd replaced the ball more favourably, Monty agreed it didn't look good. He couldn't disqualify himself – it was too late for that – but he decided it would be wrong to profit financially from the tournament. He gave his Indonesian prize money to the tsunami relief appeal, an act of charity that nonetheless did little to placate a growing band of critics from the Tour's rank and file. It was money, they would claim, that should really have gone into the pockets of his fellow competitors not to those who had suffered in the natural disaster that had struck Asia at the end of 2004. Such was the level of discontent that the matter was put on the agenda when the Tournament Committee, that included Monty and was chaired by Jamie Spence, met at the Forest of Arden in the English Midlands in the week of the British Masters later that spring. This meeting proved as uncomfortable an experience as Monty has endured as he was asked to explain himself to his peers. 'What on earth were you thinking?' was the opening gambit. He was grilled for an hour.

'The committee wanted my view,' Montgomerie said the next day while taking a break from his pre-tournament pro-am duties. 'The question that has been asked is why didn't I mark my ball? As soon as you don't mark the ball and you come back the next morning and it isn't there, there is a guestimate to where your ball was and I guestimated too far off the realms of where it should have been,' he admitted. The reason he hadn't marked his ball was 'a huge clap of thunder right behind me', he said.

'It wasn't just thunder, there was a lightning bolt and I wasn't prepared to stand in the bunker any longer than I had to while marking my ball and picking it up. I know we are only talking about a matter of seconds but at the same time you never know in a thunderstorm. So I ran off the green. You don't mess around with these Indonesian thunderstorms because you know how violent they can be. There is always talk about how they have lost five people in a year to lightning strikes. Well, sorry, I don't want to be one of them and I'd rather answer for not marking my ball than not be here to do so.'

Nonetheless, the committee took a dim view and they publicly expressed their 'dissatisfaction' with how he had acted in not marking his ball when play was suspended. 'If any player has an issue, I will speak to them and let them know the situation and it will be fine. Ask my playing partners – I was not trying to gain any advantage. Hopefully my fellow players will realise it was a complete mistake. In my haste to avoid the storm I left the ball where it lay and did not mark it,' Montgomerie reiterated.

Monty had thought that the issue had been dealt with through consultation with the players with whom he had been grouped at the time of the incident. He thought it was all over once he had been cleared by the tournament director. He felt sure it was done and dusted now that it had been investigated by the Tournament Committee and they'd issued their rebuke. He said: 'The respect of my peers and the rules of the game are extremely important to me, which is why I'm grateful the matter has been raised and I have been able to look into it. I am obviously upset that I could have inadvertently caused my colleagues to question me. I wasn't gaining an advantage and I have been cleared by the tournament director in Indonesia and that's that. I can't see the issue being raised again and as far as I'm concerned it is dead and buried.'

It was far from six feet under, however. Later in May 2005, Montgomerie was playing at the European Tour's flagship PGA Championship at Wentworth, an event backed by new sponsors BMW. It had been a strategically vital deal for the Tour at the time. On the final hole of his third round Monty hit his ball into the BMW hospitality area to the left of the fairway. He was given a free drop but after he dropped his ball it bounced over a painted line, out of the drop zone and into a more favourable lie. Wary of the Jakarta furore, he was not going to take any chances and called a referee to confirm that he would be allowed to play the ball as it lay. He would. No problem with that one, but the ghost of Indonesia was still restless. It stirred again that very afternoon as veteran tour player Gary Evans went to the media centre to tell reporters that 'there's a bit of smoke about Monty'. Evans was becoming the first player to break cover and publicly express concern over what Montgomerie had done on the 14th hole of his second round in Jakarta. 'I'm not saying that Monty is lying,' Evans said. 'But why would you give your prize money to charity? If he's so upset why did he not DQ [disqualify] himself? Give the money back to the tour and remove the world ranking points?' The fact is Montgomerie could not throw himself out of a tournament once it had been completed and there was no mechanism to remove the ranking points either.

Naturally Evans' comments were seized on by reporters and his quotes made the affair's biggest headlines to that point, providing uncomfortable breakfast reading for Montgomerie ahead of an important final round. Still outside the all-important top fifty, he needed a big finish. There was no chance of him winning the tournament. He was among the earlier starters with an opportunity to climb the leaderboard. As Monty began his round, George O'Grady came to the media tent. The Tour boss, for whom the week had been all about his new deal with BMW, was livid. The headlines had been stolen and were negative. He branded Evans' comments 'enormously disrespectful' and 'unacceptable'. Monty, meanwhile, was concentrating on his golf and when he arrived at the 18th green he had a seven-foot birdie putt for a six under par round of 66. He slotted it home and it gave him an eleventh place finish. 'I am only glad I was able to score 66 in very difficult circumstances,' he said as reporters surrounded him with microphones. 'Yes, I am hurt and I'm very glad I was able to do what I did to prove I can still do what I do best. I thought this was dead and buried.'

Not quite though, because over in the United States the American pro Kirk Triplett had failed to play all four rounds at the St Jude Classic tournament on the PGA Tour. This, combined with the world ranking points Montgomerie picked up at Wentworth, helped elevate the Scot into the world's top fifty and gained him entry to the US Open, the second major of the year. The ranking points from Indonesia had also been important and because they'd helped Monty win back his major status the story became more and more relevant. The questions kept coming. Next stop on Tour was Celtic Manor and the Wales Open. Tournament Committee chairman Jamie Spence was also in the firing line. Surely they should have taken stronger action? 'I think those who are kicking up a fuss have not thought it through properly,' Spence said. 'You cannot disqualify someone after the event and nor can he disqualify himself and hand back the points. I still have the greatest respect for Monty. He has been a great servant to the Tour and terrific for the membership.' They were welcome words of support but Montgomerie was showing signs of strain. He had clearly had enough. 'Can I just ask one thing more?' he said. 'Can we finally, finally, draw a line under this and get on with what we do best?' He missed the cut in Wales.

Monty's wishes for the affair to be put to one side were largely realised in the months that followed. There were a few questions at Pinehurst, the venue of the US Open and the site of his major debut in 2005, but he wasn't the story, finishing in a lowly share of forty-second place. The attention was elsewhere as New Zealand's Michael Campbell held off Tiger Woods to claim the title. As far as 'Jakartagate' was concerned, there was the odd muttering of discontent from players, past and present, but nothing on the record. One prominent Tour member was heard griping about Monty only for the subject of his ire to hove into view. In a swift about turn his critic greeted the Scot like a best pal. This was typical. Occasional comments questioned Montgomerie's character behind his back but were never for public consumption. The controversy seemed to have run its course and it didn't warrant mention as Monty finished second to Woods at the 2005 Open at St Andrews. It had been a big deal in golf for a while, but the story didn't truly transcend. The greater sporting public, brought up on a diet of footballers and rugby players seeking at every opportunity to gain an unfair advantage behind a ref's back, cricketers who refused to walk and tennis players vigorously contesting line calls, couldn't see what the fuss was about. In golf it is different, though. Discipline and respect for rules and referees can't be imposed from on high by governing bodies. It has to come from within the playing culture of a sport. Those who meddle with the rules lose the respect of their peers in golf. That's a far greater sanction than any disciplinary body can impose. It is why Montgomerie's errors in Indonesia were potentially so damaging to him and why, as future events were to prove, he continued to struggle in his quest for complete closure on the controversy.

8

24 SEPTEMBER 1999, THE COUNTRY CLUB,
BROOKLINE, MASSACHUSETTS

*'Of all the egos a captain has had to look after
he's right up there at the top of the Order of
Merit, but that's not a criticism. That's what
happens if you are going to have to play really
well at the sharp end'*
– **Ken Brown, Assistant Captain to the European team**

*H*e *was there as a threat. They, the fans, knew he was good,
very good, especially when he wore the badge of Europe. They
knew he should have won more, should have taken at least one of
the major titles by now. He hadn't, but when it came to the Ryder
Cup he was a winner through and through. He was the man who'd
closed out the Americans in Spain. He had made sure Europe had
now won the last two matches and he was the undisputed danger
man as they tried to make it three in a row. America had Tiger,
but the Europeans had him. He was the irrefutable leader, around
whom the team would be built. He loved it. That was his role, the
big man for the big occasion. It made him bigger and stronger and
he had never needed to be stronger, especially between those all-
hearing ears of his. Put him with anyone and he would be a threat.
The* threat. *But they'd done it before, the fans, and they could do
it again, couldn't they? They could get under his skin. They could
try. 'Sticks and stones . . .'*

Colin Montgomerie's ball had just made an unwanted splash. It had drowned in a Miami lake, just like his hopes of securing a place at the Masters. He was only halfway through the tournament but there was no chance of the win that Monty needed to give him any possibility of playing at the first major of 2008. Monty was past his prime, though still eligible for a big tournament like this one – the WGC CA Championship at Doral next to Miami airport. Perspiring and bitterly disappointed with a second round of 74, he wearily climbed the slope at the back of the 18th green to reach the recorder's hut where he would sign his scorecard. It documented a double-bogey six on the final hole, the consequence of dumping that second shot into the drink. Montgomerie's tired stride told the story. As had happened throughout his career you could see how well he had played through his body language. Chest pumped, with a confident stride, and it would be clear the course and the field had been beaten. Resigned trudge, shoulders slumped, face flushed – these are the signs that he is the one who has taken the beating. Fans didn't need to look at a leaderboard.

The latter scenario was his sorry demeanour that warm Friday afternoon as the jets roared overhead in Florida. All that was on his mind was to get the miserable scorecard signed and get out of there. Normally after rounds of 75 and 74 it would be straight to the airport, his scoring of an insufficiently good standard to be eligible to contest the weekend prize money. But in World Golf Championships strokeplay events competitors play all four rounds. There was no early exit, just a sense of more futile torture to come over the next two days.

Monty provided the easiest target for American fans and the softest story for British newspapers. It had become apparent in the incident in the second round at the 1997 US Open in

Washington when he'd climbed outside the ropes to pursue his tormentors. It remained so throughout his career and it is no exaggeration to say that Sunday reporters would bank on such episodes to solve their most problematic piece of the week, the early edition story that needed to be filed before any third round golf is played. Given the time difference in America, journalists need a story late on the second day of a tournament. The reporters then write it up to be sent on the Saturday morning to meet their first deadline. They call it the 'Monty heckling story', a stock source to fill column inches. So when the Scot is out of contention he is still worth going to see at the end of a round. Most other players are ignored in such circumstances, but not Monty. Something might happen, just as it did on this particular occasion in March 2008 when he was old enough and should have been wise enough to know better. American crowds could never resist baiting him. Montgomerie could not turn a blind eye to it.

'It's good job there's no cut,' yelled a fan as Monty headed up the hill. The spectator was swaying slightly, beer in hand but still sober enough to know his words would hurt and draw a reaction. Montgomerie should have kept his head down. He should have walked on. That's what most players would do, but not the fiery Scot. He stopped and looked up. Turning his head to his left in the direction from where the shout had come he fixed the heckler with a hard stare. They were no more than five yards apart. The impasse lasted fully ten seconds, punctuated only by another fan yelling, 'Colin, we love you, babe.' Eventually the weary Scot dismissively and contemptuously shook his head and resumed his traipse to the scorer's hut.

This was a relatively minor episode, certainly by Montgomerie's standards, but it was enough to satisfy watching reporters' note-books. It doesn't happen to other players and so he made another headline even though his golf had been unworthy of mention. The incident merely illustrated the enduring urge for American golf fans to get under his skin, even at a time in his career when he was no longer a genuine threat. The level of abuse on this occasion was at the mild end of the scale compared with what he had regularly endured at the height of his powers – and never was the nastiness greater than at the thirty-third Ryder Cup played at Brookline Country Club in 1999.

American golf was hurting. The last two Ryder Cups had been lost and an unprecedented hat-trick of defeats was beyond contemplation. Europe simply had to be put back in its place; the USA must win at Brookline. Ben Crenshaw, the two time Masters champion from Texas, was the man charged with regaining the trophy. Always a popular figure, he had played much of his career as the 'heir apparent' to the great Jack Nicklaus, but instead of multiple major wins he was best known for his near misses. Crenshaw was five times a runner up in the game's most prestigious tourna-ments and third on four more occasions. This was why his two Masters victories in 1984 and 1995 met with such universal approval, particularly his second Green Jacket which was emotionally won in the immediate aftermath of the death of his lifelong coach Harvey Penick. He was regarded as having the surest putting touch on tour and didn't have a single three putt during that 1995 victory on the treacherous greens of Augusta.

As sure as Crenshaw's ability with a putter was his grasp of the game's finest traditions for fair play, honesty and integrity.

He was a traditionalist, one of the good guys who knew what golf was all about. 'If we are to preserve the integrity of golf as left to us by our forefathers, it is up to all of us to carry the spirit of the game,' the charming Texan once said. He seemed the ultimate safe pair of hands to entrust with the traditions of the Ryder Cup. But Crenshaw wasn't just a soppy traditionalist, he was a steely competitor who saw it as his ultimate duty to steer his country back to victory. He knew that with the talent at his disposal there could be no excuse for failure.

Tiger Woods had just won his second major title, the US PGA at Medinah, and was the figurehead of the American team. He was world number one, and the man immediately behind him in the rankings, David Duval, was also in the side. Payne Stewart was the reigning US Open champion and was expected to play a big role, as was the man who was runner-up to Stewart at Pinehurst, Phil Mickelson. The Americans also had 1996 Open winner Tom Lehman and his successor as the holder of the old Claret Jug, Justin Leonard. Then there was Hal Sutton who was as tough as teak when it came to head-to-head combat. This formidable line-up of talent also included the big hitting Davis Love III, double major winner Mark O'Meara, World Matchplay champion Jeff Maggert, a future US Open winner Jim Furyk, and Steve Pate, who didn't have quite the same pedigree but was still regarded as a great team man. America were the firm favourites to win back the trophy.

Like the US team Europe had a new skipper. Seve Ballesteros had surprised many observers when he said on the night of victory at Valderrama in 1997 that he didn't want to continue. He preferred to try to play himself back into the team, but it hadn't been possible. Mark James, a plain-speaking Yorkshireman who had transformed himself from being the Tour's *enfant terrible* to its ultimate committee man, was the new captain. In his early years on tour James had railed against authority and was fined for what was regarded as disrespectful behaviour when he appeared in the 1979 Ryder Cup. As he matured, the man nicknamed Jesse decided that if he didn't like the way the Tour was being run he might as well do something about it. He stood for a place on the Tournament Committee and eventually rose to the position of chairman. It was golf's ultimate tale of the poacher turning gamekeeper.

This was a new Europe. There was no Nick Faldo, who had played for the last time in Spain. Bernhard Langer was also missing and had been disappointed not to gain a captain's wild-card pick. Instead, James had opted to go with the US-based Swede Jesper Parnevik and, controversially, the rookie Andrew Coltart. The Scot finished twelfth on the qualifying list but was preferred to the man who finished eleventh, Robert Karlsson. The Swede was heartbroken and twice asked James to explain his decision on the day it was made. The skipper admitted the process of telling Karlsson and Langer they weren't making the trip to Boston had been the most draining experience of his life.

Coltart was one of seven newcomers in that European team. Paul Lawrie had won his place with his shock victory at the Open at Carnoustie, so too had the man who threw away the chance to win that Championship on the 72nd hole, Jean Van de Velde. Sweden's Jarmo Sandelin finished eighth on the qualifying list and with two late runner's-up finishes Padraig Harrington claimed the last automatic place. There were two Spanish newcomers as well. Miguel Ángel Jiménez, an assistant to Seve at Valderrama, enjoyed a stellar season and a nineteen' year-old by the name of Sergio García had skipped his way into the side courtesy of his inspired second place to Woods at the US PGA.

So there was a huge responsibility resting on the quintet who had some familiarity with this unique form of the game. Even so, it was a pretty limited level of experience. For Parnevik, Darren Clarke and Lee Westwood, Brookline would provide their first taste of facing the US in their own backyard. Only two players in the European side had any idea of what that might involve and they were José Maria Olazábal and, of course, the continent's undisputed number one, Colin Montgomerie. 'With six rookies we had a young team, a very, very young team,' Monty recalled.

James knew that the Scot was his key player. 'A big man with a big game and personality to match,' James said. 'In Europe Monty is without doubt our Tiger Woods. We knew that at Brookline the rest of the team would look to Monty for a lead and he would give it. No matter whom he partnered it would be a good pairing and once you have a player like that it gives the rest confidence.'

Such was the captain's regard for Montgomerie he was accorded what amounted to a consultancy role within the European setup. He was James's sounding board, the 'go to' man when it came to working out awkward decisions. Monty had been consulted over the wild-card picks and played an integral part in deciding policy for the week. He had again topped the qualifying table with almost twice as many points (determined by prize money) as the second-placed player, Westwood. All that had been missing, yet again, was the major title that was surely commensurate with his talents. It was scarcely believable that a Scottish player had won a major that year and it had not been Montgomerie taking the historic step.

Now his enduring failure to land one of the game's biggest titles was starting to become a big talking point. All sorts of theories were being put forward as to why this man, who could win title after title on Tour, couldn't do it when majors were at stake. Some questioned his temperament for the big occasion while others wondered whether his stoic loyalty to the European schedule was starting to count against him with three of the four jewels in the golfing crown played for in the United States.

Nick Faldo, in an interview with the *Daily Mail*, turned against his former partner by accusing him of taking easy money by not travelling to America to take on the best players in the world. 'I don't know what he wants,' Faldo said. 'I am surprised he has not done something different as a challenge, but he likes to earn his fat cheques each week. There is no harm in that if that's what motivates you. Most of us go for ten Claret Jugs.' Faldo likened Monty to Japan's Jumbo Ozaki, a serial winner on his home tour but who had done precious little anywhere else. 'Great in his own backyard, he's comfortable, and knows he's only got to play half decent and he's going to be there. Even if he plays badly, he's the sort of guy who turns round a good score the next day and gets himself into contention. He goes out and wins a couple of hundred grand each week and goes home. I'd be comfortable if I did that every week.'

History may well have now proved Faldo correct in his analysis. 'He probably should have played more in America,' Bernard Gallacher said, looking back on Monty's career. 'But he's always been very loyal to the European Tour and he always wanted to get home on a Sunday night. To go to the States you have to go for a month at a time and he probably found it lonely over there because it is such a different lifestyle. To me he has always been a journeyman type of pro, who plays better than that. Faldo would give up weeks and weeks to practise for a major but Colin would think, "No, I'm a pro, I'm a player and I've got to play this week, earn money and keep playing,"' Gallacher added.

Nevertheless, Faldo's was an extraordinary attack on a partner with whom he had enjoyed so much Ryder Cup success. It had been published in the run-up to the Brookline match and there was also an implied attack on the standard of golf on the European Tour. James was furious with his fellow Englishman who he had overlooked for a potential wild-card selection. 'Not one person in the team room had any sympathy for his sentiments,' the skipper said.

When Faldo wrote a good luck message to the team the captain held it in utter contempt. Other letters from well-wishers had been posted on the wall of the team room in Boston, but the one from Faldo, Europe's most prolific point scorer, was dispatched to the dustbin. With friends like that, who needed enemies? And there were plenty of those in Massachusetts anyway with no shortage of hostility towards Europe in general and Montgomerie in particular.

But Monty thoroughly enjoyed the build-up to the match. He relished being the lead player. He had sat in the front row on Concorde on the journey over, a flight that broke transatlantic records by taking a mere three hours and eleven minutes. Montgomerie was the individual identified to promote the team cause; effectively he was the on-course skipper. It was no coincidence that he was seated next to captain James in the official team photographs and was at his skipper's side at the official gala dinner.

'To get the best out of him you had to encourage him to think, "You're our man here, Colin,"' captain's assistant Ken Brown recalled. 'Of all the egos a captain has had to look after he's right up there at the top of the Order of Merit but that's not a criticism. That's what happens if you are going to have to play really well at the sharp end. He needs the arm around his shoulder, that's just his personality. It's a trait of his. Some you can let go, some you need to put your arm around. They need a hug at times,' Brown added. 'Monty was a really integral part of the team. It was the match where he turned from being the man who needed help in terms of his partners, to the man who was happy to help. It raised his stature.'

There wasn't just the need for psychological boosts to ensure Montgomerie would deliver. Mark James also needed to attend to the demands of his star player's stomach. This meant swapping main courses with him at that official dinner because the big man from Troon didn't care for his somewhat undercooked lamb chops. And during practice rounds Monty would order tuna sandwiches with the specific instruction 'no chunks'. James was more than happy to oblige.

In those reconnaissance rounds Montgomerie spent most of his time with fellow Scot Paul Lawrie. The pair became good friends and it was clear that the Open champion held his compatriot in the highest regard even though it was he rather than Monty who could boast a major title to his name. There was much to admire in Lawrie's game. He could hit imperious long irons such as the lusty blows that produced a closing pair of threes in the play-off that won him the 1999 Open at Carnoustie. His short game was sharp and the reason his nickname was 'Chippy'. Monty was more than happy to take a rookie under his wing and discussed their potential partnership with James ahead of the match. 'We both had the feeling that, although Paul was obviously a very good player, he might be special under pressure,' James said in his book about the match, *Into the Bear Pit*. 'Monty was happy to play with him.' In practice rounds the European team played each other in money matches and it was the back pockets of Lawrie and Monty that bulged the most afterwards.

The European players had been told to ingratiate themselves with the home fans during practice rounds and the process had gone well. If there was any hostility from fans ahead of the match it was reserved for some of the American players like David Duval, who had suggested that match fees be paid to team members. This didn't sit well with the US golfing public, for whom the idea of representing your country was reward enough.

To no one's surprise the two Scots were put together when the serious business began and they were kept in tandem throughout the foursomes and fourball sequences. Mark James had high expectations and sent them out in the top match against Duval and Phil Mickelson. Montgomerie had engineered it for his partner to tee off on the odd holes. Paul Lawrie was therefore entrusted with the opening tee shot of the 1999 Ryder Cup. He might, at the very least, have expected his experienced and talismanic partner to be at his side as he made his way on to the tee. And that was certainly Montgomerie's intention, but he was held up by an animated conversation with Bill Clark, the referee appointed to the match. It was mere small talk, but the official seemed desperate to prolong the chat as Monty was trying to make it to the tee with his partner. Eventually Monty broke free but he was the last player to arrive. The absurdity of the situation combined with the inevitable tension of the moment reduced Montgomerie to an involuntary fit of giggles that he struggled to contain. Lawrie, meanwhile, embarked on hitting the most nerve-wracking drive of his career.

The Open champion's tee shot found the semi-rough down the right side of the fairway and as far as he was concerned it was an absolute triumph, especially as Mickelson's drive went much wider and further into the rough. Montgomerie was left to explain to his partner how the bizarre conversation initiated by the referee had so delayed his arrival on the tee.

From the very start Monty's putter was on song. He holed from around ten feet on each of the first three greens to fend off early pressure from the American pair. Assistant captain Ken Brown was not surprised. 'The thing that was noticeably different in the Ryder Cup was that Monty started to hole those ten- or fifteen-footers. He would hole those much more often in matchplay when he really needed to than he ever did as a player on the Tour. He's holed lots of putts and lots of big putts in his time, but at the Ryder Cup, that moment when he has needed that one putt, something invariably inspired him to hole it,' Brown said.

Montgomerie needed no extra motivation, but he soon had it. The atmosphere around Brookline was shifting. Montgomerie's caddie Alastair McLean almost immediately sensed that he and his boss, along with Lawrie and his bagman Paddy Byrne, were a lone quartet pitted against the whole of America. Nasty shouts could be heard from the increasingly partisan crowd as they walked down the fairway. 'Go home, Europeans' was at the milder end of the scale. If Duval and Co. had been the objects of abuse for their mercenary opinions in the build-up, now that it was underway Europe, the holders, were the undisputed enemy. The home fans would leave them in no doubt about that.

'It was a week of vociferous crowds and Monty was getting the brunt of it, which I think made him more determined to try to do his best,' Brown said. 'So he was an amazing part of the side. He was the mainstay, almost the nucleus of the whole team.'

In this top match those early putts helped grow Montgomerie's confidence and settle the nerves of his partner. It was just what Mark James wanted. He didn't just require a point from the two Scots, he needed them to set an example to the rest of his team. The first five holes were halved and then Duval drove into the crowd at the sixth. Europe failed to take advantage and lost the hole to give first blood to the home side thanks to a superb flop shot by Mickelson from the trampled rough to two feet. Within two holes American cheers had been silenced as Montgomerie and Lawrie turned one down into one up. The lead did not last, however, and the scoreboards showed the match was back to all square as they departed the ninth green.

The hostility of the crowds was inspiring Monty who in turn was cajoling Lawrie to make sure the home fans would be disappointed. Duval and Mickelson contrived to three-putt the tenth. Europe were back in front and it was a lead they would refuse to surrender. Montgomerie started to create the chances and Lawrie eagerly converted them with his assured putting touch. It was as though the two Scotsmen had been playing together all their lives and there was nothing their illustrious opponents could do in reply. By the 16th it was all over: Europe had its first point thanks to a 3 and 2 victory.

Remarkably, given the difficulty of foursomes, Monty and Lawrie didn't drop a shot all the way round. That enabled them to close the door on their opponents and shut up their fans. The Scottish duo had done precisely what their skipper had asked of them.

Mark James was proved correct in his theory that by sending out first Montgomerie and Lawrie they could play an inspirational role for the rest of the side. The captain had paired together the excitable duo of Sergio García and Jesper Parnevik. Buoyed by the knowledge that the top pair were holding off Mickelson and Duval, the Spanish/Swedish combo did the same to Tiger Woods and Tom Lehman. The Europeans won that one 2 and 1 to provide a dream start and heighten concern in the American ranks. The rookies Miguel Ángel Jiménez and Padraig Harrington bravely halved with Davis Love and Payne Stewart and Europe's only defeat came in the bottom foursomes where Darren Clarke and Lee Westwood fell to Hal Sutton and Jeff Maggert.

Europe were ahead; the favourites were trailing the underdogs. Given their relative lack of experience, the visiting team were happy to be known as the 'under-puppies'.

For the visiting 'young pups' what was a fine morning became a dazzling afternoon. Only Montgomerie and Lawrie – sent out first again – failed to win their fourball match. They were facing Love and Justin Leonard and it turned into one of the best contests in the entire match. Monty was now the top target as far as the fans were concerned and they hurled abuse in his direction from behind the ropes. Ironically, given Monty's preferred choice of sandwich filling that week, they started to call him 'Tuna', but this was down to his perceived resemblance to the well-built New England Patriots NFL coach

Bill Parcells. This was probably lost on the Scot, just as it was to anyone unaware of Parcells' unusual nickname, the origins of which stemmed from an old tuna television advertisement. Montgomerie called it 'The worst atmosphere I've ever had to encounter on a golf course; having to back off shots with all that was going on.' Montgomerie knew he was being targeted and knew why. 'They only do it because I'm a threat and if I'm a threat then that's good,' he later said, his voice high-pitched and quivering with emotion.

The deadlock in this fourball match was not broken until the ninth hole where a Justin Leonard birdie at the par five ninth put the Americans ahead. Montgomerie's birdie four holes later, where he sank a 15-footer, levelled the contest and the standard of play continued to hit the heights. At the 14th Davis Love holed a monster for eagle that broke from right to left from the back of the green and Paul Lawrie matched it with a putt across the putting surface for a half in stunning threes. It was that sort of clash; the quality of the golf was at times breathtaking.

Monty then made sure Europe couldn't lose by emphatically ramming home a three-foot putt to win the 17th to go one up with one to play. On the final green Love holed an unlikely putt to snatch a half point for the home side. Given the nature and excellence of the match it was a deserved half, but that did little to improve Montgomerie's mood, which was starting to darken as the abuse he received began to take its toll. This was, after all, golf – a game in which such crowd behaviour is totally alien. 'This is going to make me play better, not worse,' he resolved.

'It was an extremely tough, extremely tough, week for him,' Ken Brown remembers. 'He was the headline man to barrack.'

Brown believes this is where he, Sam Torrance and Mark James needed to play crucial supportive roles to make themselves visible to the players under fire. 'As often as you could you would get out there and say, "Colin, come on, just stick in there", just so he could see a familiar face. "Keep concentrating, Colin, you can beat these", that sort of thing. You'd help them through little narrow gaps, your two yards to walk through to the next tee. There was noise, noise, noise all the way through. It was a football match atmosphere. He kind of . . . not encouraged it . . . but he would say: "If you want to be like that, I'm going to get stuck in here." It was at times two players against a lot.'

In the midst of this hostility it was easy to identify Montgomerie's unique Ryder Cup DNA and the premium he has always put on success in these matches. Had this been an ordinary Tour event or a major the abuse would not have been so vocal, personal, impassioned and pointed. Yet it would be much more likely to succeed in its intention of derailing the Scotsman's progress. It would identify the temperature of one of his defining characteristics, an acute sensitivity and desire to be liked. The taunts would expose this vulnerability like a heat-seeking missile and there would be no defences. Instead there would be a ruinous explosion, the evidence of which would show up on his scorecard. But in the Ryder Cup, with the volume turned up to max, Monty could not only cope but thrive. He would allow no room for outside agencies to affect his performance. It was too important for that. John McEnroe would never let himself be distracted when playing Björn Börg, such was his respect for his opponent, and Montgomerie was the same in these biennial matches against the US. This attitude enabled him to compete at Brookline despite the atmosphere that former Royal and Ancient Secretary Sir Michael Bonallack described as a 'bear pit'. This week provided compelling evidence of his competitive desire in the face of outright hostility and how the Ryder Cup meant as much, if not more, to him than any other form of golf in his career.

And in some ways it was okay to be insulted; after all, he was the enemy. He could accept not being liked by the crowds, whereas in a regular event, where it was every man for himself, Montgomerie felt the need for respect and affection. He would struggle to cope if it wasn't forthcoming and in particular if fans started to taunt him. And knowing the likely reaction, how American fans loved to do just that.

At Brookline the home galleries had growing incentive to make the environment hostile for Europe. Their much-vaunted American team were taking a serious pounding on the first afternoon. Montgomerie and Lawrie had been held to a half, but the remaining three fourball matches were all being edged by the visiting team, who were holding their nerve admirably down the closing stretch of holes. Parnevik and García saw off Mickelson and Furyk on the final green, Jiménez and Olazábal accounted for Sutton and Maggert on the 17th and Clarke and Westwood were taken the full distance before completing a famous win over the world's top two players, Woods and Duval.

The opening day could hardly have gone better for Mark James and his team. He hadn't used Jean Van de Velde, Andrew Coltart or Jarmo Sandelin and only Olazábal and Harrington had not been required to play morning and afternoon. The tactics seemed vindicated by a scoreboard that showed Europe's 'under-puppies' ahead by six points to two. James saw no point in changing policy for the second day and went with the same foursomes pairings he had used to open the contest. The European skipper shuffled the order but still opted to send out first

Montgomerie and Lawrie with the clear hope that they could build on his side's extraordinary four-point advantage.

That Saturday morning hazy sunshine gave way to light rain as the Scots took on Hal Sutton and Jeff Maggert, the only American pairing to have won a match on the opening day. It proved another outstanding contest involving four supreme competitors. First blood went the way of Europe thanks to an excellent Montgomerie five-iron tee shot at the short second which Lawrie converted for the first birdie.

The atmosphere was again rancorous and Montgomerie was back in the familiar position of bearing the brunt. At the sixth Sutton holed a 15-footer and Monty needed to hole from six feet for a half. One spectator broke the relative quiet by yelling 'Miss the putt!'

'Just as he was about to take the putter head back an idiot yelled at him,' James recalls in *Into the Bear Pit*. 'Monty backed away, glared, settled and then drilled the ball home before staring in the general direction of the troublemaker, without once losing self-control.' James added that Monty later said to him: 'These people are too stupid to understand that type of thing only serves to make me more determined.' Assistant captain Ken Brown witnessed the scene. He said: 'When it happened on the sixth green a bloke shouted out at an inappropriate time, but Monty just ended up walking to the next tee. I've never seen him so cross, but it just drew him in deeper to say we're going to dig in here.'

The American pair didn't retrieve the single hole deficit until the par five ninth. Then both sides traded holes with a dropped shot apiece early on the inward half. At the 15th Monty hit a promising approach which had his partner urging it to 'be as good as you look'. It finished within tap-in range but was not enough to win the hole as Maggert sank his birdie chance from ten feet to keep this absorbing contest all square. The American was a steely competitor and many of the best moments of his career came in matchplay. Certainly Maggert will always remember his curling right-to-left long-range putt across the front of the 17th green for it put the Americans one up with one to play. Maggert then shut the door on Monty and Lawrie with a brilliant seven iron approach to the last. It was classic Ryder Cup stuff, the US pair playing the last four holes in three under par, but only winning by the narrowest of margins.

Sutton and Maggert were still the only US combination to register a win until Tiger Woods and Steve Pate closed out Miguel Ángel Jiménez and Padraig Harrington on the final green of the third match in the morning foursomes. The other two went the way of Europe: Clarke and Westwood revelled in each other's company and saw off Furyk and O'Meara without too many problems and the effervescent Parnevik and García claimed the all-important bottom match against Stewart and Leonard 3 and 2. The session finished level to preserve Europe's four-point advantage from the previous day.

The scoreboard was confounding the pre-match predictions but it left captain Mark James with a huge dilemma. For the final sequence of fourball matches should he stick with the players who had earned such a healthy lead or should he blood the golfers he had so far not used? If he went with the former option it would mean Coltart, Van de Velde and Sandelin would not play until the closing Sunday singles, which was far from ideal. But it was the option James chose. Just as happened the previous day the European skipper substituted Harrington for Olazábal to partner Jiménez in the fourballs and kept the other partnerships unchanged. James realised that his opposite number, Ben Crenshaw, would not be surprised by these tactics, so switched the order, sending out Montgomerie and Lawrie in the final match of the day. They were up against Woods and Pate, the only other American pair who had a win to their name.

The home team were appearing ever more desperate, staring a third successive defeat in the face. When Crenshaw issued a rallying call, claiming, 'I think we're ready, my team is sky high', in his Texan drawl, it was difficult to believe him. But in another extraordinarily tense afternoon the European captain James was forced to rely on his Monty/Lawrie partnership to vindicate his controversial tactics. Clarke and Westwood fell 2 and 1 to Mickelson and Lehman and the next two clashes went the distance.

Thankfully for James his main man came to the fore with one of the greatest putting displays of his career. Monty holed from six feet at the third to cancel out Pate's opening birdie and then at the eighth the Scot canned a delicate downhill 15-footer to level for the second time. The Scots then went ahead thanks to a Montgomerie approach from the middle of the next fairway. At the 14th Monty could not find the par five green with two drivers but got up and down for a birdie and a crucial half after the mighty Woods missed his eagle chance, having found the green with two lusty blows. Two holes later Lawrie joined in, running an approach to tap-in range to put the European pair two up with two to play.

They had thoroughly enjoyed each other's company in their previous three matches and this one was no different. An understanding and firm friendship through a mixture of inspired golf and a siege mentality had been built to keep the hecklers at bay. Lawrie was grateful to his partner for helping him through the most pressured golf of his career. It not only boosted the European cause, it assisted Lawrie as he sought to justify the tag of Open champion that many felt he had been fortunate to acquire. Montgomerie had been true to his word in being all the more determined to win in the face of the abuse being hurled by the American crowds. 'In that position I would fight like I never have before,' he later recalled. 'I holed putts I wouldn't have normally and Paul and I did particularly well.'

Walking down the 17th, Lawrie thanked his senior partner and moments later the great Tiger Woods missed the chance to take the match to the final hole when his putt from ten feet failed to drop. 'It's frustrating when you play well and still lose,' Woods admitted. Monty and Lawrie could have said the same thing in the morning but this time they had won, taking the partnership's haul to an impressive two and half points out of four. Mark James commented: 'Monty's performance all week had been enormous on and off the course. I and my assistants were all too happy to confide in him.'

Moments later, up ahead on the 18th green with Monty down on his haunches watching, the final match on the course was halved. Sutton and Leonard had come from behind and forced Jiménez, who was partnering Olazábal, to hole a match-saving putt on that final green for a share of the spoils. As happened in the morning, the session had been shared and Europe's sizeable advantage from the first day remained intact.

Leading 10-6 they needed only four more points to retain the trophy and four and half to win it for an unprecedented third match in a row. The question was from whom would those points come? The way the singles draw lined up offered little encouragement for Europe despite their commanding position. Jesper Parnevik voiced his concerns to Montgomerie over breakfast on the Sunday morning and his words carried some weight given that he was based in America and knew the opposition better than anyone else on the European team.

Ben Crenshaw knew he had to rally his shell-shocked team and exuded a positive attitude that contradicted what had happened on the opening two days. At the Saturday night news conference he wagged his finger at his sceptical audience. 'I'm a big believer in fate,' he announced. 'I have a good feeling about this, that's all I'm going to tell you.' Crenshaw enlisted the help of George W. Bush, the future President who was then Governor of Texas, to inspire his team. Bush was delighted to help. 'We're close buddies,' Bush told the *Boston Herald*. 'We're from the same town. We go to church together. We play golf together. I'm looking to say hi, to pick him up. He's a good guy. He'll get a handle on it.' On an evening of inspirational speeches from American players, wives and officials Bush quoted from the Letter from the Alamo of Colonel William B. Travis to try to motivate his country's players.

Montgomerie had witnessed the American desire earlier in the week when he unwittingly went into the wrong team room and saw a huge sign that stated: 'Losing is worse than death; you have to live with losing'. With that in mind it is perhaps easier to comprehend the apparent loss of perspective that afflicted so many of the US side and their supporters.

Crenshaw sent out his team in garishly designed patchwork shirts that bore images of former American heroes. His team were now the massive underdogs and he reminded them of Brookline's history and how it had staged the famous 1913 US Open victory of Francis Ouimet, an amateur caddie who lived over the road from the course. On that occasion the unheralded champion had overcome the odds and formidable European opposition to beat the great Harry Vardon and Ted Ray in a play-off. It had led to a massive boost for the game in the US. 'The Country Club has been good to American golf,' said Crenshaw, who first played there in the 1968 US Junior Amateur.

On that final morning there was a sense that somehow momentum had swung without a shot being hit. Partisan home fans were swarming over the course in numbers that seemed to far outstrip the tickets sold. Tom Lehman stirred them up on the first tee by conducting raucous renditions of 'Gold Bless America'. Golf had never seen the like of it before, even at Valderrama two years earlier where Europe had received vociferous support. The American players seemed to have acquired a confident swagger and, as Parnevik had suggested to Montgomerie over breakfast, there was European worry over how the singles draw had lined up, especially as they were fielding three players who had yet to play any Ryder Cup golf.

'Mark had employed a high risk strategy by running nine guys into the ground on the opening two days,' recalled Ken Schofield. 'Perhaps it was more worrying having the three guys that didn't play until the singles.'

Crenshaw sent out Lehman, Sutton, Mickelson, Love, Woods and Duval as his top six. You could make an impregnable hexagon out of that collection of names. James countered with Westwood, Clarke, Sandelin, Van de Velde, Coltart and Parnevik. It prompted an inevitable question: if the top two Europeans struggled, how would the newcomers cope against three of the best players in the world? It was asking an awful lot, but Mark James felt they were better off putting the rookies earlier in the draw rather than anywhere near what might prove the denouement. It was a big risk; there was every chance that Europe's hard-earned advantage could be quickly wiped out and if so all the momentum would be with the home team and their impassioned and inebriated fans. So it proved.

The Americans swept through the top six matches; not one of those contests made it as far as the 17th tee. Sandelin was beaten 4 and 3 by Mickelson, Van de Velde was trounced 6 and 5 by Love and the brave Coltart fell 3 and 2 to Woods. The atmosphere was growing ever more menacing. The Scottish newcomer was on the ninth hole when a marshal told him his blind tee shot had gone into the woods. In fact, it was in the rough, just a few feet from the fairway. Coltart had to hit three off the tee, but then his first ball was found lying incongruously plugged in the rough seconds after the five-minute time limit was up. 'That's tough,' he said. 'You've just got to get on with it, and you've just got to try and play.'

Montgomerie had been sent out in tenth place in the order. James felt his might be the match that could decide the trophy and that is where he needed his strongest player. Monty was up against US Open champion Payne Stewart and was defending his unbeaten record in Ryder Cup singles play. Stewart was one of the game's true gentlemen and the golfing world was united in mourning his loss when he was killed in a plane accident later that year. As the atmosphere at Brookline grew more hostile, Stewart repeatedly called for order to allow his opponent to play in what proved another tense and close contest. 'Payne was fantastic with his own crowd for me,' Montgomerie later recalled. 'It meant so much to him to be on the Ryder Cup team but he was more interested in the integrity of the game than he was in his own performance. It showed the quality of the man.'

The nadir came on the ninth tee when Monty was about to drive. A drunken fan yelled: 'Miss it, you c**t! You European c**t! Go home!' It was perhaps the most sickening moment of spectator misbehaviour ever witnessed on a golf course. Montgomerie's father James could take no more and left the course, disgusted at the way his son was being abused. This served only to increase the player's distress. As the miscreant was thrown out, Monty, his legs shaking in fury, turned to the crowd and warned them that if anyone else followed suit they would end up going the same way.

Monty was not alone in being targeted. Darren Clarke received a sarcastic 'Good shot!' when he missed a chip and his 4 and 2 defeat to a pumped up Hal Sutton made the score 10-10. David Duval had already wrapped up a 5 and 4 thrashing of Parnevik and celebrated in ludicrous style, skipping about the green with double fisted salutes that only served to wind up further the passions of the baying crowd.

Montgomerie resolved to dig deeper, but, still shaken, missed from four feet on the ninth in the wake of the vile abuse he had received on the tee. He had been three up and now his lead was down to one. With scoreboards all over the course indicating that Europe were in free fall, Monty somehow managed to win the 12th to double his advantage. But Stewart sensed the glory might be his for the taking and claimed the 14th and 15th to leave the contest all square with three to play.

The overall situation was changing rapidly and, directly in front of Montgomerie and Stewart, José Maria Olazábal was suffering. He had earlier built a four-hole advantage against Justin Leonard but the 1997 Open champion was surging back. Furthermore, Steve Pate and Jim Furyk had added two more points for America and although Padraig Harrington had won the 'all-Irish' clash with Mark O'Meara and Paul Lawrie had dispatched Jeff Maggert in the bottom match, America now needed just half a point to regain the trophy. There were only two matches left on the course and Olazábal would have to win to give Montgomerie the chance of keeping the Ryder Cup in European hands.

But the Spaniard had failed to find the bogey that would have put him five up after eleven. He had then dropped shots at the next two holes to see his advantage halved and Leonard's putter came alive to win the 14th. At the next the American drained another long putt to level the contest. Like Monty's match with Stewart it was now all square with three holes to play. It remained that way as they reached the 17th. Both Olazábal and Leonard found the green in two, even though the Spaniard had been angered by another heckler as he played his second shot. Nevertheless, he was marginally closer to the hole than his opponent, though both seemingly had only outside birdie chances.

From the fairway behind Montgomerie watched, knowing that if Leonard won this hole the American would be one up with one to play, effectively guaranteeing the half that would give the Cup back to the home team. All of the American players and wives gathered at the back of that 17th green, the fermenting crowd strained against the ropes desperate for a glimpse of the action. Reporters crouched low, commentators whispered into their microphones. Leonard was first to putt . . .

Ron Jones, BBC Radio Five Live: 'Oh, it's gone in and everybody, all the Americans, come tumbling on to the green . . .'

Mark James: 'Leonard unbelievably sunk his putt and all hell broke loose. The Americans were celebrating because they thought that was it.'

Sam Torrance: 'The US should be ashamed. It's about the most disgusting thing I've seen and this is not sour grapes. The way they ran across the green was disgraceful. Tom Lehman calls himself a man of God but his behaviour today has been disgusting.'

Colin Montgomerie: 'I couldn't believe what I saw happening on the seventeenth green. I felt sure that when the celebrating finished they would all walk to the next tee, but then I saw José Maria standing there on his own trying to make a putt and I thought: "This is unbelievable."'

Ben Crenshaw: 'I've never seen such an indomitable spirit from our guys.'

José Maria Olazábal: 'The bottom line is that the whole world saw what happened and the whole world is going to judge what their behaviour was like. All we ask is respect from our opponent.'

When Leonard's ball went into the hole any remaining decorum on that feverish afternoon in Massachusetts went out of the window. The celebrations were premature: Olazábal still had a putt to halve the hole and take the match down the last. Montgomerie was all square with Stewart and helpless back down the 17th fairway. The green had been invaded as the American players and wives sought to chase after the ecstatic Leonard. Some witnesses claim they had run over the line of Olazábal's putt. Video evidence suggests that wasn't the case as Leonard wheeled away from the position from where the Spaniard would eventually play. Regardless, they were unprecedented scenes that showed just how desperate the USA were for victory. 'Payne and I looked at each other as if to say, "That's strange", and I said to him, "Sorry, is that it?" because it seemed like it was. The green was a mess and I felt it was a very, very odd situation,' Montgomerie told me later. 'I think a team running on to celebrate a victory is okay (once it has been completed) but the days of supporters running on are a thing of the past. Put it this way, they won't be running on the green when I'm the captain, I can assure you.'

America's win duly arrived as Olazábal's long-range attempt to match his opponent's feat understandably failed in its mission to prolong the contest. Leonard was one up with one to play; a guaranteed half-point meant that the US would reach the magic number of at least 14½ points at the completion of their match. In a display of extraordinary defiance, Olazábal managed to birdie the closing hole to avoid personal defeat, but it was ultimately of little consolation to the dejected but dignified Spaniard.

The trophy was switching hands, but Montgomerie had a record to preserve. He had never been beaten in singles and this was no time to surrender a statistic of which he had become increasingly proud. They halved the 17th and on the last Montgomerie found the green in two and his opponent was 15 feet away in three shots. Stewart offered the Scot a half as they made their way up to the green, a gentleman's draw given that the contest was all over. Monty wasn't interested; he still wanted to win his match. He had been denied that opportunity against Scott Hoch in 1997 by his captain's sportsmanship and it still rankled. 'He wants points and he wants it on the record that he's won most points, otherwise he would have halved with Payne Stewart at Brookline,' noted his former skipper Bernard

Gallacher. 'He's a different animal in the Ryder Cup; he has this determination to follow it through.'

Stewart was ready to celebrate 'the comeback of the century' with his team-mates and once Monty indicated that he wanted to putt out the American offered his hand. The US player conceded to give a win to the Scot that took his haul for the week to a fine three and a half points. Stewart's concession was a rare moment of genuine sportsmanship from the Americans on an otherwise shameful Sunday afternoon and it meant that having come from 10-6 down they had won by 14½-13½ points. Stewart's gesture left an indelible mark on Montgomerie's memory, made all the more poignant by the American's untimely death later that year. 'I'll never forget when he won the 1999 US Open at Pinehurst, the first thing he said was that he was in the US Ryder Cup team,' Montgomerie remembered. 'And he was thrilled about being in the Ryder Cup team, even more than winning the US Open. It meant so much to him to represent his country. It was a shame the way it finished. He'd had enough, I had had enough, and he picked up my ball at the last, I'll never forget that. I look back at Brookline with memories; they're not all fond, but that match with him I will always think of with fond memories.'

Even though the 1999 Ryder Cup had ended in overall defeat for Europe, Monty had delivered in exactly the way his captain had hoped and in so doing the Scot endured the worst crowd excesses ever witnessed in golf. 'As far as the heckling I took is concerned, well, I now use it as a motivating factor and as a compliment because it must mean that I can play this game quite well,' he said. 'I cannot tell you the number of occasions I had to back off a shot. Personal attacks should never happen.'

Montgomerie's caddie, Alastair McLean, who had nearly

been arrested as he tried to beat a traffic queue with an illegal manoeuvre on the way to the course that morning, offers a telling account of how well his boss coped. He told Norman DaBell in *How We Won the Ryder Cup*: 'He comes under a lot of fire from the press and public that he doesn't handle himself well, but nobody in the world could have handled himself better than he did that week, especially that last day. It was unbelievable what he went through, how he survived it.'

America had the trophy, Europe had the moral high ground and Monty had his unbeaten record. 'He's a wonderful golfer in every way,' Ben Crenshaw commented. 'He's shown it many times in many places and he certainly lifts the players with him. You could say a lot of things about Colin, but he's a tremendous golfer.'

Montgomerie would later recall it as his finest performance to date on the other side of the Atlantic. 'I've played well in Europe over the years, I suppose. But in America that was the best I've played, yeah,' he said. Monty also had high praise for the way he had been handled by his skipper. 'Mark really was a brilliant captain and especially when he talked to you at Brookline. It was the best part of the day for everyone concerned. It was a shame that we just came up half a point short.'

For many observers that final day was the lowest point in the Ryder Cup's history, but television ratings soared and Ken Brown, a beaten captain's assistant, is convinced it was a great occasion for the future of the competition. 'This was the all-American comeback from the dead, and they were lucky to be only four points behind going into the final day,' he said. 'It was brilliant for the Ryder Cup even though it hurt like hell for us.'

The match capped a decade of Ryder Cup action that had seen the event grow and grow. It had served some of the greatest sporting drama of the 1990s and Montgomerie had been at the heart of much of it. There was a huge sense of anticipation for the next contest, the first of the twenty-first century, which would be staged back at the Belfry. Europe couldn't wait for the chance to win back the trophy, America couldn't wait to try to defend it and Monty was looking forward to building further his Ryder Cup legend. But they would all have to hang around longer than expected before the opportunity came along.

9

'That was the best moment, when that ball was
mid-flight, that I have ever had in my professional
career' — Colin Montgomerie

*N*o *longer number one. His back was dodgy and he hadn't*
won for more than a year. But the sun was shining and
there was nothing wrong with his shoulders, still broad and strong
enough to bear the responsibility of leadership. The fans had
cheered him and laughed with him. They had roared him to the
first tee. He had a job to do and he was up to the task. It was a
very important role, one for which he had been hand-picked. He
was nervous; his hands were shaking. His team needed a fast start
and he had to set the tone. The trophy was in American hands
and they seemed reluctant to let go. It would have to be prised
from their grip and it was his job to loosen their hold, and do it
quickly. He felt the admiration. He was the man, the player
enjoying the week of his golfing life. It was hard not to smile from
ear to ear as the starter announced his name in the autumnal
sunshine. A bashful grin would suffice. Then a deep breath followed
by the sweetest of swings. This drive would go for miles . . .

The grandstands stood tall but it would be a while before they
would rock to the sound of European roars. The marquees

were in place and the wait seemed to be almost over. In the West Midlands of England it was nearly time to repair the Ryder Cup and restore its spirit after the pummelling the event had suffered through the bad blood of Brookline. In a few short days the European team had an appointment with its desire to win back the trophy that had been ripped from its grasp by that almighty comeback from the USA in Boston.

It mattered greatly two years earlier when national pride lay in the hands of a dozen golfers. But now the game had been rendered meaningless. The world was in shock and America was grieving in the wake of the terrorist attacks of September 11 2001. There was no way that the US could think about something as trivial as a golf match and their opponents fully understood. It was no surprise and a source of much relief when the decision was taken, five days after the planes flew into New York's Twin Towers, to postpone the 2001 Ryder Cup for a year. The stands and the tents were dismantled with dignity, to be rebuilt twelve months later.

So Colin Montgomerie and the other twenty-three players who had won selection for the match were made to wait before playing in the thirty-fourth Ryder Cup, the first to be staged in an even-numbered year. Officials from the PGA of America, European Tour and PGA had decided that the players who had qualified or been selected for the 2001 match should be the ones who would play a year on, regardless of current form. They would also wear the original official team colours. This would be the 2001 match in every respect, apart from the date it was played.

As expected, Sam Torrance graduated from a vice-captain's role at Brookline to take over from Mark James as Europe's skipper and two-time US Open champion Curtis Strange was appointed to lead the visitors. 'I don't think cancelling or post-poning is giving in to terrorism,' Torrance said when the decision was taken. 'I think it is reflecting the enormity of the horrors we have seen.'

The delay meant the captains occupied their roles for three years and the circumstances meant that they faced unique challenges. The biggest of these was leading players who had lost form. Normally they would be managing golfers who had been playing well enough in the recent past to earn a qualifying spot or a captain's wild card. They should be players who were not lacking in self-belief. But golf is a transient game and confidence can be lost more quickly than the time it takes to be gained. A few of the players had gone from strength to strength, most notably Tiger Woods, who had successfully defended his 2001 Masters title and earned a second US Open crown. He had also won the WGC American Express Championship the week before the Ryder Cup.

Others had less cause for self-assurance. When the teams had originally been assembled every American was in the top 24 in the world and each of the Europeans occupied places in the leading 55. Twelve months on and Hal Sutton had plummeted from 21st in the world to 125th and the 2001 Open champion David Duval had slipped to 93rd on the PGA Tour money list. Europe had been hit harder. Rookie Paul McGinley's ranking had fallen to 71, two more newcomers had suffered hangovers from their year of qualification – Phillip Price was down to 119th and Pierre Fulke 88th – and most dramatic of all had been the fall of Lee Westwood from 17th in the world to only just inside the top 150. The aggregate ranking of the American team had slipped from 118 to 346 and Europe's had ballooned from 284 to 611.

Montgomerie had not suffered too much, but the statistics suggested he was no longer the player he had been. In 2001 he won twice on the European Tour in eight top ten finishes. The following season yielded no victories before the Ryder Cup and although there had been a respectable amount of cheques there was an increasing number of missed cuts creeping on to his record. His inconsistency was perhaps summed up best by his four rounds at the Open Championship at Muirfield. Montgomerie opened with a frustrating 74; he was all smiles after a superb second-round 64, only to card a miserable 84 in atrocious Saturday conditions which meant his closing 75 was of little consequence. Yet another major had slipped by.

More worryingly, there were a couple of withdrawals through injury. The Scot's back was playing up. He managed only one round at the season-opening Johnnie Walker Classic in Perth and the same thing happened at the WGC NEC Invitational in Seattle a month before the match at the Belfry. 'I've got a problem and I've got to deal with it,' he said when he arrived for the Ryder Cup. 'It's self-help right now, unfortunately, that's the toughest way.' The good news for his captain Torrance was that the 'self-help' was doing the trick and he was fit to play. 'I wouldn't have travelled here if I wouldn't have been fit to play five times. But there were times over the last two months where I really thought I was going to have to take the rest of the year off.' Torrance knew all too well the importance of Monty to his team and made provision for a massage table to be erected in the player's hotel bedroom.

Montgomerie was no longer the undisputed European number one. Lee Westwood had ended his run of seven Orders of Merit in 2000 when Monty finished sixth on the money list and he was fifth highest earner in 2001 when he ended up behind Darren Clarke, Padraig Harrington and Thomas Björn in the Ryder Cup qualifying table. It was the lowest qualifying position of his career in the matches to date. But in the context of these biennial clashes with the Americans, Montgomerie's stock had never been higher. His heroics at Brookline in nurturing the debutant Paul Lawrie in the face of such outright hostility from the US crowds had become the stuff of legend. It had been witnessed first hand by Torrance in his role as a vice-captain and it was little wonder that he repeatedly referred to his friend and compatriot as his 'rock'.

Monty was delighted to be playing under the new captain, whom he had been so keen to partner at Oak Hill back in 1995. Being asked to deliver for Torrance was an additional motivating factor. 'Winning this would be nice to sort of finish off Sam Torrance's career,' Montgomerie told reporters. 'It means an awful lot to him. He's a very emotional man and I know him very well. He's not just from the same country as me, he's from the same county [Ayrshire] and I know what it means to him. It would be nice to finish off his career with a win for his sake.'

Being appointed captain was the pinnacle of Torrance's career. The mustachioed man from Largs was one of the most popular figures in European golf, both in and outside the locker room. He had acquired his own place in the history of the matches by holing the winning putt on the final green at the Belfry in 1985 to condemn the Americans to their first Ryder Cup defeat in twenty-eight long years. As the ball dropped his arms spread wide and the tears of elation began to flow. It meant that much, as did his appointment to lead his continent. 'It's enormous, it's everything you ever wanted in golf . . . it's fantastic,' Torrance said.

Torrance didn't just use the extra year of preparation time to foster a formidable team spirit; he also turned his attention to the setup of the Belfry course. It is the home captain's prerogative to adjust the playing characteristics better to suit his team. Remembering that the Americans could boast the big-hitting Woods, David Duval, Davis Love and Phil Mickelson, it made sense to try to take the driver out of their hands. Torrance instructed the green-keepers to grow in the rough to narrow the fairways beyond the 280-yard mark where their balls would be landing. He felt that the visitors would be better equipped and better practised at dealing with long rough around the greens, so he shortened the grass in these areas to remove the American flop shot from their armoury. By doing this he nullified those high-flighted chips from around greens that are routinely played on the US Tour. And on the greens he believed that Curtis Strange's team would relish fast, slick putting surfaces, so the instruction was for them to play relatively slowly by professional standards.

Right up to the week of the match Europe's captain tinkered with the setup, using his players as sounding boards to try to create the optimum playing conditions to suit his side. After the team convened on the Monday of the match he took his two senior playing lieutenants, Montgomerie and Bernhard Langer, to one side to discuss the length of the rough. They advised shortening the grass and the mowers were dispatched to reduce its length from four inches to three and a half. Perhaps the logic was to make the Belfry less like a US Open course; perhaps it was simply the preference of two ageing players, one with a dodgy back, the other suffering from a sore neck. Maybe they didn't fancy a week hacking out of the long stuff?

Montgomerie had let it be known that he was keen to be

reunited with Langer in foursomes and fourball play but Torrance was keeping an open mind. 'The fact is you could pair Monty with anyone,' the captain recalled. His talisman was in upbeat mood and the reason was the simple fact that he was there. Montgomerie had been so concerned that his troublesome back would rule him out of his favourite week on the golfing calendar that he had called a meeting at head-quarters of his management company IMG a couple of weeks ahead of the Belfry clash. Monty, his coach Denis Pugh and sports psychologist Hugh Mantle were in attendance with his personal manager Guy Kinnings to discuss their strategy. Monty was at his wits' end over whether he would be able to play and the prospect of taking the rest of 2002 off was one of the options discussed. Eventually they decided they should wait to see how he fared at the American Express event and with each round that he played at Mount Juliet Montgomerie's form and fitness improved. He was able to make the call that his captain had so desired and expected. The 'rock' was fit to play and confident there would be no damaging erosion even if he was asked to play in all five sequences of matches. It was as though a tremendous weight had been lifted from Monty's shoulders and he was ready to relish what proved the most enjoyable week of his golfing life.

Torrance was keen to make his fellow Scot feel special and openly talked up his influence even though he was no longer the number one player in the European team. It was an astute piece of man management from a clever captain and Mont-gomerie sent out positive signals to remind the Americans that he was still a genuine threat. 'I don't have the number one tag and I think that's quite good,' Monty told reporters. 'It's a more relaxing position I'm in. It's the first time since

New boy on parade: Monty (*back row, second left*) embarking on his Ryder Cup career at Kiawah Island in 1991.

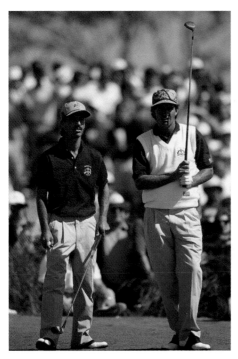

Kicking up a storm: Monty didn't think much of Corey Pavin (*left*) and Steve Pate's (*right*) provocative Desert Storm caps in 1991. Pavin would go on to captain the US against Monty in 2010.

A legend is born: But had a tiddler on the 17th dropped for Mark Calcavecchia, Monty's unbeaten singles record would never have even begun.

Master and apprentice: Nick Faldo and Monty's partnership bloomed in 1993 at the Belfry, but Faldo chose not to pick his former teammate for the 2008 match.

Legless: Bernard Gallacher didn't need a drink, such was the intoxication upon winning at his third attempt as captain in 1995.

Captain Seve Ballesteros was an ever-present force in 1997, however his sporting gesture cost Monty outright victory against Scott Hoch.

Reigning in the rain in Spain: Monty steps up to take centre stage for Team Europe after guaranteeing victory at Valderrama.

They think it's all over … it isn't quite: The American team celebrate Justin Leonard's bombshell by invading the green at Brookline in 1999. But Olazábal was still to putt.

His finest hour: Monty leads the way to European victory at the Belfry in 2002. In the background the scoreboard turns to a sea of blue.

Strong as rope: That's how 2004 US captain Hal Sutton (*inset*) thought his dream team pair would prove. Unfortunately for him Tiger Woods (*left*) and Phil Mickelson (*right*) failed to gel.

Finishing the job: Monty never holed a putt to win a major but he did close out victory in 2004 for captain Bernhard Langer (*inset*) at Oakland Hills.

On the same side: Sandy Lyle (*left*) was a captain's assistant in 2006 at the K Club. There was never any chance of him performing the same role in 2010 after he accused Monty of cheating.

The agony: Monty's face is a picture of anguish as he attempts to hole the winning putt against David Toms in 2006.

The ecstasy: Or is it just relief? Monty celebrates on the way to three successive European victories.

Rain stops play: Rivers of rainwater cover the 18th fairway at Celtic Manor as suspended play on the first day of the 2010 Ryder Cup adds to the tension.

Cometh the hour…: An anxious crowd urge Graeme McDowell's birdie putt into the 16th hole knowing that, if it drops, Europe will almost certainly regain the Ryder Cup.

No 'I' in team: Colin Montgomerie with the Ryder Cup surrounded by his victorious 2010 squad. (*From back-left to front-right*) Luke Donald, Lee Westwood, Martin Kaymer, Peter Hanson, Colin Montgomerie, Padraig Harrington, Ross Fisher, Ian Poulter, Miguel Ángel Jiménez, Francesco Molinari, Edoardo Molinari, Rory McIlroy, Graeme McDowell.

Monty's Manor: Victory as captain of Europe confirms Montgomerie as one of the greatest figures in Ryder Cup history.

we came here in ninety-three that I haven't had that position. And I think that it did bring the pressure on, being the number one player in Europe. Now I don't have that pressure and stress. I'm more relaxed because of that.'

This was significant because the cumulative effect of not punching his formidable golfing weight in the majors had taken its toll. Ever more Montgomerie was becoming known for his tetchy demeanour when things went against him. He always struggled to hide emotions when his golf let him down and 'Monty meltdown' stories were common occurrences. That week at the Belfry there was a different Monty as he sought to make himself the most popular figure in the European team. In one practice round he came to the par three 12th hole. He'd put himself in an awkward spot close to the galleries. 'I had a horrible lie and I didn't fancy it. So this guy in the crowd thought he did,' Montgomerie said. 'I gave him my club and he hit it stiff! Of course I had to have a go and I chipped up and missed the putt. Steve was his name and now he's one up!' Never mind that a mere fan had outplayed one of Europe's finest golfers; the crowd loved what was the most fantastic piece of public relations imaginable. Montgomerie also felt his actions benefited the players around him. 'There are a lot of people and the stands are full and it can get quite tense, even for the rookies, I suppose, as well.'

As one of the two most experienced players in the European team, Monty knew the roles that had been identified for him and his fellow senior citizen Bernhard Langer. 'Of course Bernhard and myself would be seen as on-course leaders and it is a nice position to be in. It's a position that I like and thrive on. Rookies have come up to me already and asked certain questions and certain ideas about what's what. And it might be a little frightening to ask certain questions, but they can ask me. I feel that I have that sort of on-course role; obviously not an off-course role because that is down to the captain.'

For these reasons and the fact that he had practised with him, many pundits were expecting Montgomerie to be paired with the fragile Westwood, with whom he got on well. But when the pairings for the opening fourball matches were announced, Sam Torrance sprang a couple of surprises. He preferred the effervescent Sergio García as Westwood's ally and heeded Montgomerie's preferred option, which was to be put with Langer. 'They've both got a wealth of experience, they're both playing great,' the skipper commented. 'They were actually a couple of my floaters, they could have gone anywhere. The other teams gelled together so well I didn't need to split them up, so it was great to be able to put them together.' Montgomerie and Langer were sent out third behind Darren Clarke and Thomas Björn and the García/Westwood combination. Padraig Harrington and Niclas Fasth were the final pairing. Monty and Langer would face Scott Hoch and Jim Furyk, a tough and uncompromising pair of whom the Americans had high hopes.

The night before the match began Langer, who had been nursing his own neck and back problems, tried to get off to sleep. But he lay in an awkward position and soon realised he had aggravated his injuries and his neck began to seize up. He made a late-night call to his captain to alert Torrance that there might be a problem and a frantic search to locate physio Dale Richardson followed. Only the next morning did Langer declare himself fit. He and Monty weren't the only ones struggling to be ready for action. Langer's caddie Pete Coleman had broken his shoulder earlier in the summer when he tumbled from a stepladder while picking blackberries and had defied doctors' orders when he returned to his duties ahead of schedule. Coleman needed to pace himself during the practice rounds and Torrance's regular bagman, Malcolm Mason, had deputised for him during a couple of them.

Monty, meanwhile, had a relatively new caddie in Andy Prodger. They had been working together since May 2002, when Montgomerie parted from his long-serving bagman, Alastair McLean. The move was not without controversy because Prodger switched bags at the Benson and Hedges tournament, also staged at the Belfry, without the blessing of his previous employer, Phillip Price. Any ill feeling between the Welshman and the Scot seemed to have been put behind them by the time they returned to the West Midlands course, especially as they were now team-mates.

Montgomerie was delighted to be spoken of as an on-course leader, but there was no doubt who was in charge of his partnership for this fourball match. Monty was more than happy to leave the decision-making to his methodical German partner. By letting Langer play the senior role, the Scot was again showing the relaxed demeanour that was his trademark that week. What Langer said went. This included the lining up of putts, decisions on which player would hit first and the identification markings applied to their balls. Most players mark their ball with a felt-tipped pen to provide an additional distinguishing feature, but Monty would never bother. Langer instructed Coleman to apply markings on his and his partner's golf balls to ensure there would be no mix-ups.

Their contrasting approaches to the game provided a source of strength. Monty was laid back, relaxed and freewheeling;

Langer was intense, organised and precise in word and deed. It made for a perfect combination on the course. Although Furyk and Hoch played nicely enough, they never stood a chance. The European pair were two up after eleven holes and at the next Monty, who has always enjoyed putting on relatively slow greens, slotted home a 16-footer that put them three up for the second time in the match.

Two holes later Langer effectively ended the contest. Never the most demonstrative of players, the two-time Masters champion was indicating that his birdie putt was going to drop with the ball still travelling towards the hole. The downward thrust of his hand heralded yet more roars from the home fans and the ball duly disappeared. One hole later it was all over on what was turning into a superb morning for the home team.

Montgomerie and Langer's 4 and 3 win yielded Europe's second point after Westwood and García had secured the first by beating David Duval and Davis Love by the same score. Moments later, up ahead at the 18th, Darren Clarke and Thomas Björn edged home in a tense contest with Tiger Woods and Paul Azinger. Furthermore, Europe were threatening to go through the morning unbeaten. Padraig Harrington was convinced he had secured a half in the bottom match as he putted across the final green and stared with utter disbelief when his ball horseshoed out to allow Phil Mickelson and David Toms victory by the narrowest of margins. Nevertheless Europe were 3-1 ahead after a highly encouraging start to their quest to regain the trophy.

Sam Torrance saw no reason to change any of his top three pairs for the afternoon foursomes. His only alteration was to bring in the steady Paul McGinley to replace Niclas Fasth as

Harrington's partner in the anchor match. Montgomerie and Langer were again sent out third and this time their opponents were Mickelson and Toms, the only successful Americans in the morning sequence.

In practice the Scot and the German had decided Montgomerie would take the tee shots on the odd numbered holes but when it came to the match they switched roles. The decision was the result of more analysis than when Nick Faldo had unilaterally decided to change the batting order with Monty in 1993. This change followed dispassionate evaluation of their relative strengths. Montgomerie could be relied upon to hit long irons with supreme accuracy while Langer's forte lay with his wedges. The short par four tenth provided the perfect example of why Monty should tee off on the even numbered holes. With the tee set further back, fewer players were prepared to take on the green with a driver or three wood. The hole called for a lay-up with an iron followed by a delicate wedge to the pin. The par three 12th would require a long iron that Montgomerie would be better qualified to hit. So the tactics of the practice round were thrown out for what proved a thrilling clash that went the full distance.

The European pair picked up from where they had left off in the morning, tapping into a well of confidence that was being constantly replenished by the enthusiastic support of the home crowds. They moved smoothly into a three-hole lead and still held the advantage with four holes to play. Elsewhere, Clarke and Björn were struggling against Hal Sutton and Scott Verplank but Sergio García and Lee Westwood were again proving to be an inspired combination and were holding at bay Tiger Woods and Mark Calcavecchia. The bottom match looked to be heading the way of the visitors with Harrington out of sorts and McGinley, on his debut, struggling against Stewart Cink and Jim Furyk.

To preserve their healthy lead, Europe could have done with the point that Montgomerie and Langer looked on the brink of securing. But then Europe's two oldest players started to run out of gas. At the 15th Langer pushed his drive and made finding the green in two on the par five impossible for his partner. Mickelson hit the putting surface with the Americans' second shot to set up a hole-winning birdie. The lead was down to two and the visiting pair sensed they could make more inroads. At the 16th a trademark Mickelson chip-in from the edge of the green provided a hole-winning birdie. Monty and Langer were rocking and in what was a rare occurrence that week a look of indignant concern played across the Scot's face as the players moved on to the penultimate hole. Still they were ahead, but only by a single hole and the momentum was definitely with Mickelson and Toms. Monty's worries were justified as he and Langer failed to match the US pair's third successive birdie at the par five 17th and they went to the last all square.

Montgomerie hit a superb tee shot over the water and into the centre of the fairway. 'A lot of pressure,' acknowledged Sam Torrance. 'Gone from three up back to all square and you stand on that last tee, you definitely need bicycle clips. He hit the most beautiful tee shot. He's a class act, Colin.' Meanwhile, Mickelson's tee shot ran through into the right-hand edge of the rough. Advantage Europe, but Langer then pushed his long iron approach to the right of the green. The diminutive Toms needed all his strength to muscle his approach from a diffi-cult lie on to the front of the vast home green. The pin was cut at the back on the highest of the three tiers and he had left his partner with what appeared a monstrously difficult putt. When the players arrived at the green Mickelson left his putter in his bag. He felt he could get the Americans' third shot closer by chipping. There were audible gasps from the galleries as he took his wedge from his bag to play their third shot from the tightly mown putting surface. Montgomerie, meanwhile, was surveying an awkward pitch from the right of the green. The outcome of the match would depend on the success, or otherwise, of these two wedge shots.

Mickelson is a master of the short game. He is probably the only player in the world who would consider taking on a shot such as this with so much riding on it. As he made contact with the ball a huge divot of lovingly manicured turf flew before it – now the gasps were from the green-keepers. The fans were concentrating on his ball which flew to the back of the green some 15 feet from the hole. Now it was Montgomerie's turn. If Europe could get up and down in two it would possibly be enough to earn them victory. The Scot played a bold shot that narrowly missed the right edge of the hole, but it raced on a further ten feet. Now it was down to the putters of Langer and Toms. The American was first to go and he charged it three feet by, effectively ruling out a European defeat. Langer's putt for victory also failed to drop and it was a bogey five. Mickelson still had work to do, because the putt for a half was no gimme, but the three-times Masters winner held his nerve and, somewhat anti-climactically, the match ended in stalemate. 'It was a big half point for us because we weren't really in the match at all until the last few holes,' Toms later claimed.

Having been three up with four to play, the European pair were understandably frustrated not to have converted the advantage into a win. But Monty's reaction, 'at least we didn't lose', was a clear indication that he was very much in a 'the glass is half full' state of mind. His captain agreed. Torrance said: 'I was glad to get half a point. In foursomes when the momentum has changed it is very hard to get it back again, especially if there is only one hole to go. It was a great half-point.'

The afternoon foursomes session was edged by Curtis Strange's Americans 2½-1½, leaving Europe ahead by just a single point at the end of a typically enthralling day of Ryder Cup golf. It had been just what the match needed after three years of dwelling on the unsavoury events of Brookline. 'The people have been wonderful, very fair,' Mickelson confirmed. Tiger Woods, who endured a miserable day losing both his matches, went further: 'I think this is much more how it should be. It's much more bipartisan. There are no comments at all from the fans and they appreciate good shots from both sides and that's the way the Ryder Cup is meant to be played.' Complimenting the spectators in this way was a smart move from Woods, who had disappointed thousands of ticket holders on the eve of the match by choosing to practise early in the morning before the gates had been opened to the public.

Unlike the first day, the second began with the alternate-shot foursomes. The order of the different formats is dictated by the home captain and Torrance had gone away from the accepted norm. His feeling was that Europe would be more successful in the better-ball format. 'I always thought, start with your strength and finish with your strength.' He was also keen to make sure that all twelve of his players would play before the final-day singles so there would be no repeat of what happened at Brookline when Europe gave three rookies their first taste of the Ryder Cup when the pressure was at its most intense. So Pierre Fulke and Phillip Price were brought in and sent out first ahead of Westwood and García, the trusted Montgomerie/Langer partnership and Darren Clarke and Thomas Björn, who were sent out last.

Langer had requested to miss one session, so knew that he would be replaced in the afternoon after their match against the two American Scotts – Verplank and Hoch. There were echoes of the previous afternoon as the European pair made a strong start only to be pegged back. Monty and Langer were one up after four holes and two up after ten. The Americans then won the 11th when Verplank holed a huge putt and then the 15th and it was still all square with two holes to play. At the 17th the home duo made the decisive breakthrough. Langer struck a superb seven iron to within six feet of the hole to prompt a massive roar from the home fans. Emboldened, Montgomerie was never going to miss the chance to put Europe ahead again. He duly obliged, but only after absorbing detailed analysis from his partner on what was required. They initially thought the putt would borrow from the right lip but Langer noticed the criss-cross patterns on the putting surface left by the green-keepers' mowers. 'One goes this way and one comes the other way, and the majority of the one mower went sort of left to right across the line,' Langer recalled. 'That covered most of the ground from his ball to the hole, so we changed it from right lip to maybe right centre, almost straight. I think that was a wise thing to do.' Such attention to detail allied to the enduring accuracy of Montgomerie's putting stroke ensured that they made the most of Langer's stunning approach shot. A par at the last slammed the door to keep Europe ahead.

Between them Langer and Montgomerie had been an

impregnable force. At no stage in their three matches together were they ever behind. 'I was thrilled to be paired with him,' Langer said of Monty. 'We just seem to gel well together. In the fourball we did extremely well. Whenever he wasn't quite there I came in and when I was gone, he was there. It worked out wonderfully.' Langer also recognised the importance of keeping Monty's spirits high when things went against them. 'If I see that he has a tendency to get down I won't let him. I've got to tell him, "Come on." We don't worry about what's happened, whether we lost a hole or won a hole. We look at the shots we face until it is over. That's all you can do.'

Monty was equally thrilled with his German partner. 'The whole team would love to play with him. I was lucky enough to have him. I think the whole American team would love to have him as a partner, as well. The way Pete Coleman and him work together is fantastic.' The Scot was also grateful for the way Langer kept his mental attitude in the right place. 'He slows me down. I've got great admiration and respect for him and you need both of these in a partner. We've played together seven times and we have lost only once. We have a super record.'

Clarke and Björn had already lost heavily to Woods and Love and the plucky rookies Fulke and Price went down 2 and 1 to the dependable Mickelson and Toms. Westwood and García maintained their 100 per cent record by closing out victory over Cink and Furyk at the 17th and it meant that Europe led 6½-5½ heading into their perceived strong suit, the afternoon fourballs.

Monty knew that he would have a new partner for the afternoon and Torrance, in his autobiography, *Sam*, reveals that when told he would be paired with Padraig Harrington,

Montgomerie said he preferred to play with Paul McGinley. Firmly the skipper told Monty that Harrington would be his partner. 'He's perfect for you,' the skipper said and didn't hang around for any further discussion. The Irishman had been out of sorts on the opening day and had practised with his coach, Bob Torrance, Sam's dad, until darkness fell the previous evening. He spent the morning on the range as well to get his game back into shape and the hard work paid dividends. Sam's refusal to bend to Monty's wishes was the starting point for another famous partnership.

If Monty had been happy to play second fiddle to Langer there was always going to be a role reversal here. Harrington didn't expect anything less. 'Monty and Langer had a tremendous record and I was brought in because Bernhard wanted a rest,' Harrington recalled. 'Monty was playing fantastic, as he always does in the Ryder Cup. So I said to my caddie [Dave McNeilly] that we'd got one job to do, we were there absolutely in a support role. We just had to keep Monty happy. If we kept him happy he would keep playing well and if we threw in the odd birdie to back him up that would be fine, but our most important job was to keep him happy between shots.'

While Harrington had the morning to prepare for the match, Montgomerie had a mere twenty minutes between leaving the closing green and heading to the first tee. He made the journey with confident strides, unbeaten with two and half-points out of a possible three and with Europe clinging on to the narrowest of leads. This match promised to be a tough test because the opposition was the undefeated pair of David Toms and Phil Mickelson. They were Curtis Strange's most dependable combination, but they were also the ideal adversaries as far as Monty was concerned. There was a definite feeling of unfinished business after the way the US duo had fought back to claim that half-point on the first afternoon and the Scot used it as a motivational tool.

To say the new partners hit it off would be a major understatement. They dovetailed superbly, with Montgomerie claiming a birdie at the second and Harrington contributing two more birdies in the first five holes while Monty was effectively drawing breath after his morning exertions. Both players' games fitted perfectly and it was a seamless transition for the experienced Scot. Another aspect that helped this process was Harrington's intelligence and intuitive feel of how to treat his partner, recognising what made him tick. The key was making Montgomerie feel happy between shots and to keep him mentally fresh by distracting him from the golf and the size of the occasion. Harrington feared, though, that this policy was in danger of backfiring as they made their way down the fifth fairway. 'Monty had hit a three wood off the tee and that particular club had been in his bag for about ten years,' Harrington said. 'It was the famous one with the red shaft. My caddie then decided to talk to Monty about the club being in his bag for such a long time. He went on to explain to Monty about the ohms of electrical resistance that club must have generated if each hit he had made counted as one ohm. This is in the middle of the Ryder Cup! Monty was looking at him aghast, like he was totally mad, as if to say, "What is this man going on about?" All this as he made his way down the fairway but it suitably kept Monty's mind off the golf and he did play fantastic. He realised that we were going to keep him talking and never let him get down on himself. If you do that he will always play well,' Harrington said.

Two up after seven, Monty stretched the advantage at the

next holing for birdie from 15 feet. By taking control of their match he and Harrington were boosting their team because the other three fourball matches were desperately close. The longer it looked likely that this match would yield a European point the more it heaped pressure on the Americans in the other games. Equally, it meant that Montgomerie and Harrington were performing under intense pressure because there were no guarantees of any other points coming their side's way that afternoon. Mickelson and Toms were keen to signal they weren't beaten yet and the back nine turned into a tense tussle in which the home pair, Montgomerie in particular, had to play brilliantly to stay in front. At the 14th the Scot astounded the galleries by holing from 35 feet. Suddenly Mickelson's 15-footer was for a half and when he missed it the Americans fell two down again having arrived at the green harbouring realistic hopes of levelling the contest. Monty and Harrington preserved that two-hole advantage until the 17th where a mere half would suffice. Montgomerie hit a superb third shot to the right fringe of the green on the par five. Both American opponents carved open their own birdie chances, but they would be redundant if Monty could hole his putt. As the ball set off on its journey it seemed destined to finish in the hole. So sure was Monty that he had secured yet another Ryder Cup point that he began to step away in celebration, only to see the ball horseshoe out of the hole.

It meant that the Americans were still alive, but only if one of them could hole out for birdie. Toms went first and missed and then, inexplicably, Mickelson left short his attempt when golf's oldest adage of 'never up, never in' should have been burning his ears. Monty and Harrington had won and as far as the Scot was concerned he had played the Ryder Cup golf of his life. Asked whether his play had ever been better in a fourball match, he said: 'No. And had to be so. We were playing the number two and number six ranked players in the world. David Toms is an underrated player and we don't know much about him in Europe. And of course with Phil you can't be sure what will happen around the greens, he's a magician. I think we did well to hold them off.

'Padraig did awfully well. He was looking forward to playing after losing both games on the first day and he came out firing on all cylinders and he was a great partner to have. To have that confidence in a partner is huge. I never felt that I was on my own. It's terrible to feel that way, but I didn't feel that,' Montgomerie said.

Harrington added: 'Colin was making stacks of birdies. I knew if I backed him up a little bit we would be good enough.'

Mickelson described his European opponents as 'sensational', adding: 'After we halved number one in par there was a birdie in the groove all the way through fourteen and somebody birdied at least one. It was a wonderful match.'

It proved the only home success that afternoon. Jesper Parnevik, in his first outing, partnered Niclas Fasth to defeat on the final green against David Duval and Mark Calcavecchia and Sergio García and Lee Westwood were frustrated to finally run out of steam and fall to Tiger Woods and Davis Love, García kicking his bag in frustration as he departed the 18th green a beaten man. The bottom match featured Darren Clarke and Paul McGinley against Scott Hoch and Jim Furyk and was the third match of the afternoon to go the full distance, this one ending all square. It had been America's session and, having trailed since the opening morning, Curtis Strange's team had at last fought back to parity.

Despite letting slip the lead it was important for Europe to remain upbeat. Sam Torrance tried to exude calm as he faced the massed ranks of reporters in the media centre. 'We're tied for the lead going into the final day and that's always good,' he said before adding his famous line: 'They've got one Tiger, I've got twelve lions.' Montgomerie also sought to set a positive tone with the kind of analysis that marked him out as a future captain. 'We have a great team spirit and I think we just have to go for it now. We have to say, okay, eight-all, they're not ahead and they're a very strong team, the Americans, and we look forward now to winning the singles series, and we haven't done that often. We did it at Oak Hill. We did it here in eighty-five. We need to do it again.'

It was now time for the captains to gamble, to assemble their final hand and the order in which they would play their cards in the final-day singles. Whichever skipper made the correct decision would be the one holding the trophy come Sunday evening. As Montgomerie said: 'Sam has an important task to get the order right. Sometimes we have felt that the order hasn't been the way we would like it and the draw hasn't come out the way that we would like it to. Hopefully, this time it will.'

Torrance knew what he needed – six and a half points. Nothing more, nothing less, and he wanted to get them quickly. When the draw was published Montgomerie, who had just returned from a back massage, scanned it keenly, trying to see who he would be up against and at what point he would join the fray. But he struggled to find his name. Initially he was expecting to be put around seventh or eighth in the draw, the sort of position that traditionally decides the match. He was wrong. He was out first and the reason his name didn't jump out at him was because he was the only player of the twenty-four on the handwritten sheet who had not been referred to by his surname. Instead, Torrance had simply written 'Monty' as the name to lead off Europe's quest to regain the trophy.

Montgomerie's was the first name in a top-loaded order, meaning Torrance, a renowned gambler, was sending out his biggest stars first to steal the initiative and who better to play the lead role? 'Number one,' the matter-of-fact Scot said of his compatriot. 'He was number one for seven years and he's doing it again this week. He's been quite incredible, considering what he's been through the last few months with his back. He's as good as it gets. That's why he's number one tomorrow.'

Behind Monty Europe's batting order had the new continental top dog Sergio García next, followed by Darren Clarke, Bernhard Langer and Padraig Harrington. Those five European big guns would face, respectively, Scott Hoch, David Toms, David Duval, Hal Sutton and Mark Calcavecchia. Europe liked the look of this because their opposing captain had taken a different view from Torrance. Curtis Strange wanted to reserve his top players for the final matches; Tiger Woods was out last against the out-of-form Jesper Parnevik and in the penultimate match Phil Mickelson would face the Welsh rookie Phillip Price. The danger for America was that their top two players might play matches that would have no bearing on the overall contest, especially if the home team's big boys did their stuff early in the order. 'You know I'm not sure what to think,' Strange admitted on the Saturday night after the draw had been published. 'I've never seen someone front-load like this.'

'Curtis has his way of sending out his boys and I have my way,' Torrance countered. 'If it comes down to the last two matches he might be looking favourite. If it doesn't . . .' Torrance just left the thought hanging, raising his expressive eyebrows to maximum altitude to leave no one in any doubt that he was very comfortable with the look of the line-up.

His back had held up. He'd come this far as an unbeatable force. Never behind. The rock was solid and Langer and Harrington had provided secure foundations. Now he was on his own. The solitary leader and he loved the role, loved the responsibility that had been put on him. He could cope; he could thrive. He was nervous, he was shaking, but he wanted to seem relaxed and the fans adored him. They had cheered his every move and he had given them great cause to react in that way. He was one man in a team, but seemed the centre of attention and he had no problem with that. The putter was on song and the hole still seemed the size of a bucket. It was time to lead, let it flow from him and have some fun . . .

Montgomerie relished his early start. Normally you want a lie-in on the final day of a tournament because it means you will be teeing off among the leaders last out. This was no normal week and Monty knew he could lay the foundations for a famous win if he sustained his form of the first two days. Rarely had he felt so at ease on a big day such as this. Huge crowds had gathered at the practice range, the 7,000-seat grandstand was packed, when he arrived for his warm-up. The Scot has never been one for pounding balls on the range; all he requires is to hit a few to get the feel for his rhythmic swing. He wanted to show just how relaxed he felt and repeated his stunt from his earliest practice round by getting the crowd involved. He invited a spectator on to the range to hit a few balls. Standing next to him was Monty's coach Denis Pugh. 'Colin genuinely was showing his nerves at this point. He said he didn't fancy hitting any shots right now,' Pugh recalled. 'I said to him in a joking fashion that either he should hit some shots or I hit and I think it's much better if you hit. So he said: "What about if one of them hits?" So he already had it in his mind. He hit one or two shots to loosen up and on the third one he hit the 50-yard sign and the crowd went crazy. He turned and took a theatrical bow and this chap said: "Well, it took you three goes!" Monty responded by saying, "If you think you can do better, come on down." It wasn't a worry until I saw who it was. The guy clearly wasn't a golfer, he looked like he had just finished his breakfast and he was about to take Colin's sand wedge with grease-laden fingers. He was quite a character and I gave him the sand wedge because Monty was quite happy about it and the first shot was terrible, the second shot was terrible, the third one he just got airborne and he got a boo from the crowd. He was quite a character and we never saw him again. The next half a minute or so I was rigorously dunking Monty's sand wedge in the water and wiping the grease off the grip.'

Montgomerie knew what he was doing as well. He was signalling that he was brimful of confidence for his clash with Scott Hoch. As he departed the range, one of Europe's later starters, Paul McGinley, was arriving. The Scot made sure to wish his Irish team-mate the best of luck. It was a smart move.

All week he had tried hard to give the impression that he was in total control of his golf ball and of his emotions. Only those closest to Montgomerie knew any different. Denis Pugh recalls his final conversation with the player moments before he headed to the first tee. 'He was on the putting green and I was just talking with him as we normally did. He liked to talk about anything, just to be distracted, his favourite football team maybe, stories on TV, a joke or something like that. But on this occasion he asked if I had any coins in my pocket because he had forgotten a ball marker. It was a bit of a role reversal, because usually I was asking him for money! Anyway, as he pulled his hand out of his pocket to show me he had no coins there were about half a dozen tees jumping around like snakes in his hand because he was trembling. I said: "Colin, you look a little bit nervous", and he looked at me and said: "Yes, I am, but do you want to know the good news? I've hit a lot of really good golf shots when I've been nervous.'"

As convention dictates the away side has the honour on the first tee and Hoch struck a respectable drive into the edge of the semi-rough that bordered the left side of the fairway. Up stepped Monty, with his famous three wood, the Callaway that had generated so much golfing electricity down the years. The roars of appreciation echoed across the English countryside. 'It was like a boxing match,' Pugh remembers. Montgomerie could barely suppress a proud but bashful smile in response. 'Ivor Robson, our starter for 35 years, had never felt that atmosphere on the first tee. He had to announce my name twice because it wasn't heard the first time. His clipboard was shaking and it wasn't windy and I thought, "Oh my God." I was very nervous at this point, thinking: "This is just unbelievable."' He channelled all the brewing emotion and flowing adrenalin into the most sublime swing that effortlessly propelled his ball a country mile down the centre of the fairway. 'That was the best moment, when that ball was mid-flight, that I have ever had in my professional career,' Montgomerie told me eight years on from that extraordinary tee shot. The watching Sam

Torrance galloped after Monty as he strode purposefully off the first tee. One last word of encouragement from the man who had instructed his team '*Carpe diem*' – seize the day. The skipper's opening batter had sent his ball careering past Hoch's ball. Size isn't everything and it isn't how, it's how many – Hoch would have been tempted to seek solace in such clichés, but it must still have been a sickening sight.

The American did well to recover his composure and hit the better approach shot. Monty was somewhat wrong-footed because he had a mere 104 yards to the flag and didn't commit fully to his sand wedge shot that crept on to the front of the green. It was the Scotsman rather than the Scott to putt first from around 35 feet.

Carpe diem; Montgomerie stroked his putt, aiming to the right. It took the borrow, it had perfect strength and it fell obediently into the hole. It was going nowhere else and it was a savage blow. Hoch's putt for a half refused to take the borrow from the right that the American had envisaged and Europe were ahead at the very first opportunity. Blue was on the board from the off; captain's orders followed to the letter. 'We never looked back,' Montgomerie said.

Pugh, remembering his conversation regarding those pre-match nerves, stationed himself at the back of the driving area on the second. 'As he came on to the tee he smiled at me, a wink of the eye and said: "I told you so", and I knew then that the day was going to be a short one for Scott Hoch,' Pugh said.

Of course it was only one hole and there were still seventeen to go, but Montgomerie was an unstoppable force when the momentum was with him. He wanted to do it for himself and he needed to do it for his team. The putts just kept on falling and Hoch could do nothing about it. At the turn Monty was three up. Torrance, who was stationed at the first tee to see off each of his players, was waiting to offer a final good luck message to Phillip Price who was up against Phil Mickelson. The skipper caught sight of Monty departing the ninth green which is also close to the clubhouse. Torrance sprinted over; he wanted Hoch to see him because earlier in the week the American had been critical of the way Europe's skipper had set up the tenth hole they were about to play. According to Torrance, this might sow more negative seeds in the American's mind, but more important to the captain was the demeanour of his on-course leader. Montgomerie was 'striding ahead, taking giant steps for Europe'. Furthermore, his commanding position was having the desired effect on his team-mates. Europe were ahead in four of the first five matches, indeed they took the lead first in eight of the twelve matches that day. It was all flowing from Monty.

At the 13th Montgomerie played a wedge approach shot that almost spun back into the hole. Although it didn't drop it was enough to put him four up with five to play. One hole later, the short 14th, the burly man clad all in navy blue with the greying hair unleashed a gorgeous tee shot to 15 feet. The shell-shocked Hoch pulled his left and from there was only going to make par at best. Monty stepped up and knocked in yet another birdie, his sixth of the match and his last in this extraordinary week because it sealed an emphatic 5 and 4 victory. He had claimed a stunning four and a half points out of a possible five, he had put his team ahead again and he had provided just the start Torrance had anticipated when hatching his master plan.

'I played Monty three times and I cannot believe how well he putted,' Hoch later said.

'It was nice to beat someone of Scott Hoch's ability, because he is a tough man,' said Montgomerie, who raced off to support the rest of the team. He wasn't disappointed despite García falling to Toms at the last and Clarke only taking a half from his match against David Duval. By the time those matches were over Harrington had completed a straightforward win over Calcavecchia and Langer disposed of Hal Sutton with the efficiency he had shown throughout a week in which he claimed three and a half points from a possible four. Thomas Björn weighed in with a 2 and 1 win over Stewart Cink and Europe were on the brink.

There was still no guarantee of glory, though. Still too many matches that could go either way. Price was making a mockery of the world rankings and was firmly in charge against Mickelson in the penultimate match, but could he hold his nerve against such an illustrious opponent? There was plenty of pressure on him because Lee Westwood had fallen to Scott Verplank, but Price, playing the calibre of golf that had won him his place on the team a year earlier, completed a famous victory at the 16th. It meant Europe were just a point away from the magic number of 14½ and with Niclas Fasth one up with one to play against Paul Azinger the end looked in sight. That was especially the case because the American found the bunker to the left of the closing green and the Swede was in good shape to make the par that would surely be enough. Azinger had other ideas, however, sensationally holing from the sand and repeatedly and animatedly high-fiving with his caddie in celebration. He had snatched a half that thrust the spotlight on Paul McGinley and Jim Furyk who were watching back on the 18th fairway.

The Irish rookie had just birdied the 17th to level the match and needed a half to win the Cup for Europe. If Furyk snatched a win it would all come down to the tight contests between Woods and Parnevik and Pierre Fulke's tussle with Davis Love. It was too close to call.

Both McGinley and Furyk missed the green in two, amid scenes of growing excitement. The 2002 Ryder Cup was getting the climax it thoroughly deserved. McGinley pitched his third shot to nine feet before Furyk very nearly emulated Azinger's feat of holing from the same bunker. It slipped past by a matter of millimetres to leave McGinley with a putt to secure the half-point that would win the Ryder Cup. For most of their match both golfers had felt like bit-part players. The roars were elsewhere as Montgomerie, Harrington and Langer had been closing out their matches. The Irishman had been playing to a depleted gallery as he struggled to hang on against the doughty Furyk. But after that crucial birdie at the 17th all eyes were now on McGinley as he settled over the putt. 'Of all the people to ask to hole this putt, the last one you would ask to do it would be Paul,' Harrington later said. 'Not because he is a bad putter, but because he is the unluckiest putter I have ever known,' his Irish team-mate smiled. Not this day he wasn't and, besides, he didn't need luck, even though he'd been wished it by Monty at the start of the day. The ball disappeared and the stands erupted. The European team jumped for joy, the tears flowed from the captain and McGinley was thrown into the lake in celebration. The little man from Dublin had finished what Monty had started and the trophy was back in European hands.

Torrance deserved great credit for his inspired stewardship. His man management had been superb in ensuring he got the best from disparate characters who ranged from the fragile

Westwood to the bubbling García, the timid Price to the moti-
vated McGinley, the methodical Langer and, of course, to
Monty, a persona so complex no single word does it justice.
The Scot was relaxed when the norm at the time was for him
to be uptight, he was in tune with the spectators when ordinarily he would often be at odds with galleries; he was so happy
to be led by Langer but by the end was emboldened to do the
leading himself. 'He just led them to the water,' Torrance said.

Montgomerie was top points scorer. 'My most enjoyable
Ryder Cup. I did like being under Sam Torrance,' Montgomerie
said. 'We all did it for him and to see him jump as high as
Paul McGinley did when he sank that putt was fantastic.' This
was Monty's sixth Ryder Cup and he was thirty-nine years
old. He had yet to win a major championship and he had
that unwanted tag of being the undisputed best in the world
not to have secured one of the big four titles. Now fans, press
and players were starting to speculate for the first time that
it might be the Ryder Cup that would provide his legacy,
rather than the calibre of tournaments he won. 'Possibly,' he
conceded. 'You like to think the major championships are
more important, in a way, but I've always liked team competition and I've always thrived on that competition more than
I have the [individual] game of golf. The competitive nature
in me comes out in these matches.'

Europe partied long and hard in the Belfry's main bar
that night. Lee Westwood was the master of ceremonies and
led the singing. The only players missing were Monty and
Langer who had to be cajoled to come and join the celebratory throng which then prompted many a rendition of
'We Love You Monty, We Do'. The player himself has never
been much of a party animal. 'In fact afterwards there was

more a sense of deflation than elation for Monty,' Denis Pugh remembers. 'It was as though Monty and Langer took the view "job done". They enjoyed the doing of their jobs rather than the aftermath and only made token appearances at the party.'

Nevertheless, the next day, when Montgomerie and his wife Eimear departed the Midlands in his Bentley there was no wiping the smile from his face. I know because I happened to be driving in front of them as they drove out of the gates and witnessed what appeared a total sense of glee and complete satisfaction in my rear-view mirror. And whenever Monty glances back at his career, he undoubtedly sees the 2002 Ryder Cup as the week of his golfing life.

Seven years later he would endure one of the worst weeks of his career and it had nothing to do with how well he hit the ball.

10

Sandy Lyle had been looking forward to appearing at the 2008 Open. It offered him a return to the limelight, a reminder of former glories, and he was entitled to be there as a past champion, a winner of golf's most treasured prize. A long time ago, perhaps, but one of the rewards is that they invite you back until you're fit for your pension. He was just fifty. And he remained popular, forever remembered for that bunker shot at Augusta at the last hole in 1988, a seven iron to set up a famous birdie that brought lovely American sunshine into cold British homes. Our lad had done it, taking one of those famous green jackets. Throughout his career Lyle's reputation remained unchanged – a lovely man, a real gent and a champion at the highest level.

At Birkdale he had his son caddying for him and was no doubt keen to show him that the old man could still do a bit against the best in the world. That was his reward for being an Open winner, to be allowed still to test himself against the best. But his son would have his work cut out caddying in these conditions. A howling wind carryied with it a stinging, cold drenching rain, the stuff that comes at you sideways and crawls inside your waterproofs and shoes. It enveloped you in an inescapable, grim, chill damp when it was supposed to be high summer. Those grey clouds hung overhead; they would not be there for long, but would be quickly replaced by more, scudding in from the Irish Sea and ready to deposit yet another dose of misery. It seemed as if there was an endless supply rendering an already tough course almost unplayable.

This was Lyle's thirty-third Open and he'd never seen a morning like it. Actually, he couldn't see much at all. He was wearing glasses and focusing through the rain-spattered lenses was nigh on impossible. This was miserable. The ball was going all over the place. The wind was howling. The rough was long and wet, very wet. He couldn't see anything through misted glasses; he couldn't find the centre of the club when he swung. The shots started to hurt. His left knuckle went numb and if it hadn't it would have been throbbing because it had been a problem for a while. After ten holes it was unbearable. Lyle had never been a quitter, but there was this white image apparent through misty lenses and it was the clubhouse. A warm, dry sanctuary. He was 11 over par. He was never going to win the Open and he certainly wouldn't after this start. He wasn't a quitter, but he'd had enough and he didn't need to prove anything to anyone. Not even to his lad on the bag. He quit. And those clouds kept coming, depositing yet more misery.

The fallout was brutal. A sea of critical headlines – 'Pampered pros not hungry enough' – that sort of stuff – followed. Sandy Lyle felt obliged to write a letter of apology to Peter Dawson, the Chief Executive of the Royal and Ancient who run the Open. Members of Lyle's family were reduced to tears by the hostility of the media reaction to his walkout from the world's most historic and prestigious tournament.

Fifty-one weeks and two days after the two-time major winner had departed midway through his first round at the

2008 Open, two journalists sat in a media tent in Scotland. The *Independent*'s James Corrigan and a colleague were there to cover the Barclay's Scottish Open at Loch Lomond, one of the prettiest venues on the entire European Tour. But their minds weren't on this tournament, let alone the bonnie, bonnie banks of the loch. They were looking ahead to the following week when the eyes of the sporting world would be elsewhere in Scotland; Turnberry on the Ayrshire coast and the home of the 2009 Open Championship.

This is when golf correspondents come to the fore, emerging from the shadows of Wimbledon and the regular diet of football and cricket coverage. Column inches are suddenly devoted to their curious ball and stick sport and it is their job to fill them with features and stories. To this end Corrigan and a couple of fellow reporters were keen to talk to Lyle, to revisit his walkout at Royal Birkdale twelve months earlier. They wanted to get his side of a story that had generated the worst headlines in the otherwise popular player's long career. He had suffered heavy criticism for not staying the course, for quitting in the foul conditions. The American Rich Beem had also walked in early on that miserable first day on the Lancashire coast, but there was a sense that Lyle, as a past champion, had let down fans and fellow players alike. He'd tossed away an opportunity to compete in the event that most golfers would give their proverbial right arm to play. It wasn't the done thing, especially for someone who had pretensions to be a Ryder Cup captain.

There was much to explore in a story on Lyle twelve months on from the lowest point of his career and it would make an ideal piece to be used in the build-up to the 2009 Open. But never did the correspondents think it would be the interview that would set the news agenda for Open week. Nor did they envisage that it would reopen old wounds and ruin Montgomerie's dream of a triumphant week competing as a Ryder Cup captain in the world's most prestigious championship in his native Ayrshire.

'It's a good place to get them, at Loch Lomond,' Corrigan said of players who are suddenly in media demand because of the proximity of the Open. 'We'd spoken about it before and had discussed that it would be a good thing to do given Lyle's walk-off the year before. The questions were to centre on that. His answers were always going to be used in the week of the Open.

'We went out of the press tent and we were looking everywhere for him and we saw Wobbly [Phil Morbey, Ian Woosnam's former caddie] on the range. We asked him, "Have you seen Sandy Lyle?" He said, "Yes, he's over there." He was actually just about five yards away from us!' said Corrigan, who is an exceptionally talented writer, a sharp journalist and does self-deprecating Welsh wit to a tee. Lyle was practising at the far end of the range. He has always been one of the most approachable men in the game, happy to give time to reporters, and he readily agreed to talk. 'What we were looking for was stuff about how he walked off at the Open and whether he regretted it, about his sisters crying at the coverage,' Corrigan adds. 'The Ryder Cup wasn't really on our minds, but I said to him, "Did you think the walkout had any bearing on not being picked as [2010] captain?" He said he didn't really know, you'd have to ask the committee about that. And then he went into Monty.'

The Dictaphones under Lyle's nose continued to turn their tapes and record every word Lyle said. Not even a keen breeze that occasionally distorted the recording could disguise the fact that the quotes being given were in news sense absolute dynamite. Lyle said: 'You would have to ask the committee about that. But you've got Monty with his situation where he was dropping the ball badly overseas. And that is far worse than someone pulling out because he has got sore knuckles. It's a form of what could be called cheating.'

And there it was – the C word, the great golfing taboo, the word that no one had dared use in connection with Montgomerie even when the Jakarta furore was at its height four years earlier. As the BBC's voice of golf, Peter Alliss, put it: 'If you're known as a cheat in golf, golfers ostracise you. You can be a womaniser, you don't pay your taxes, a whiff of BO – but he cheats at golf, oh Colombus, we don't want him in the club.'

This was astounding. Sandy Lyle was calling Colin Montgomerie a cheat. It was big news, massive, and all because of the use of that word. Lyle then added: 'If anything was going to be held against Monty you would think: "Yeah, that's a case where he is breaking the rules." There have been a few times where he has been called in to see videos.' Here Lyle was referring to the 2002 Volvo Masters in Spain where Monty was asked to view footage that suggested he had addressed a moving ball. It was thoroughly examined and no penalty was imposed. Montgomerie went on to share the title with Bernhard Langer.

The reporters knew that they had a big scoop on their hands and they knew when it would have most impact. Not during the warm-up event, the Scottish Open, but in seven days' time, when the sporting focus would be on golf, when Tiger would be in town, when we become a nation of golfers – Open week.

'We were always going to keep it for then, because the interview was based on the Open,' Corrigan said. 'We were later accused by one American journalist of sitting on it just to use it at the time when it was most explosive, but that wasn't entirely the case. Granted, if we'd used it straight away it wouldn't have had the prominence. It all went off, didn't it?' Corrigan is convinced Lyle was feeling huge resentment that he'd been overlooked for the Ryder Cup captaincy and it came spilling out in the interview. 'It was something that had been welling up inside him, you could see. I think he would have gone further if we'd pressed him. We actually reined back a bit. If we'd had one of the tabloid boys with us I reckon we would have got a lot more out of him.'

The two reporters sat on the story for a week, but they did leak it to two tabloid journalists because one of them had been involved in the earlier plan to talk to Lyle. Another commitment had prevented him from being present at the interview. While an out-and-out exclusive scoop is often a reporter's dream it is more frequently the case that quotes will be shared in a collective back-scratching exercise. It's a form of insurance policy to ensure the paper you serve isn't left out of the loop when significant stories break. They like to hunt in packs and for those in the know on this occasion there was a strict embargo on when the story could be used.

Tuesday of Open week, two days before the greatest tournament of them all was due to start, Colin Montgomerie planned a late-afternoon practice session, followed by a few holes to reacquaint him with the demands of links golf. He knew Turnberry well. His golf academy is there and the spectacular course is only a short drive south from Troon where his dad still lives. This is Monty territory and in years gone by he would have been centre of attention. This time, though, his form didn't warrant a refloating of the eternal question of whether this could be the week he would break his major duck. Although he was Ryder Cup captain, for once he would not be the story. Jakarta was long since gone – finally dead and buried – and as the Scottish anthem goes 'in the past now it must remain'. As a story it had been subsumed by his finish as runner-up at the 2005 Open, then victory at the Alfred Dunhill Links Championship that October en route to an eighth Order of Merit. There was also his marriage to his second wife, Gaynor Knowles, and, of course, his appointment to lead Europe. All of these momentous occasions had passed with barely a murmur about the events of the second round of the 2005 Indonesian Open. He was apparently happy and settled. Even if his golf hadn't been great, there was much to enjoy in his life as he readied himself for his twentieth Open appearance, the first major for which he had been eligible in 2009. Indeed, he was looking forward to coming into the Open 'under the radar'. He might just rise up and be a contender again! But once the newspaper print runs began for that fateful Tuesday, it was never going to be a likely scenario. This battered Flower of Scotland would have to think again.

'Monty Is a Cheat' screamed the *Sun*, adding: 'It's Open Hatred'. The *Mirror* yelled 'Monty Is a Cheat; Scots at War'. Scotland's *Daily Record* went for: 'Lyle in Monty Cheat Blast'. The story was everywhere. James Corrigan in the *Independent* had given a more measured account of their conversation with Lyle, but the tabloids had gone for it with both barrels, suggesting the quotes had been given 'last night'. This is nothing more than a journalistic tool to give the words more immediacy rather than any kind of time reference to when they had actually been said. The stories arrived without warning for Montgomerie and even though Lyle had given the interview he hadn't seen them coming either. Asked whether he thought Lyle had had any idea of the impact of the words he'd used when he'd chatted with reporters at Loch Lomond, Corrigan said: 'He didn't have a clue.'

Tuesday of Open week is always busy. It is when most players try to fulfil their media obligations and one after another the big names, Tiger Woods included, troop into the press tent to discuss their prospects for the week. Each half-hour slot is allocated to the players judged most newsworthy, but the schedule had been drawn up well before this dramatic turn of events. No one had anticipated any great demand for quotes from Sandy Lyle or Colin Montgomerie. Woods, the world number one playing his first Open for two years, was the guy we would want to hear from, surely. Not any more.

Lyle was keen to talk. He needed to set the record straight and his request for a late-afternoon slot in the interview room was granted by the R and A media manager Malcolm Booth. By the appointed hour there was standing room only in an interview area built to house golf's largest travelling army of reporters. 'Who's the only other player who can fill a media room like Tiger? This oughta be good,' boomed the deep American voice of the colourful veteran radio announcer Bob Bubka.

Lyle sat at the top table flanked by his experienced agent, Rocky Hambric. There was a palpable air of anticipation as the two-times major winner unfolded a piece of paper upon which was written a prepared statement. Lyle began to read it aloud: 'In my frustration over continually being asked about the incident at last year's Open Championship I regretfully brought up another old incident, one that has long since been resolved. I was trying to make the point by comparison that neither of these incidents had anything to do with the selection of the current Ryder Cup captain. I deeply regret making this comparison and apologise to Colin for involving him in my own issue. I sincerely hope that nothing more will be made of this issue. I hope our friendship is still there. I feel especially bad if I have jeopardised his preparation for the Open Championship.'

It said all the right things to diffuse the situation. Typically, Lyle had been man enough to say that it had been his fault and to say sorry to Montgomerie. He should have left it there, but Lyle felt he was a big enough man to endure more scrutiny and to field questions. Bad decision.

He was soon talking himself into more trouble. Reporters used to dealing with slick media operators well versed in damage limitation tactics couldn't believe what they were hearing. Lyle had said he was 'gutted' by the way the papers had treated his interview, but then said: 'I think big headlines calling Colin a cheat are totally out of context. It's been well documented, it's all on video. It's not like I'm pre-fabricating [sic].' In other words: 'I'm not making this up, he did it.' So did he regret what he'd said about Jakarta? Lyle replied: 'I'm only going from what other people have said and it was a pretty poor drop. It was one of his mistakes. I didn't make him do the mistake. It was his mistake and it will probably live with him for the rest of his life. It'll be cropping up. I can't do anything against that.' You could hear the spade digging ever deeper ... and deeper. 'There was a rain delay. They stopped play because of bad light and returned the next morning. Apparently he was in an extremely bad position. You've all seen it anyway. I don't think you need me to say it, but the problem was the drop wasn't close to where it should be. And of course TV doesn't lie.'

Lyle's account was riddled with errors – the reason for play being abandoned and saying that Monty had dropped rather than replaced his ball – but the biggest mistake was revisiting the subject at all. He had undone the apologetic opening statement good and proper. The *Daily Telegraph* would later ask: 'Will somebody please save Sandy Lyle from himself?' If ever evidence had been needed that Lyle was unsuitable for the job of Ryder Cup captain this was it. His lack of media savvy was there for all to see and it is impossible to lead Europe without being blessed with at least the ability to know when it is best to shut up. But this story was as much about the man who was the Ryder Cup skipper, not just the bloke who'd been overlooked. Lyle was anxious to see Montgomerie, be a man and explain his side of the story face to face. For his part, Monty wanted nothing to do with him and this prompted scenes that would have been at home in a West End farce.

He didn't want to be there, locked in the room at the back of the pro shop in the clubhouse with his manager. He wanted to be on the course making a plan. A plan of attack to show them he wasn't finished, that he could still contend at an Open. But Lyle had been speaking, speaking to the press in their tent and saying sorry to him. Some apology. He'd got it there, the whole transcript, there in black and white. He'd come there, to the office at the back of the pro shop, from the range. He'd been working on his game, his tempo, his rhythm. Same swing, always, just softer for a lower flight – useful on a windy links – harder for higher. Light hands, don't grip too tight, you wouldn't get any release, complete the backswing. There wasn't much release here. The press were outside, so was Lyle. Just 20 feet away, now he was talking to a player called Storm – that was appropriate. The skipper had come back to the clubhouse past the academy that bears his name. The press had told Lyle he was back. Lyle apparently wanted a word; Europe's leader didn't notice because he was on the phone. There was lots to discuss, but not with the press. Another phone went off, what was the ringtone? Ah, the theme tune to 'The Good, the Bad and the Ugly'. You couldn't make it up. Lyle hung around at the back of the clubhouse, the reporters thought he looked like a naughty schoolkid. Then he went round the front. Another fifteen minutes passed, the skipper's meeting with his manager was over. They saw each other, the captain and Lyle. Their eyes met momentarily across the car park. Lyle didn't follow, he went. For the skipper it was time to get on to the golf course.

Montgomerie's manager, Guy Kinnings, was left to do the talking. 'Monty was surprised to read the comments by Sandy and didn't plan to dignify them with any response,' he said. 'However, he welcomes Sandy's apology although his subsequent comments remain concerning. It is strange that something that was resolved so long ago has been brought up again and a particular shame that this has happened at the Open.'

Usually Montgomerie is more than happy to be centre of attention, but not on this occasion. He didn't address the controversy until his practice round on the eve of the Open when he revealed that he was relying on advice from Sir Sean Connery who told him to think about creating a metre of space around him to hold at bay the outside world. From there he could 'disappear inside a bubble of concentration'. But it was clear Monty was livid with the disruption Lyle's comments had caused to his Open preparations. 'I came down here to play golf and was hit with this,' he said. 'Because he's not being

234

Ryder Cup captain, please don't take it out on me. I know he's disappointed, that's obvious. But please, don't take it out on me. I just think it is so sad after I had supported his candidacy for the Ryder Cup captaincy through the whole process. Why does he feel the need to take it out on me? Is it my fault the committee decided they wanted a younger man?' One intrepid reporter asked whether there was any chance of a vice-captain's role for Lyle at Celtic Manor. 'I think you know the answer to that one' was the curt reply.

Monty began with a one over par 71, seven shots behind the first round leader, Miguel Ángel Jiménez. Lyle was round in 74. Neither player was threatening a challenge. Lyle continued to talk his way into trouble. 'We all know Colin, he's a bit of a drama queen' to Five Live's Rob Nothman did nothing to quell the row. But by this time it was clear the relationship between the two Scots had broken down irretrievably. Monty fired a second round 74 and missed the cut. He said the row had ruined his Open and reiterated that Lyle had no chance of serving as one of his vice-captains. 'I thought it was rather amusing when he said he hoped it doesn't jeopardise his vice-captaincy position. I thought it was very, very funny,' he said without a trace of humour in his voice.

The 2009 Open was the biggest golfing occasion since Montgomerie's appointment as Ryder Cup captain. It had, of course, no real bearing on the match but he had become a figurehead for the European game and this was the week when the eyes of the sporting world were on his sport. He had cancelled an appearance at the Association of Golf Writers annual dinner on the Tuesday night, the evening after the story had broken. It was a story that had reaffirmed Monty's position as the most talked about man in European golf. Some seven months earlier he had been talking up Lyle as the right man for the job that he himself was eventually given. People wondered then whether Lyle's Birkdale walkout would count against him. Monty had said: 'I think you are talking to someone who sometimes regrets what I've done in my career. One so-called mistake shouldn't affect him as a Ryder Cup captain and the respect he has from the rest of the players.' Lyle could not or would not articulate similar sentiments when he was asked to speak and it led to this unsavoury and unnecessary controversy that clouded a high-profile period in Montgomerie's captaincy. The two players met a fortnight later at Hazeltine in Minnesota at the US PGA Championship. It was a perfunctory meeting arranged by the European Tour and the upshot was an agreement that neither would speak of the row again. They probably wouldn't speak to each other again either, but it was at last closure on an incident that dated all the way back to 2005.

It should never have resurfaced; closure should have come with Monty's appointment as skipper. The body that appointed him to the job was the same Tournament Committee that had investigated the Jakarta incident. An abiding memory from the day he was put in charge of the effort to regain the Ryder Cup was of the *Daily Mail*'s golf correspondent Derek Lawrenson chasing after Monty when he had completed all his interviews. There was one more question to be asked: the *Mail* man wanted to know how much it meant to be backed by the people who had sat in judgement after the Indonesian incident. 'It means more than anyone can imagine and that is why I feel so emotional,' Monty answered. 'To go from that situation to your peers standing and clapping as you say "yes" to the captaincy, it means everything.'

That should have been closure; it should have been dead and buried then. Monty had done nothing new to warrant it resurfacing. The committee had decided that whatever had happened in Indonesia was not sufficient to prevent him leading his continent. He was the best man for the job, the most suited to win back the trophy. Yes, a mistake had been made, but it was gone as far as they were concerned and he was still fit to be a leader. A career's worth of heroics, leading off and closing out matches against the best that America could throw at him more than qualified him for the role.

11

'You know when you've got a partner like Monty, just let him do his stuff'   – Padraig Harrington

He had done this thousands of times. Four feet, maybe five, that was all. Just had to make it disappear. This was big. Not sure how big, but he sensed an important moment. How important? How big? The cameras were trained on him, the commentators were whispering urgently. He could feel it from the crowd, the players – his team-mates, all gathered around watching and hoping. He could feel their support and their will, but he was in a lonely place. Right now he was on his own in golf and in life. It was down to him. He had started the job and done it well, like the leader he remained despite needing an invitation to play the role. They had depended on him on Friday morning and he had delivered. He had turned the American dream into a nightmare. Set the tone to keep his continent on top. Now it was Sunday afternoon, the end was in sight, the trophy was staying with them. All that was needed was confirmation. He might just be the man to deliver it. How fitting. All he had to do was make the ball disappear, just like he'd done thousands of times before ...

Colin Montgomerie's pursuit of golfing success was always relentless and knew no barriers. Nothing could get in the way. It brought him huge reward, multiple victories and millions of pounds. He had a wife, three children and all the trappings. The luxury mansion in Surrey that boasted a post-code to covet, a fleet of top-of-the-range cars and recognition as one of the very best players on earth. But it came at a cost. The passionate desire to be the best, the abhorrence of losing and the constant need to travel in pursuit of glory led to a loss of perspective. His family life suffered and so the period that followed that glorious week at the Belfry in 2002 became the most painful of his life. His marriage to Eimear became increasingly strained as Montgomerie found himself in an ever more vicious cycle. The more tense his domestic life, the more erratic was his golf. The worse he played the more his home life suffered. He went through 2003 without a tournament victory. It was his first barren year in more than a decade and he finished it in lowly twenty-eighth place in the European Tour's Order of Merit. This was the Chelsea or Manchester United of golf finding itself in a relegation scrap. The following season, despite winning in Singapore in March 2004, was little better with just three more top ten finishes.

This was the year that his marriage reached breaking point and he and Eimear separated. The collapse of what had been one of the more visible marital relationships in British sport meant that Montgomerie spent more time in the gossip columns than he did in his usual domain at the back of news-papers. Then again, there wasn't much to write about regarding his, at best, patchy golf.

Back in 2002, given his commanding performance at the Belfry, it was inconceivable he would not be one of the first names on the European team sheet for the defence of the

Ryder Cup two years later. Much had changed in the inter-vening period and it became increasingly clear that he would struggle to qualify automatically for a team that would be led by someone with whom he had enjoyed so much success in these matches, Bernhard Langer.

The Montgomeries split soon after the 2004 Masters in the April of that year. 'It's clear I've been through a personal tragedy,' Monty told reporters as he sought to put behind him his troubles off the course. There was little sign of encour-agement in his play as he strove in vain to contend throughout the spring and his loss of form was a source of concern for the new captain. 'First of all we need to understand he's gone through a very, very difficult time in his life,' Langer acknowl-edged. 'Thank goodness I never had to go through it, but I've seen other players and almost everybody struggles when that happens. It's just hard to block out.'

Langer's hope was that the apparent certainty of the split would mean that Montgomerie would be able to find a way to concentrate fully on his golf again. 'There's no doubt he has been a fantastic player for a very, very long time, a great guy to have on the Ryder Cup team and I'd obviously love for him to make the team.' The captain spoke to Monty on the phone that spring when most of the European season lay before them and was encouraged by what he heard. The Scot, who was then approaching his forty-first birthday, was still desper-ately keen to be a part of the European defence of the trophy. The question was whether his golf would be good enough to warrant a place in the side.

Montgomerie's form in the majors had been utterly miser-able in 2003 and was just as bad in 2004. He didn't contend and there was no sign of him making the breakthrough his career needed and warranted in the game's most prestigious tournaments. By the time the US PGA, the last major of the year, came into view in August 2004, there was still little indication of the consistency of old in his game. Monty agreed to be interviewed by Radio Five Live at his golfing base at the Wisley club in Surrey shortly before heading to the Scandinavian Masters and then Whistling Straits for the final major of the year. So distant was he in the qualifying table it seemed he would need to win at least one of them to have a chance of claiming an automatic place in the European team. 'I can tell you whether Bernhard Langer is going to give me a wild-card pick,' unprompted, Montgomerie said over the phone as the final arrangements for the interview were made.

'Really, you can?'

No, he couldn't; he was joking.

This exchange did serve to highlight the issue uppermost in his thoughts, though. Monty hadn't heard a word from the captain and was in the dark. This worried him greatly. The very fact that he was going to need selection was bad enough, and the total absence of an encouraging vibe from the skipper compounded his disquiet. There were other worries, too. On the day of the interview he was heading off afterwards to buy a new bed for the London flat that was his new home as a single man. The prospect of now dealing with domestic matters because he was fending for himself filled him with a dread that almost equalled his fear of missing his favourite golf event.

'I sensed he should be picked and would be picked for the Ryder Cup but he didn't fully believe it because of what he was going through,' Monty's coach at the time, Denis Pugh, remembered. 'He was very up and down, it was an emotional roller-coaster for him.' Montgomerie encouragingly finished fourth in the Scandinavian Masters but was a miserable seventieth at the US PGA. Time was running out to impress the captain, who was keeping a deliberate distance from all of his prospective picks.

If the criterion for selection was based on reputation alone Monty would have been a shoo-in, but the player knew he needed to show form as well. The team was finalised at the end of the BMW International Open in Munich at the end of August 2004 and the tournament constituted Montgomerie's last chance to shine. He felt he should make a change to provide an impetus and decided to re-employ the caddie with whom he had enjoyed most success. On the Sunday before this final qualifying tournament Montgomerie called Alastair McLean. The conversation began with prolonged small talk and then Monty said to his fellow Scot: 'There's a reason I'm calling.'

'Yeah, I thought there might be . . . yeah, yeah, great. Come on, let's see what we can do,' replied McLean, who had split from Adam Scott, the Australian who had been his employer in the two years since he had last carried Montgomerie's bag.

On the Thursday morning the reunited pair arrived on the first tee to begin the opening round of the BMW tournament. They played alongside Luke Donald, an America-based Englishman of high promise and who was in the Ryder Cup reckoning after a tweaking of the rules that meant he would be eligible for selection despite his US base. Montgomerie was heard to say to Donald: 'Do you think we'll be okay?' as they waited to tee off. Some witnesses took this to be a reference to their likely need for a captain's pick, but in fact it was a reference to the threatening clouds overhead. Montgomerie was wondering whether they would need to use their water-proofs.

With McLean carrying his clubs – and his rainwear – Monty was transformed. He knew he required a successful week and, as ever, a victory was the ultimate goal. It always has been, even when he was well past his prime and preparing to captain his team in 2010 at Celtic Manor. 'I want to be able to stand before my team as a winner in my year of captaincy,' he said. He had no such need; it didn't matter a jot to the players he led and it was a ludicrous contention, but it served as a constant source of motivation for Mont-gomerie the player as he competed on the European Tour. The need for a win in Munich back in 2004 was far greater and he opened with a superb 67, equalling his lowest round since taking the Caltex title in Singapore six months earlier. Suddenly he was bubbling with enthusiasm and crediting his caddie for the upturn in his form. 'I've always put huge emphasis on who carries my bag around a golf course and I've missed Alastair McLean the last two years,' he said. 'I feel very confident with Alastair there.'

Rounds of 70 and 68 followed to keep Monty's name on the leaderboard heading into the final day, the Sunday that would conclude with the announcement of the European team. It was a nerve-wracking day for several players and Ian Poulter, Paul McGinley, Paul Casey and David Howell achieved the results required for automatic spots in the team that travelled to Oakland Hills in Michigan for the defence of the Ryder Cup. Montgomerie finished with a 68 to move to 16 under par and a highly encouraging third place behind the champion, Miguel Ángel Jiménez. It could hardly have provided a better or more timely reminder to the captain who needed to wait until the final reckoning before knowing which of the form players of the year would still be in need of a wild card.

It came down to a choice of two players from three: Montgomerie, Luke Donald and Freddie Jacobson. At a packed news conference shown live across the world, Langer confirmed that Monty had indeed done enough and would be joined by Donald, the recent winner of the Scandinavian Masters and Europe's rising star in America. Langer's only slip was to announce the Scottish veteran as 'Colin Montgomerie from England' and amid bemused looks from the assembled media the German skipper quickly corrected himself. 'I'm sorry, but he's lived in England long enough,' he smiled.

'Colin has given us a great performance this week,' he went on. 'To play that well knowing he still had to show me something. I gave nobody the nod and I did that for a reason. I wanted the guys to try as hard as they could until the very last putt and show me what they are made of. And I'm very proud of him the way he played. We know he's had some very difficult private times, which probably hurt his golf game for several months, but I think and I know he's over it a little bit. He's coming out the other end and most importantly I think he will rise to the occasion,' Langer said. 'We know there are players who crumble under pressure and there are others who thrive on it and I think he is one of those. His record proves that. He was my first pick for those reasons.'

So Monty was on the plane to the Oakland Hills Country Club in Michigan, which would play host to the thirty-fifth Ryder Cup. Upon being told the good news he said to his captain he would do everything in his power to make sure the trophy would be with them for the return journey. He wasn't there just to make up the numbers either. Langer thought that so long as the Munich form could be sustained Montgomerie would be capable of playing a pivotal role.

Unfortunately when they arrived in Detroit three weeks later Monty's game was all over the place, much to the concern of the captain. Denis Pugh had travelled with the team but was there 'more as a support mechanism for Monty than as a coach'. It was Langer who made the most significant contribution to fixing his talisman's game. After an early practice round in which the player had no idea where his ball was going, the captain reasoned he was moving his hips rather than leading off his swing with his arms. Having always held Langer in the highest regard, Montgomerie was more than happy to heed his skipper's advice. Within a few shots on the range Monty had rediscovered his stock fade, the left-to-right flight path that gives his golf its ultimate control. Seasoned watchers of the European golf scene could quickly sense that he was a different animal from the one that had scratched around for the past two years on tour. Suddenly he had a real presence and exuded confidence. This was partly due to the technical change suggested by Langer, but was also down to the unique mindset Montgomerie acquired during a Ryder Cup. 'The feeling of being picked by Bernhard turned him into the sort of character that would say I'm going to show the captain and the world that I was the right man,' Pugh said. 'He did act very positively and there was a degree of acting at every Ryder Cup, but it was acting to make sure he was the very best Monty.'

It was still an awkward week because the players' wives have a prominent role at the functions that take place during a Ryder Cup. Monty was on his own and his team-mates knew it. 'The feeling of going there as a lone individual had quite an effect on him and the way the other players treated him was to almost join up to become collective Mrs Montgomeries,' Pugh added.

More important was the Scot's golf, and his game was in a semblance of shape. Definitely not at the heights it reached in the years during which he was dominating the European game, but certainly of a standard in which his captain could have faith. This belief was apparent when the pairings for the opening sequence of fourballs were announced.

The American captain, Hal Sutton, went with an audacious ploy, putting together the world's top two players, Tiger Woods and Phil Mickelson. They had never been a partnership in Ryder Cups or Presidents Cups, the latter the biennial match the US play against a Rest of the World team. Woods and Mickelson were viewed as rivals rather than partners but they were the best two players in the world. The Radio Five Live breakfast show presenter Nicky Campbell drew a comparison with the newsworthy tensions at the top of the British government at the time by dubbing them the Tony Blair and Gordon Brown of golf. Sutton recalled: 'I knew it was chancy to put Tiger and Phil together but you know they paired Palmer and Nicklaus in days gone by and I felt like it was a statement maker and if it went well it would be great and if it didn't go well it might not be so good. The world needed to see those two together and they personally needed it as well.'

The American skipper had also failed to keep a lid on his plans. Europe had an inkling that Sutton would make this bold move of sending out his big guns first. Sutton admitted that it had been his plan from the moment he was appointed to take over the captaincy from Curtis Strange. So Langer was quite aware of the need to forge his own 'dream team' to counter the illustrious American pairing. His choice was Colin Montgomerie and Padraig Harrington and it set up the most eagerly anticipated opening match the Ryder Cup had ever seen. 'We were sent out as a partnership because we played together in 2002,' Harrington recalled. 'The word came out that Hal Sutton was going to pair Tiger and Phil and they were going to be unbeatable. Myself and Monty were a partnership from the Ryder Cup before and we genuinely wanted to have a go at them. Part of it is because we were in a position where we had nothing to lose. How can Tiger and Phil possibly be beaten playing together? And, sure enough, myself and Monty were just loving it. The opportunity to lead out in the first match was brilliant for him. He loved the chance to go out there and beat Tiger and Phil.'

The entire first hole at Oakland Hills was surrounded by fans standing three or four deep well before the arrival of the players. Harrington wanted to show he was in a relaxed mood, to convey a feeling that Europe had nothing to lose from this match and an awful lot to gain. He also wanted to transmit this feeling to his partner and as they made their way to the tee they chatted and smiled.

The television cameras were trained on America's skipper. Hal Sutton had donned a Stetson. Was he a captain or a cowboy? Given the way the match panned out, there became more compelling reasons for this question than just his choice of headgear. His top two players were not giving off any signs of camaraderie, barely acknowledging each other as they arrived on the tee. The portents were not good for the home side and their fans.

Montgomerie teed off first. 'He absolutely couldn't wait. He has to hit the first ball,' Denis Pugh said.

It was a slightly anti-climactic tee shot that found a fairway bunker but there was no embarrassment because none of the four players could locate the fairway. Opening shots in this contest are regarded as the most nerve-wracking in the game, even for its very best exponents. This one, given the personnel involved, seemed to have even more riding on it. 'I had a little lump in my throat on the first tee shot, to be honest,' Montgomerie admitted. 'Because to be standing where I was after coming through the four months I had was something. Just real emotion there. I said I was going to have a smile on the first tee, to myself really more than anybody else. I took a look across at Woods and Mickelson and I thought, "Right, I've got back into the arena that I feel I belong in." I was proud of myself for that.'

The hoards followed as the players set off to locate their balls and Monty hit the best of the second shots, propelling a 165-yard seven iron from the sand to within 12 feet of the hole. Moments later he was putting for a win. His stroke was as confident as it had been the last time he had putted against America. There was the extra follow-through that always seems to come to the fore in the Ryder Cup, that additional nudge of authority, and his ball duly obeyed its forthright command. An opening birdie and Montgomerie had put Europe ahead at the very first opportunity. If ever there was a sign that Monty's unique ability to seize a Ryder Cup moment was still intact this was it. 'It was no surprise,' said Pugh.

Harrington then won the third hole and the American 'dream team' already appeared in disarray. They trudged independently with apparently no time for each other. Woods, as has so often been the case in Ryder Cups, was shorn of his usual commanding presence and Mickelson seemed at odds with the prospect of partnering Woods the person as well as the woods in his bag. The left-hander had switched club manufacturer, signing a multi-million-dollar deal with Callaway in the run-up to the match. It was a move that stunned American fans because it is rare for a player to make such a dramatic switch mid-season and especially when a big event is just around the corner.

By contrast, Montgomerie and Harrington were in perfect harmony as they strode confidently, two up after just three holes. 'I made sure he was enjoying it because when he enjoys it he plays great,' the Irishman said of his partner. 'I've got to say I was very much the back-up role but I was happy to play that. You know when you've got a partner like Monty, just let him do his stuff.'

Mickelson birdied the seventh to provide the first home cheers of the morning, to halve the arrears, but the European advantage remained at one hole as they turned for home. Although Harrington claims to have played the less glamorous part, it was his golf that was rock solid and it provided the perfect foil as Europe regained their two-hole advantage. A Monty birdie at the 12th put them three up, a lead they continued to hold until Mickelson sank a long putt to win the 16th and keep the match alive. It was never going to be enough, though, and Montgomerie tapped in at the par three 17th to close it out and secure an opening point for Europe that felt like a whole lot more.

'It was tough for Phil and Tiger to gel together,' said Harrington. 'They had two totally different games and it was very frustrating for them and they knew that Monty and I were going to give them a tough game that day and they had to perform.'

Looking back on that victory, Harrington's partner observed: 'This wasn't a gift. Woods and Mickelson, they weren't on form as a team but they weren't bad individually and we did remarkably well. It was a great win and I think it sent a message down the whole team. Padraig and me winning was worth more than just a single point.'

Hal Sutton admits Europe put their strongest partnership against his top two. He believed Monty and Harrington would constitute the European equivalent of his supposed 'dream team'. 'Yes, I did. I knew it was going to be a great match. You know Colin's a great competitor and so is Padraig. They were putting the best players out there against my leading pair,' Sutton said. As for putting Woods and Mickelson together, he admitted: 'I wouldn't do it again, but it was the right thing to do at that time. I don't think it did any good on a whole lot of fronts but it did stand a chance of doing some good.'

The fact that Montgomerie and Harrington were never behind offered a huge boost of confidence to the rest of the European team. They were the players with the smiles on their faces. They had won over the home fans during practice rounds when they happily signed autographs and posed for pictures. Bernhard Langer had outmanoeuvred his opposite number by instructing his players to do this. Sutton was abiding by the protocol that said neither side would indulge the fans in this way. The Europeans had already won the PR game. They were the good guys and were ensuring no repeat of the hostility thrown at them at Brookline in 1999, the last time they had played a Ryder Cup in the US.

Behind the top match the cigar-toting duo of the in-form Miguel Ángel Jiménez and Darren Clarke romped to victory over Davis Love III and Chad Campbell and Sergio García and Lee Westwood did the same against David Toms and Jim Furyk. The Americans' only success was to claim a half from the match that pitted Chris Riley and Stewart Cink against Paul McGinley and Luke Donald. Europe had surged through the opening session of fourballs, claiming three and a half points from a possible four and the catalyst was the beating of the much vaunted Woods/Mickelson combination.

For the afternoon foursomes Sutton gave Woods and Mickelson the chance to atone but this time they were spared facing the Montgomerie/Harrington partnership. Instead they were up against the two best friends on the European Tour, the irrepressible Darren Clarke and Lee Westwood. Stablemates around whom the influential International Sports Management agency was built, they travelled, practised and partied together. Just as Monty and Harrington had done in the morning, they relished the prospect of taking on the top two players in the world in the alternate-shot format. It was an opportunity not to be missed, especially for Clarke who counted Woods among his closer friends. Their match was a tighter affair than in the morning with the European pair fighting back from being three down after seven holes. It is remembered for a particular moment of ignominy for the American partnership on the 18th tee. Mickelson sprayed his three-wood drive way left, almost out of bounds, on a 500-yard closing hole. It effectively left his partner dead and Woods looked on with an expression of utter contempt. It is hard to imagine such disunity ever being apparent in any European Ryder Cup partnership. Mickelson's drive cost the American pair any chance and Westwood and Clarke were able to record a one-hole victory that meant the partnership that was supposed to be America's trailblazing catalyst garnered nothing for its team on the opening day.

By the time the Europeans had claimed this highly encouraging point, Montgomerie and Harrington had already breezed to their second win of the day. The Scot and the Irishman beat Davis Love and Fred Funk 4 and 2. Having defeated the top two in the morning, no obstacle was going to be big enough to deny the European combination, even though the Scot admitted feeling fatigue after the rigours of the pre-lunch victory. This indomitable spirit was typified by Monty on the eighth hole when he demonstrated his underrated imagination and short-game skills to deny the Americans the chance to claim a potentially momentum shifting hole. Harrington's approach to the uphill plateau green skipped through to the raised portion at the back of the putting surface. The pin was located towards the back as well so Montgomerie had little room in which to work. Even the most delicately struck shot from this position above the hole would race past the flag and leave a long putt for a half. Monty quickly made up his mind. He could see the shot. It would need him to aim in the opposite direction to the hole. So he played away, chipping the ball into the semi-rough and letting the tangly grass and gravity do the rest. The ball trickled out of the rough, barely moving before taking the slope at minimal velocity and then trundled down towards its target. Montgomerie's ball came to rest stone dead; he very nearly holed it. Any American optimism was snuffed out by a moment of sheer golfing genius. It was a signal that there was no way the Europeans would be denied a full point from this match and so it proved.

The only US success in the entire day was victory in the top match of the afternoon session where Jay Haas and the effervescent Chris DiMarco accounted for Jiménez and the debutant Thomas Levet 3 and 2. When Sergio García and Luke Donald recorded their 2 and 1 victory over Kenny Perry and Stewart Cink, Europe had completed their greatest opening day in Ryder Cup history. They led by five points, an extraordinary advantage that left Sutton's strategy in tatters. Bernhard Langer had completely out-thought his opposite number, anticipating his moves and using his best players to counter the home plans. Central to that had been taking care of Woods and Mickelson. 'What we get for the two wins is two points, but it's probably worth three or four,' the European captain said. 'It was huge psychologically, a huge blow to the Americans and a huge help for the Europeans. I'm just thrilled it turned out that way for us.'

It was huge.

Sutton had no choice other than to split up Woods and Mickelson for a second day that had the Americans under massive pressure. Woods was paired with the rookie Chris Riley and Mickelson was unceremoniously dropped. Either or both of the top two could have been left out given what had happened on the first day, but there was no way an iconic figure such as Woods could realistically have been dumped by his captain. Mickelson's wayward drive at the last the previous evening made him ripe for the role of scapegoat, especially as it was abundantly clear that he had yet to come to grips with his new equipment.

Langer also had to worry about who to leave out, but for the best of reasons because so many of his team were playing well. He'd used nine of his twelve players on that first day and the lead was such that the remaining three, Ian Poulter, Paul Casey and David Howell, who were all making their debuts, could be given their first taste of Ryder Cup action on the Saturday morning in relatively pressure-free circumstances. But all things are relative for there is always pressure at a Ryder Cup.

Casey and Howell were paired together for the fourballs that began the second day while Poulter was put alongside Darren Clarke. Only one European pairing from the same sequence the previous day remained intact: Padraig Harrington and Colin Montgomerie. The Irishman felt that having led off on the first day they would be better placed to go out last on that Saturday morning. He discussed it with his partner before the pairings were handed in and Montgomerie said he would have a quiet word with the skipper to make the suggestion. Langer was happy to oblige and so they occupied that strategically important last position in the draw and they were pitted against Stewart Cink and Davis Love, a less glamorous but far more effective partnership than the one they had played the previous morning.

In the top match the animated Chris DiMarco desperately tried to stir to life the shell-shocked crowd, encouraging them to roar louder and inspire their team, but it was only to limited effect. The continued brilliance of the Europeans saw to that. DiMarco partnered Jay Haas and they faced Lee Westwood and Sergio García. DiMarco's gesticulating did fire up the fans and early in the match there was more hostility than had been shown the day before. García, himself sometimes guilty of excessively inspiring European support, felt the need to ask DiMarco to 'keep it friendly' after the home fans had cheered a shot from the Spaniard that found water. It was a tight match and the Europeans birdied the 16th to make it all square with two holes to play. It remained that way on the final green where García holed an outrageous par putt that curled a mammoth distance before dropping. Westwood had been lining up his own putt for par from around ten feet but it was no gimme and it was now rendered redundant by his partner's inspired play that gave Europe a half-point.

It was important that the visiting continent didn't lose that match because Poulter and Clarke had already fallen to Woods and Riley and Montgomerie and Harrington were struggling against Cink and Love. Monty was running out of steam, playing ragged golf, and his Irish partner couldn't carry him. The Scot had been out of sorts from the moment he arrived on the range that morning. 'He even asked me not to watch him warm up, which he'd never done before,' recalled Denis Pugh. 'There was a sign there that not all was right with him.'

Eventually, Cink and Love eased to a 3 and 2 win. Monty admitted the defeat had been his fault. 'I've never said sorry to a partner before in any of these matches, but I did there,' he said. The defeat heaped the pressure on the rookies Howell and Casey who were playing Jim Furyk and Chad Campbell, desperate not to hand a surge to the home side.

The key moment came at the par three 17th where Howell had a tee shot that his caddie Mick Doran felt needed to be a five iron to make the 203-yard journey uphill to the pin. With the match all square the Englishman pulled a six iron from the bag and, what's more, he mishit it. But it flew and bounced the required distance. Howell's ball finished five feet from the hole. It was a stunning blow made under huge pressure because the momentum was turning the way of the home side. Only a player as self-deprecating and honest as the engaging Howell would have admitted to not making a pure contact. Mishit or not, it was still voted European Tour Shot of the Year. At the time there was no better putter on Tour than Howell and he duly knocked in what was still a tough birdie putt (perhaps that should have been the shot of the year) and it meant the rookies were one up with one to play. Casey then stepped to the fore and blasted a monster of a drive off the final tee. His approach finished 30 feet from the flag on a similar line to the one García had successfully putted and Langer raced over to advise his young charge. Casey was able to choose the right spot, but his putt ran on nearly five feet and he did well to hold his nerve and stroke it through his shadow for the par that clinched a morale-boosting point. It meant that Europe, despite losing the session 2½-1½ still led 8-4 heading into the afternoon foursomes.

For the first time in thirteen years and thirty matches, Colin Montgomerie was rested that Saturday afternoon. He knew it was coming. He was forty-one and appeared to have aged more that year than in any other in his life because of the stresses and strains of his domestic situation. His golf had been sporadic, inspired on the first morning but not dependable enough for foursomes after an exhausting three matches already completed. 'Individual Ryder Cup means nothing to me,' he said when asked for his reaction to being dropped. 'It's a team event and that's why we are here.' The decision to rest him was made with his full agreement, but it was still an emotional moment and led to an unfamiliar role in the afternoon. What to do? Monty headed to the range, but he has never been a fan of spending too much time there and he soon headed out on to the course to offer support to the eight men charged with preserving Europe's handsome lead.

Not only did they do that, they stretched their advantage. The US simply could not match the spirit of their opposition, never mind their ability to hole crunch putts. The difference in attitude between the sides was illustrated by the American rookie Chris Riley who had starred in winning alongside Woods in the morning but didn't fancy playing again in the afternoon. It was easy to understand his captain's frustration. 'Chris was heavily on my mind and I told him, "Look, man, I hate to use this line, but I as a forty-two-year-old fat man in ninety-nine went five straight matches, so I'm sure a thirty-year-old flat belly that's hyper can go four, can't ya?" He kind of stuttered and said, "Well, I guess if you really want me to." So I backed off and thought if he doesn't want to go then I'm not sure he can help us as much as somebody who is really energetic about going out there.' Riley was duly dropped.

Mickelson was drafted back in and in partnership with David Toms, the man with whom he had enjoyed success at the Belfry two years earlier, he provided the only home cheer. They defeated Levet and Jiménez 4 and 3 but the rest of the sequence was one-way traffic and it was the sound of Europe's adopted anthem 'Olé, Olé, Olé' that echoed across Oakland Hills that Saturday afternoon. Clarke and Westwood thrashed Haas and DiMarco and Harrington and McGinley eased past Woods and Love. García and Donald's final-hole victory over Furyk and Fred Funk made it a glorious afternoon for Europe that left them just three and a half points short of winning the trophy for the second match running. Such was the manner of Europe's domination and the mood of the players and their fans it was impossible to see how Hal Sutton could come up with a batting order that could prevent European glory.

He wasn't at his best. The team had done brilliantly but he was nervous, worried, concerned. Sure, Europe were going to keep the Cup. There was no way these Americans could turn it round, but he feared he couldn't make his usual contribution. It felt strange being here on his own and having needed a pick to make the journey. Unsettling. Day one had been brilliant even though he didn't play his best. Inspiration and adrenaline made him able to make his telling contributions when required. Always the way at a Ryder Cup, but this time not as consistently as in matches gone by. Europe were too strong this time, they didn't need to depend on him like they used to. But he still had a job to do. Someone would have to close out this thing. Could he still do it? He never lost on a Sunday . . .

Hal Sutton was out of his depth, foundering in the tide of European domination. There was none of the upbeat, blind confidence of Ben Crenshaw five years earlier when he had the 'feeling' that fate would deal the US a winning hand on the final day when it needed a massive comeback. This time America, trailing 11-5, required an even greater turnaround and in his attempt to engineer it Sutton used the bluntest of tools. There was no subtlety in deciding the order of his players. He knew he needed early points and believed the only way to do that was to send out his best first. Taking no heed of the individual form of his team that week he relied on the ranking lists to decide who was best. Sutton simply sent them out in the order in which they had qualified. Woods first, Mickelson second, Love third and so on.

As the week had gone on the American captain's press conferences became ever more tense as his decisions attracted increasing scrutiny. This less than subtle approach to the singles merely attracted yet more. British tabloids had been chipping away throughout the week and after the miserable start made by Sutton's team he had been asked if he wanted then to give up hope of his side achieving a win. On the Saturday night after the singles line-up had been announced, Sutton was asked to explain why he had put out Woods and Mickelson first. Surely it would have been better to invert his order because they were two of his weakest players that week. Sutton had no answer. 'You're full of great questions, aren't you? Aren't you the same guy that asked me, would we concede? You know what, when you're asked such stupid questions, you remember a face. So, no comment,' Sutton said, shaking his head.

Bernhard Langer had been much more calculating and canny in deciding his order. On the Saturday evening he spoke to Darren Clarke and Paul Casey as they sat on a buggy watching the action. The captain said he was thinking of sending out first one of those two players and quick as a flash Clarke indicated that it should be the rookie Casey who should play the leading role. All three were convinced the Americans would lead off with Tiger Woods and, as Clarke celebrated dodging a bullet, Casey knew he was about to be preparing for the biggest match of his life.

It panned out as Langer had expected and Casey led off for Europe against the world number one. It was also clear that the skipper wanted to claim the required three and a half points quickly. Europe's number one, Sergio García, was placed second in the order, the dependable Clarke was next, followed by David Howell, Lee Westwood and then sixth Colin Montgomerie. He was nicely tucked away, but ideally placed to close out the match if he could overcome the resolute David Toms.

During breakfast on the Sunday Monty discussed with Lee Westwood the point at which Europe's overwhelming superiority that week would be turned into victory. The consensus was that it would probably fall to the fifth or sixth man. It could be either Westwood or the experienced Scot stationed midway down the list. Outwardly Monty exuded confidence about his clash with David Toms, but this belied the truth. 'That was the singles match he probably feared most in his Ryder Cup career,' Denis Pugh recalled. 'Toms was a proven quality player and a major winner. Colin wasn't playing well and he was doing it all on instinct and guts. I think there he genuinely thought he might lose his unbeaten record. He wasn't confident going into the match and he wasn't easy to be around. He was uptight, but the great thing about Monty is that there was no way he was going to let anyone know.' Montgomerie even allowed Pugh to watch him warm up ahead of the match.

The Scot was going to have to depend on the power of positive thinking as he headed to the first tee and reaped instant dividends with an opening birdie after a superb wedged approach shot. It provided echoes of day one at Oakland Hills and, of course, the final day at the Belfry two years earlier. But Toms would not roll over and be beaten in the same way as Scott Hoch had done in 2002. The American levelled with a birdie at the third, but then at the next missed a short putt for a half that might have been conceded had this not been the Ryder Cup. Monty's golf wasn't great, but he was scrambling to keep his nose in front. His caddie Alastair McLean commented: 'It was real piss-you-off matchplay golf', and Toms ruefully recalled: 'It seemed like he made every putt he had to make.'

Montgomerie was two up after six and at that stage he was the only European in the top six who was ahead. He managed to secure a gutsy half at the next thanks to a wedged third shot after having only been able to hack out of a fairway bunker following another errant tee shot.

Elsewhere Europe, buoyed by Monty's positive start, began to turn the tide back in their direction. Casey was always behind against Woods, who eventually won 3 and 2, but García raced away from Mickelson to win by the same score. Two and half points needed. Darren Clarke grabbed a half against his good friend Davis Love. Immediately afterwards they enjoyed a cigar together to demonstrate the great spirit between them. Two points needed. Howell was already toast against Jim Furyk, the European rookie falling 6 and 4. Still two points needed. Then Lee Westwood edged home on the final green against Kenny Perry. One point required and next in was Monty, although Ian Poulter was in command against Riley and might secure the winning point first.

The television cameras were on Montgomerie, though. He'd been involved in a tense struggle in which Toms had hit back from being two down after eight. By the 11th the American had made it all square. Monty reassumed the lead one hole later, sinking one from ten feet before Toms missed from six – a sickener for the US player. At the 13th Monty halved from ten feet, but at the next blew up to leave the match back at all square. It was starting to become clear that he might be the man who would win the cup for Europe, but he was oblivious to the fact. He did know, though, that his proud, unbeaten record in Ryder Cup singles was hanging in the balance.

At the 16th McLean was concerned by Montgomerie's second shot which would be played from the left rough with water to the front and right of the green. The caddie suggested Monty should aim a little left of the flag for safety. As the shot came out it took no heed of the bagman's judicious caution and flew straight at the pin, but with no damage done. It finished 15 feet past the hole. This was the Ryder Cup, this was Monty, this was his kind of moment. The birdie putt was never going to miss and Europe's 'rock' moved one ahead again. He then needed to work hard on the penultimate green to hole a curling four-footer for a half after a brave chip. It meant the unbeaten record would remain intact. He was one up with one to play but Europe still needed that single point to be sure of winning the match. The eventual outcome wasn't in much doubt, but everyone watching knew how appropriate it would be for Europe's veteran talisman to be the one who completed the job.

Not that Montgomerie was fully aware of the situation. He had a sense that a big moment might be in the offing, but his sole purpose was to beat Toms and garner a full point for his team. He was pumped up. His three-wood tee shot on the last finished just a pace short of the bunker that sat 310 yards from where he had driven. Toms hit his second shot just to the right of the green. Langer was down the fairway with the man with whom he had shared so many memorable times in this competition. Yet another was looming large.

The captain had already seen Clarke and Westwood come down the last and knew that the best place to aim was to the right half of the green and that is precisely where Montgomerie lined up to hit, but his approach ran through the back. For the third shots it was Toms to play first and he chipped to 15 feet. Monty faced a devilishly difficult shot that required him to putt through the fringe before sliding across the putting surface. He judged it wonderfully and the ball rested four and a half to five feet from the hole. Courageously, Toms holed his lengthy par putt to ensure a fitting climax. Monty would have to sink his putt for the win that would clinch the Ryder Cup for Europe.

Montgomerie and McLean took due note of Toms' putt because it showed that his ball broke the opposite way to the overall slope of the green. By now Monty could sense this was a very big moment. As he settled over the ball he tried to compose himself. Four, maybe five feet, that was all. He says he told himself over and over again, 'You've done this thousands of times before.' He was saying those words as the putter head rested behind his ball. Then a deep breath, the putter went back and through, striking the ball holeward. It had to disappear, the script demanded it.

The ball covered the four to five feet quickly, but could it obey this compelling storyline? Europe's fans collectively held their breath, desperate to see it vanish. It did, in a moment of sheer sporting magic. Pandemonium across the course. Monty could add another one to the tally of the thousands of times he had performed such a task, but never before had he done it in such a high-profile setting.

This was Monty's major moment. It never happened with one of the game's most prestigious titles on the line, but appropriately it did in the event that ultimately defined his career. 'That was the nearest thing to holing one for myself, but I was doing this for my team,' Monty said when I asked him if that was the closest he had come to the feeling of holing a putt to win a major.

Montgomerie turned away in a celebration that betrayed sheer relief more than joy. 'Fate played its part and it was me who was given the opportunity to hole the winning putt and I took it,' Montgomerie later recalled. 'God knows how, but I did.'

Job done and done better than even he could have dared imagine, given the uncertainties of his life in 2004. Langer was the first to hug him and Monty's reaction was to thank his captain for the wild-card pick that had brought him to Oakland Hills. Langer said he'd just witnessed the reason why the Scot had been selected. A jubilant Montgomerie was at pains to stress it had been a team effort. 'We had strength at the top, we had strength in the middle and we had strength at the bottom. That's the first time I could ever say that,' he said. 'Lee Westwood and I had a chat in the morning. He was five and I was six and it was about that time we felt we could win. It just happened that it fell to me, but it doesn't matter who holes the putt.'

It did for the script, however. This had been the perfect ending.

'I was hoping David would miss his putt, I must admit that,' Montgomerie went on. 'That was a hell of a putt he holed and it made me have to hole mine. I'm glad mine caught the left side of the hole!'

So was his Ryder Cup scriptwriter. There was only one error: 'When I dropped the putter I went straight to Bernhard Langer and forgot to shake the hands of David Toms and his caddie,' the Scot admitted, 'I'll always regret that.'

Europe had romped to victory. Simultaneously, Poulter was guaranteeing a half on the 15th that effectively meant Europe would have an unassailable lead regardless of whether Monty holed his putt but no one around the 18th was aware at that moment. 'Monty knew he had to do something he was capable of doing, which was knocking it in,' Denis Pugh remembered. 'The TV people made sure it was the deciding putt through their sense of drama.' And given Montgomerie's history in the Ryder Cup there was no one better to provide the crowning moment.

'It was a great finish for Colin to hole that putt to win the Ryder Cup,' said Poulter, who went on to confirm his win over Chris Riley at the 16th. He remains unconcerned that he wasn't credited with the crowning moment. 'It was a buzz for us all. Officially my match wasn't over and to me it doesn't matter. I couldn't really care either way. Colin holed the putt and his match finished at that specific moment and it was a fitting moment.'

For Europe it was party time. A sense of euphoria flowed through the team despite defeats for Luke Donald and Miguel Ángel Jiménez. Thomas Levet edged past Fred Funk, Paul McGinley, in the anchor match, beat Stewart Cink 3 and 2 and when Padraig Harrington sank the winning putt against Jay Haas he became the fourth European to close out a victory on the home green. It was another appropriate finish; after all, the Irishman had played as big a part in setting Europe off on the right course as the man who had so emotionally confirmed the victory. Harrington's win took his continent's tally to a record-breaking 18½ and the United States of America, the nation that for so many years had so dominated the history of the Ryder Cup, had been utterly humiliated.

It had been a superb team effort, brilliantly managed by the captain Langer, but there was no doubting who was receiving most of the acclaim. The man who had started the job with his opening birdie on the Friday morning, the man who had shut the door on any lingering US hopes on the Sunday afternoon, the man who had come good just in time to be there – Colin Montgomerie.

As the flag was replaced in the hole on the 18th green after Harrington had made sure the record books would be rewritten, Westwood's caddie, John 'Scotchie' Graham, scampered forward. He had plans for that flag and removed it from the pole. It was passed around the European camp and everyone was asked to sign it, apart from Monty. He was to be the recipient of what was now a priceless memento, one that meant as much as the many individual trophies he had collected throughout his career.

All sorts of messages were scrawled on it to confirm the esteem in which he was held by his team. They included, 'Monty, you are the bollox' from the cheeky chappy of the team, Ian Poulter. 'Did you spell it with an X?' he was asked. 'Yes,' he said with a smile as he remembered a compliment that was as Poulteresque as could be.

At the press conference that ended proceedings that Sunday evening in Michigan, Europe remained in understandably high spirits. The genial Frenchman Thomas Levet acted as his team's master of ceremonies with an introduction for each of his team-mates. For Monty he was succinct: 'Mr Ryder Cup, the mean machine. Don't play against him in the singles – you lost already.'

Inevitably Montgomerie attracted many of the questions, given the prominent role he had played, and especially after receiving his wild-card pick. He revelled in the attention, but just as his mantra had been throughout the week he wanted to stress the importance of Europe's team ethic. 'It doesn't matter who holes the winning putt,' he maintained, before continuing with an unusual turn of phrase. 'I've often said, this to me personally means bugger nothing. My personal record means nothing. I'm here as part of a team and whenever I play in the Ryder Cup, I'll always be that.

'I wouldn't have been able to make this team if it wasn't for the eleven guys plus Bernhard giving me their support over the last few months.' Monty then went on to thank them publicly for that fortifying influence 'in enabling me to get on to what I do best in life, and that's play golf'.

At this point, Montgomerie was visibly moved as the rest of the team spontaneously rose to salute him with a standing ovation before the watching media. Yet again, even with his personal life at such a low ebb, the Ryder Cup had provided the platform that enabled Monty to make himself the centre of glorious attention. And it felt as though this was the legend going out on the ultimate high, as the player who set the seal on his team's recordbreaking victory. But he had other ideas and could see no reason why that elusive major victory should not still be within his grasp.

12

18 JUNE 2006, WINGED FOOT GOLF CLUB,
MAMARONECK, NEW YORK

This was it. The wait was about to end. Such a wait. You could count them; fifty-seven majors played, fifty-seven majors lost. Some not by much, but all of them defeats. This was different, though. It had all fallen into place. Fairways and greens, fairways and greens, that's what you needed here in New York and there was no one better at finding them. Time and again, into the fairway and on to the green. The slowish putting surfaces helped, too, but you also needed a bit of luck. He'd never won any event without a bit of luck on the way. Well, how about that moment on the 71st green when that snaking putt from miles away dropped in? That was a break. The ultimate sign it was going to be his day, surely. A major at last. What a forty-third birthday present. Just had to get the drive away at the last. That was the difficult bit. Made it look easy. Mickelson was in trouble; this was there for the taking. The US Open. Always said this was the most likely one. The one that best suited his game. With his driving he was always one up on the rest at this event. His accuracy, he could handle those narrow fairways and brutal rough better than most. And he'd just proved it. Perfect drive, ideal spot for a trademark fade to the pin cut in the right half of the green. The hard part had been done. Just had to knock it on to the green. It was all falling into place. Just needed Vijay to get his ruling and play his shot. He had to wait for Vijay, and wait and

268

wait. Was it a six or a seven iron? Don't forget the adrenaline.
It was pumping now. He could knock it on, no problem. What
was Vijay up to? He wanted to hit, really wanted to hit. He still
had to wait. What if he made a mess of it . . . ?

Monty was back. His heroics in closing out victory for Bernhard Langer's team in 2004 proved a watershed moment in
his resurgence. In the aftermath of his marriage break-up
earlier that year he had plummeted to eighty-third in the world.
It had taken the special nature of the Ryder Cup to inspire
Colin Montgomerie's golfing recovery. The desire to prove to
Langer that he was still good enough to play for his continent
had made it a necessity. There was no alternative and once he
had been invited on to the plane to Oakland Hills he let no
one down. Monty had performed at the very start of the match
and at its denouement and it did wonders for his confidence.
It told him he was still a player, that there was substance behind
his claim that he was not finished yet.

The remainder of 2004 was relatively quiet but there were
encouraging signs in his play. At the turn of the year he
embarked on a relentless schedule aimed at taking him back
into the world's top fifty. The climb back was on and he began
the Caltex Masters in Singapore at the end of January 2005
with a sparkling 65 that paved the way for a runner's-up finish.
Then he was eleventh at the Heineken Classic at Royal
Melbourne, fourth in Dubai, sixth in China at the TCL Classic
and, fatefully, fourth at the Indonesian Open, the tournament
that had sparked all the controversy over how he had replaced
his ball after that thunderstorm. Amid the furore that followed
his results began to dip, but he was back in the elite fifty in
time for the US Open in June 2005. Then he was second at

the European Open and runner-up to a dominant Tiger Woods at St Andrews in the Open Championship. 'I won the tournament for the rest of us,' Monty quipped after perhaps the least painful of his runner-up finishes in a major.

Still he marched on. The St Andrews prize money had boosted his pot sufficiently to rekindle thoughts of another Order of Merit title. He was shooting up the money list and there was much to play for in the remainder of the year. Top ten at the WGC NEC Invitational in Akron, Ohio, showed he could still compete in world-class fields in the US and he bettered that performance with a share of third place behind Woods in the WGC American Express Championship at Harding Park in San Francisco. That tournament followed an emotional win at the Dunhill Links Championship where he played with the actor Michael Douglas in the pro-celebrity format. It is no hit and giggle event, though. There was serious prize money on offer and Monty banked around £500,000 for edging out Kenneth Ferrie on the final hole at the Home of Golf. If only he'd been able to experience that winning feeling at the same St Andrews venue three months earlier.

There was still plenty to play for because now it was down to a race between him and the US Open and World Matchplay Champion Michael Campbell for the Order of Merit crown. Monty duly wrapped it up with a third-placed finish in the season-ending Volvo Masters. 'This one feels like it means more than the other seven money list titles, given where I've had to come from,' Monty said.

After clinching the Harry Vardon Trophy, the prize for winning the money list, for a record eighth time, Montgomerie flew home from southern Spain in reflective mood. His attitude was that it had been a job well done, he had responded positively to the pressure and duly delivered. He has never been one for extravagant celebrations. 'On board that plane he was very quiet and reflective. He might have had one glass of champagne but that was it. The overwhelming feeling was one of relief and release rather than jubilation', his then coach Denis Pugh recalled. Montgomerie has also looked back at what was the catalyst for his 2005 success and pinpoints making the previous year's Ryder Cup team. 'If I hadn't have been selected I wouldn't have won the Order of Merit. That selection by Bernhard Langer was vital for my career. I was forty-one at the time and it was not looking good.'

The sizeable cheques banked after the Dunhill Links and Volvo Masters at Valderrama gave Monty a flying start to the year-long qualifying period for the 2006 Ryder Cup. He would not be needing a captain's pick to appear in Ian Woosnam's team at the K Club. Monty admitted to being able to 'walk a little bit taller' into the locker rooms of the European Tour having secured that Order of Merit title at the age of forty-two. The new season began just one week after the old one had been completed and the goal now was to secure a place back in the world's top ten. Montgomerie made a flying start by winning the Hong Kong Open when his closest rival, South Africa's James Kingston, double-bogeyed the last. Thereafter Monty found it more difficult to sustain momentum but there were still enough high finishes to remind the world that he remained a force in the game. His golf clicked with four rounds in the 60s at the 2006 Wales Open where he finished fourth before heading off to Austria for his fifth consecutive week on Tour. A closing 75 there cost him a top ten finish but there was still plenty left in the tank as he headed to the US Open at Winged Foot in Mamaroneck, New York.

The course for the second major of the year set up well for the Scot. Typically narrow fairways were lined by heavy rough that put a high premium on accuracy from the tee. The greens were bumpier and slower than usual and that helped too because it neutralised the skills of the better putters and Monty didn't regard himself as one of those. He opened with a one under par 69 which was good enough to lead. Following his second-round 71 he lay in second place but after beginning his third round with four straight bogeys his hopes were in free fall. Monty dug in, birdied the fifth and salvaged a 75 that left him three shots off the pace heading into the final round. The characterful way he had responded to those dropped shots at the start of his third round emboldened him. The Scot said he had needed to dig deeper than ever before to keep alive his chances. A three-shot deficit could be overturned in no time on that treacherous piece of New York real estate and he knew he had a big chance on the final day.

It turned into one of the most dramatic closing rounds ever seen at a US Open and Montgomerie was at the heart of the excitement. Throughout he hung around on the fringes of the leaderboard. It looked as though this was going to be another of those majors where he would come up just short, but he continued to hit fairways and greens and his only dropped shots were courtesy of three putts on the tenth and 14th holes. No disgrace, either, on those bumpy putting surfaces. Whenever he is asked about what it takes to win a major, Montgomerie always says that a slice of luck is required. 'I've never heard a winner say he was unlucky.'

Whether it was luck or judgement, Montgomerie's big break came on the 17th. Along with Phil Mickelson, Padraig Harrington and Jim Furyk, Monty was one of those harbouring hopes of victory and all the leading players were experiencing difficulty on the closing holes.

Montgomerie's approach to the 17th didn't look as if it was going to yield the birdie he so desperately needed. Time was running out and he was looking at a huge putt, as long as, if not longer than, those that he had crucially sunk en route to vital Ryder Cup singles wins against Lee Janzen and Ben Crenshaw. Just as he had done on those occasions he judged it to perfection, the ball dropped and so did the jaws of the watching galleries and, indeed, of the player himself. Suddenly and unexpectedly he was tied for the lead of the US Open with one hole to play. His rival, Mickelson, bidding for a third successive major victory, was in trouble on the 16th and for all the world it looked as though a par at the last would be enough to end Monty's quest for a major. All those near misses stretching back to the 1992 US Open, where he had finished third to Tom Kite, all those worldwide victories that needed the validation of a major – they could all be put to bed with one simple par at the last hole at Winged Foot.

Except the 18th at Winged Foot does not yield simple pars. It is a 450-yard beast called 'Revelations' with a devilishly difficult tee shot to a narrow target area guarded by a bunker on the right edge of the fairway. The hole moves from right to left, the opposite direction to the stock flight of a Monty drive. Miss the fairway and locating the green from the rough or sand with a second shot is nigh-on impossible. 'This is it for Monty,' former Tour player Jay Townsend told listeners to Radio Five Live. 'The crucial thing is the drive. If he hits the fairway he wins the US Open.' Monty was pumped and put a superb swing on his drive and the ball flew into the heart of the fairway. It was voted European Tour Shot of the Month for June 2006. It was a piece of nerveless brilliance. Montgomerie's playing partner Vijay Singh was less fortunate and carted his ball into the tented village. The Scot was unconcerned. He'd done the hard bit and strode off purposefully to ready himself for a second shot he was perfectly equipped to execute. Monty arrived at his ball full of confidence. Singh would be first to play and needed a ruling on where to drop his ball.

Montgomerie was 172 yards from the hole which was cut in the right half of a plateau green. It was the perfect pin position: he could aim to the left and use his regular fade to fly the ball into the right half where the hole lay. Monty could not have asked for a better scenario but Singh was waiting for a ruling. Harrington had finished with a third consecutive bogey and was out of it, Furyk was clinging on to his hopes and Mickelson was struggling. 'It's amazing what runs through your little mind at that stage,' Monty admitted. The atmosphere in the crowd was feverish. They recognised Montgomerie was now favourite. 'But I had to wait,' Montgomerie recalled. 'Fourteen minutes before Vijay Singh was sorted out. Negative thoughts started to creep into my head. I defy anyone not to have negative thoughts when they have to wait fourteen minutes to play the biggest shot of their life.'

Eventually it was Monty's turn to play. He had a six iron in his hand for about a minute as he had waited, but the wind had died down. The ball was flying a long way in steamy upstate New York and a seven, which for him usually flies 164 yards, would easily be boosted to 172 by the conditions and adrenaline of the moment. He pulled the seven iron from his bag. 'It was the right club,' he still contends. But it wasn't the right swing. He caught the ground first and the ball heavy.

'What a time to hit a shot like that,' he said as the ball embarked on its journey. It wasn't a trip to the promised land of the green. It fell short and right of the putting surface in thick rough. 'If my drive had been the shot of the month, that seven iron was the worst shot of the month,' Montgomerie admitted. The advantage he had earned was gone in one imprecise blow. He hacked it on to the green, but a long way from the flag. His composure had gone and he charged the par putt he thought he needed for a win and for good measure missed the return. Double bogey, when par would have been enough. Two putts would have given him a play-off.

Mickelson messed up the 18th as well and, thanks to a chip in at the 17th and a nerveless up and down at the last, the unlikely Australian Geoff Ogilvy edged in at five over par – one shot better than Mickelson and Montgomerie, for whom this was a fifth runner's-up finish in a major and easily the most painful. 'Until I win one, Winged Foot will stay with me forever,' he admitted.

'Other chances I've had in majors other players have done well. This is the first time I've really messed up' was his instant response. He even attempted to be humorous, adding: 'Which is okay. You're entitled to a couple of mess-ups on the way.' He was trying to hide the hurt he was feeling, the distress and anger that had manifested itself when he'd pushed past a state trooper at the back of the 18th green en route to the recorder's hut. 'Disaster' was another word used. The beaten Mickelson concluded: 'I'm such an idiot' after his own 72nd-hole capitulation and the gracious Ogilvy admitted: 'I think I was the beneficiary of some charity.'

It hadn't been willingly given. Mickelson, at least, already had three majors – two Masters and a US PGA – in his locker.

Monty had no such crutch for comfort. Throughout his career he had converted these opportunities to win. At that point he could boast thirty-nine victories worldwide, but when the chance came in a major he could not take it. If he had done so we would regard him quite differently. He would be seen as somebody who had finally fulfilled his undoubted potential on golf's biggest stage and in America's backyard. His reputation as a choker in the biggest events would have been banished. Montgomerie would be remembered as much for individual achievement as anything else. He didn't win, though, and this was yet more compelling evidence and ammunition for the critics who said he didn't have what it took when the greatest prizes were on offer. His failure to win at Winged Foot, however, put even greater emphasis on the arena that truly made his career – the Ryder Cup.

13

*'Monty is the guy who has put the biggest dent in
us over the years, we'd have to single him out'*
– Stewart Cink, US Team Member

*He would have loved a major. Of course he would and this
miss would stay with him until he got one. But it was 2006
and a Ryder Cup year. A bonus, that was how he saw the Ryder
Cup right now, and he wouldn't have traded any of the success
he'd had playing for Europe for a major. It meant that much,
and with each year that passed without a major trophy in the
cabinet he was more defined by his deeds in this team arena.
That unbeaten record in singles meant so much. Said so much.
About his bottle. You try holing a putt with eleven team-mates,
colleagues, rivals – they were all of those – depending on your
stroke remaining secure. That was bottle. They thought he might
be skipper for this one, at the K Club. Talked about it after he'd
closed it out for Bernhard two years earlier. He was still a player,
though, and a leader.*

Having turned forty-three the week after Winged Foot, Montgomerie comfortably qualified for the Ryder Cup at the K Club
in Ireland. Of those eligible to play for Europe, he collected
the fifth highest number of world-ranking points. The captain

was Ian Woosnam and he was delighted to have Monty making his eighth consecutive appearance. With the recently widowed Darren Clarke and his big mate Lee Westwood gaining captain's wild-card picks, the European team looked very strong. There were only three changes from the side that had completed the record-breaking win at Oakland Hills. Miguel Ángel Jiménez, Ian Poulter and Thomas Levet had been unable to hold on to their places. A resurgent José Maria Olazábal was back, the qualifying table had been topped by the rookie Swede, Henrik Stenson, and seven years on from being left out by Mark James, another Swede, Robert Karlsson, had emphatically played himself into the team.

By contrast, the American team was more a 'who's that?' of golf rather than a 'who's who'. Of course, Tiger Woods and Phil Mickelson were there for the new skipper, Tom Lehman, but figures like JJ Henry, Vaughan Taylor and Brett Wetterich were hardly household names. On the range ahead of the match Monty actually needed to have pointed out to him the identities of some of these American players. A sign that Montgomerie was of a different generation? Most certainly, but also an indication that American golf did not possess the strength in depth of old. With home advantage and a record-breaking win from their last clash there was no way that Europe could be considered anything other than firm favourites to win the cup for an unprecedented third match in a row. 'I believe it's our strongest team we have ever put together,' Montgomerie said on the eve of the match. You could also sense his delight at having the opportunity to have another go at the Americans. 'I enjoyed the putt at the 17th hole at Winged Foot, I must admit that was good. I didn't enjoy the next hole. I enjoy personal success, of course you do. But I do enjoy this more than any other, yes,' he said when asked whether he preferred the Ryder Cup to any other week of the golfing year.

Woosnam had put behind him the controversy of his wild-card selections and the criticism that had followed from Thomas Björn. His objective in the week of the match was to nurture Europe's famed team spirit and to build the team around the grieving Darren Clarke.

The captain had also brought into the setup a team psychologist, the unorthodox Jamil Qureshi who worked with several tour players as well as football teams and corporate clients on mental attitude. A former county cricketer, Qureshi had never played golf, but was there for anyone in the side should they require help. As an accomplished entertainer and magician, he was also able to assist in team-bonding exercises. This included providing the entertainment at a team dinner on the Monday evening of Ryder Cup week, the key time for forging unity among the dozen individuals who would represent Europe. For Qureshi, Monty made the perfect stooge. He asked the assembled players, wives, girlfriends and officials to do a twenty-second sketch of Monty. Then from a pile of forty he drew out four and correctly identified the artists as Sergio García, Paul McGinley, Padraig Harrington and captain's assistant, Peter Baker. Qureshi admitted the task had been made more difficult because most of the cartoons depicted Montgomerie with a big, curly hairstyle and a scowl. The joke had been at Monty's expense but it had brought together the team. They thought it was hilarious. 'He took it brilliantly,' said Qureshi.

'I chose Monty to stand up because he has real personality. He's always a very big part of the team and people would express more if they are drawing something or someone that has real character,' Qureshi went on. 'It would reveal more about how they viewed him as they expressed it in their drawing. The other thing I noticed was his willingness to take part. He sort of raised his eyebrows to show a sort of reluctance, but he was still really keen to take part. You could see Monty understood his essential part in the team. He demonstrated a high degree of perception regarding what makes good teamwork. He saw the value, setting the tone of the meeting and the dynamics of building a team.' It had been more than a mere exercise in entertainment and by simply standing up to be drawn Monty had played his part. 'I work a lot with business and in the corporate world and there you expect the best bosses to have a good knowledge of team dynamics. I don't expect that at all from golfers, but Monty showed a very highly developed sense of what makes a team.'

No one doubted Montgomerie's value to the side but few could understand why this should be, given the unorthodox path of his individual career. 'What is it about this event that transforms this strange and often aloof individual into perhaps the finest team player in world golf?' asked James Corrigan in the *Independent*. 'Why does the pressure that almost always cripples him when he is on his own in the cauldron have the complete opposite effect when there are others in there with him? How does one of the most muttered about characters on the European Tour suddenly become the most popular one for three days every two years?'

The simple answer is that he always delivered. He brought points and that's what any captain needs. 'The reason he does well is because Monty's thermostat is perfectly set for the Ryder Cup,' contends Qureshi. 'There must always be a level of pressure and stress. Too much or too little would inhibit him.'

Qureshi is also convinced that this influence percolates through the team. 'He's a winner who creates other winners by simply being around. He's not a mentor, he doesn't necessarily put an arm round the shoulder of a rookie, but he has a presence that allows you to feed off it. I remember him leaning on the bar on one elbow, legs crossed, all he needed was a smoking jacket. Monty was at ease with himself and the Ryder Cup surroundings and that transmits itself. Other players have said this to me. Monty knows the Ryder Cup, he's a bit like a barometer of how the team is doing. If he's calm and confident it is utterly reassuring because he knows what it takes to win.'

The Monty Qureshi describes is the one we see at a Ryder Cup. It is not the same character that turns up to majors. 'Although we will target all of the Europeans, Monty is the guy who has put the biggest dent in us over the years,' said Stewart Cink. 'We'd have to single him out.'

To no one's great surprise Monty was handed the task of going out first again with Padraig Harrington, for whom this was a huge week playing the first Ryder Cup to be staged in Ireland. It was also no shock that they were up against Tiger Woods and that the world number one's partner was Jim Furyk, with whom he had forged a formidable combination in the previous year's President's Cup. Making his way to the tee just before the 8 a.m. start, Monty gave a short interview to Five Live's Nicky Campbell. 'For all those people listening at home, sitting in their cars in the morning traffic jams, can I just say you can breathe at the moment. I can't,' said a clearly nervous Monty. The previous day he'd made a slight alteration to his swing because the practice rounds had not been too encouraging.

Woods walked on to the tee poker-faced and looking

determined to avenge the tone-setting opening morning defeat of two years earlier at Oakland Hills when he had partnered Phil Mickelson. The tee sat amid a packed horse-shoe stand. The weather was miserable and the roar from the Irish fans to greet the players was deafening. It was an extraordinary occasion. Even the usually unflappable European Tour starter Ivor Robson was affected. His hands were shaking as he handled his papers and when it came to announcing the first match he erroneously said it was a foursomes contest. Monty jokingly made to leave the tee, suggesting he would leave his partner to play Europe's opening drive, but there was no escape because the opening sequence of matches in the 2006 match was fourballs. As ever, the visitors would hit first and Furyk split the fairway. Woods confidently teed up his ball. Here was the world number one, golf's ultimate iceman when the heat is on and the temperature is always set to maximum on the first tee of a Ryder Cup. Woods melted. His three-wood drive flew straight left into a lake. 'I didn't even know it was there,' Montgomerie later said of the water hazard. The Scot went with a driver and split the fairway, Harrington had found the trees and the opening hole was a shootout between Monty and Furyk. The American won it with a composed birdie.

Woods was clearly unsettled and dashed off to a portable toilet on the second, only to find his caddie, Steve Williams, already using it. The world's top golfer was kept waiting by his bagman who eventually emerged with a sheepish grin. The pit stop seemed to offer little relief; Woods continued to play as though out of sorts and it was Furyk who held Montgomerie and Harrington at bay through a tense front nine.

For the European pair there was continued frustration on the greens. Neither could buy a putt and once Woods eventually settled with a fine shot into the short eighth the Americans started to take control. Furyk holed an extraordinary long-range putt with five feet of break judged to perfection to put the Americans two up. They then won the 13th and were three up with five to play. Monty birdied the 14th to cut the arrears. Two down, before Harrington pulled Europe back to within a hole and set up an exciting finale. Alas for Europe neither player could find the putt that would win either of the closing holes. They were both halved and the Americans drew first blood to cheer their captain, Tom Lehman. 'That was a big point,' he said.

It was America's only full point from the morning session. Cink and Henry managed a half with Casey and Karlsson in the second match but Europe swept to victories in the remaining two with wins for the Spanish duo García and Olazábal over Toms and Wetterich and Clarke and Westwood edging home against Mickelson and DiMarco in the bottom match. That contest had begun with Clarke smashing the drive of his life off the first tee after a rapturous welcome. His wife Heather had died from breast cancer the previous month and the welcome given to the Ulsterman had his caddie, Billy Foster, and partner, Lee Westwood, fighting off tears as Clarke unleashed his opening drive. 'I don't know how I managed to do that,' Clarke said.

Westwood needed a new partner for the afternoon because Clarke was understandably rested and Woosnam paired the Englishman with Montgomerie to be sent out third against Mickelson and DiMarco. It was a surprise pairing as neither player had spent any time with the other in practice. Woosnam admitted he'd decided on the combination 'very late on' that morning. 'They go together so well,' he said.

'I'd never played with Monty, but Woosie asked him who he wanted to play with,' said Westwood. 'And he said me, which was nice.'

Monty had the partner he wanted and they found themselves embroiled in a tense afternoon in which Europe sought to build on their advantage from the morning. The first three matches all went to the last green. Harrington, in an all-Irish pairing with Paul McGinley, halved with Chad Campbell and Zach Johnson, while David Howell and Henrik Stenson shared their match with Stewart Cink and David Toms.

There was a mighty tussle going on to wrest the initiative, and if Westwood and Monty could edge home in their match it would surely stay with the home side. The change Montgomerie had made to his turn away from the ball on the eve of the match was paying dividends with much-improved ballstriking, and in that afternoon contest his touch on the greens returned as well. Westwood drove the ball long and straight, while DiMarco tenaciously kept the Americans in the match. Behind them Sergío García and Luke Donald had their noses in front against Woods and Furyk. It wasn't looking so encouraging for the new Monty/Westwood combination, though. Coming to the final tee they were one down and needed to win that last hole. On the long par five, Montgomerie's excellent second shot found the edge of the enormous home green. A two-putt birdie was going to be enough to give the Europeans the half-point. Westwood was putting from 100 feet and he hadn't needed to strike a putt of any consequence since the fifth hole. 'He said to me, "Thanks, Monty. I've got a thirty-bloody-yard putt with a six-foot swing."' Montgomerie laughed. Westwood did exceptionally well to put it to eight feet and give Monty the sort of moment he enjoys most.

'Lee hit a fantastic putt,' commented captain Woosnam. 'The pace of that green is a little bit faster going down towards the water.'

Montgomerie, a loser in the morning, did not fancy a similar outcome after lunch. He wanted to reinforce his side's advantage. He wanted to hole this eight-foot putt. As he hunched over the ball his hook-nosed face was a picture of calm determination. Just the right amount of 'pressure and stress' and the thermostat setting was spot on. The ball disappeared, Europe had their half and with the bottom match won they led 5-3 at the end of the first day. 'Monty: how many times have we seen him hole that left-to-right putt coming back? He's got such courage,' said Woosnam. 'You know; what a man to have on your team.'

The European skipper was thrilled with the start his side had made. Seven of the eight matches had gone to the final hole and Europe had earned the lead and used every player in their team. They had all been blooded and the scoreboard was a reflection of their strength in depth. So was the fact that Woosnam could afford to leave out Montgomerie from the second day's morning fourballs. Monty hadn't expected to be dropped and was disappointed. 'I think he wanted to play all five,' said his caddie Alastair McLean. In Monty's absence the session, like the first two, went the way of the home team. The only disappointment was the continued struggle of Harrington on home soil as he and Henrik Stenson lost to Scott Verplank and Zach Johnson on the 17th. Clarke and Westwood more than made up for it with their 3 and 2 win over Woods and Furyk and García and Olazábal won by the same score against

Mickelson and DiMarco. The top match featuring Casey and Karlsson against Cink and Henry was halved. By Saturday lunchtime Europe led by seven and half points to four and a half and Monty was ready to re-enter the fray.

Woosnam had no reason to break up his foursomes partnership with Westwood and it was their ability to avoid defeat again that proved such a sickener for the American team. Paul Casey and David Howell thrashed Cink and Johnson, a match ended by Casey's hole in one at the 14th, while Woods and Furyk were too strong for Harrington and Paul McGinley. Europe had the edge in the afternoon, though, because García and Donald had beaten Mickelson and Toms. It meant that Chad Campbell and Vaughan Taylor would have to beat Montgomerie and Westwood for the visitors to avoid falling even further behind.

It was all square at the turn before the Americans moved ahead at the next with a par. Europe hit back with Westwood's 15-foot birdie putt at the 12th and the home pair went ahead at the 15th when Taylor found water. But Westwood's approach to the 17th went long and they arrived on the last tee all square. Both pairs found the par five green in two and both two putted. Monty's three wood had carried 250 yards to find the putting surface 15 feet from the flag. It was one of his best shots of the week, but Westwood was unable to convert the chance to win the match. It still felt a far bigger half for the Europeans because it guaranteed they had won another session and they were on the brink of retaining the trophy. They led 10-6. 'We're very close, we are,' said Montgomerie. 'Every game I've played has come down to the 18th. I've lost one and halved a couple.' As the senior figure in the side he went on to volunteer his own analysis of what had been a remarkable two days for Ian

Woosnam's team. 'That's five points out of six that our wild cards have had without a loss. I think that has totally justified Woosie's selections of Darren and Lee. We are a fantastic team and a unit. We want to win all five sessions for the first time ever.'

Europe had not lost a Ryder Cup since Brookline in 1999. Then they had also led 10-6 going into the final day. 'That wasn't ten-six; that was ten-nine overnight,' Montgomerie said. 'We had three rookies that had not played before and they happened to draw three top Americans in Tiger Woods, Phil Mickelson and Davis Love. This is very different, this is ten-six. We have only two rookies [Stenson and Karlsson] and they have played well and everybody has played twice and everyone's got at least half a point. So this is a very different situation and it's also being played in Ireland not in Boston.

'And, make no mistake, there's no complacency in our camp at all. We must try to counteract whatever the American team have in their thoughts,' Monty added, sounding evermore like a captain of the future.

Montgomerie wondered who his name would be up against in the singles draw. He knew that Woosnam wanted him out first to ensure the momentum remained with Europe, but he had a nagging worry that the world number one would be waiting for him. Monty had outscored Tiger Woods when they had played together in the third round of the 2005 Open at St Andrews, but his proud, unbeaten record in Ryder Cup singles would be subject to the most intense scrutiny if Lehman decided to open his batting with his top player.

With some relief the Scot surveyed the draw. It wasn't going to be Woods, it was David Toms, the man he had beaten to secure the Cup at Oakland Hills. The weather in Ireland was atrocious. It was pouring with rain as Montgomerie arrived on the first tee to be greeted by a tumultuous Irish ovation that had the Scot going over to the crowd to thank them for their support. Once the match was underway, Monty seized the initiative by winning the third and fourth holes with birdies. From then on it was just a case of holding his tenacious opponent at arm's length, which he succeeded in doing. By the time Monty reached the 18th tee he was one up and his singles record remained. Never been beaten on a Sunday at a Ryder Cup in eight matches. But he wanted more; he wanted the win. With water to the left of the green and a bunker to the right, the Scot was looking at a 240-yard second shot which in theory was on the limit for his three wood. Alastair McLean advised aiming right to take the water out of the equation and Monty took heed. He belted the three wood right out of the middle of the club face and it flew an astonishing 255 yards. He'd hit it too well. The ball found the sand to the right of the green and he was left with the most awkward of bunker shots to be played from a sodden surface. The shot was about 35 yards and he was hitting towards the lake. Toms was on the green in two. Monty had no margin for error and hit a magical shot to around seven feet. Toms putted inside, but was out of the reckoning if Montgomerie could hole his putt for victory.

Watching on television was Monty's old Walker Cup teammate, Peter McEvoy. There was a split screen image; the bottom half showed Monty's putter head behind the ball, the top half showed the player's face. McEvoy said: 'This is the moment I talk about to youngsters coming through the amateur game. Monty has such an agonised look because it means so much to him. At the point that his putter head makes contact with the ball it is utter agony. I can only liken it to the horror expressed in the picture *The Scream* such is the anguish of the moment, the desire to hole the putt. That's where you have to go to if you want to be the very best, that's how much you must want it.'

Montgomerie wanted it all right.

Sure enough, as he had done so many times in the Ryder Cup he seized the moment. In it went, his sixth victory in eight singles matches, and don't forget that he probably would have beaten Hoch but for Seve's sportsmanship at Valderrama. Again he'd gone to the place that was beyond him in the majors, and enhanced further his Ryder Cup legend.

By holing out, Montgomerie set Europe on their way that rainy Sunday afternoon in Ireland. Casey and Donald added comfortable wins and when Henrik Stenson wrapped up a 4 and 3 win over Vaughan Taylor the home side had won again. The only pity was that Stenson won too early to allow Darren Clarke, the spiritual heartbeat of the team, the opportunity to sink the winning putt. Had he done so it would have been as appropriate as Monty's role had been on the final day two years earlier. Even so, Clarke closed out victory over Zach Johnson amid extraordinary emotion on the 16th green. There wasn't a dry eye or throat in the vicinity as the Guinness flowed with the tears. It was party time. Howell had won, Olazábal and Westwood as well, and when Paul McGinley arrived on the 18th green one up on JJ Henry a record-breaking win was in sight. At this point a streaker sprinted into view and dived into the lake just as Henry was about to putt. Sportingly, McGinley conceded the American's long-range putt and the match was halved. It meant Europe matched but didn't beat their record-breaking nine-point winning margin of two years earlier. 'I'll have a word with Paul McGinley later,' Woosnam joked after, saying: 'This is the pinnacle of my life. I've won tournaments around the world, I won a major, I've been number one in the world and I've got to say this is the proudest day in my life.'

Montgomerie was equally satisfied. 'Ian thought it was good I went out first and it was important I got off to a good start and got some blue on the board early, which I did from the third hole onwards and I never let it get back to all square. I am very proud to be part of this team. Tom Lehman's father came up to me and said that this is the best European team that's ever been assembled, and I have to agree with him.' A reporter asked why. Quick as a flash Monty retorted: 'Because we're bloody good.'

Woosnam knew that Montgomerie had played a vital role on and off the course in this triumph. This was Monty's sphere and there was a certain injustice that the nerve and control he had for the environment had not manifested itself in the biggest individual events on the golfing calendar, the majors. Woosnam said: 'If ever there's anybody that deserves to win a major tournament, it's Colin Montgomerie. Never been beaten in a singles in a Ryder Cup, ever.' At this point Sergio García said, 'Hear, hear', and the rest of the jubilant team burst into spontaneous applause.

He didn't know it at the time, but his Ryder Cup playing days were almost certainly over. In eight contests Monty had been on the winning side a record-equalling five times. He played thirty-six matches and won twenty of them. He lost only nine, a truly extraordinary record that showed he reserved his most effective high-profile golf for this arena.

But this was surely the end of an era. The next time Colin Montgomerie would be involved in a Ryder Cup it would be as a captain, charged with the task of regaining the trophy.

14

*'I don't think any captain has had the difficulty
that I have had here in trying to select a three out
of a possible ten'*   **– Colin Montgomerie**

*It had been hard; tougher than he could have imagined, just
getting to this point. There had been stuff in the papers, and
the players hadn't followed the agenda he wanted either. He had
three picks. He needed more, although his task might have been
easier if he had had only two, like previous skippers. He had
known all along that he might have made life harder for himself
asking for that extra selection. But that's what he had always
done: made life harder for himself. Only one thing to be done
now: get his head down and get on with it. He'd always done
that as well, regardless of what people might have been saying
about him. It had been bloody hard, though, make no mistake.
And that's what he had to do now – make no mistake . . .*

Colin Montgomerie strived hard to make sure the K Club victory
would not be his last Ryder Cup as a player but his runner-up
finish at the lucrative French Open was his best result in 2008.
Otherwise he never genuinely threatened to be a member of
Nick Faldo's team. The captain told Monty that he was not one
of his wild-card picks in a mobile phone message that was, tact-

fully, full of praise for his Ryder Cup career. Monty kept the voicemail for some time after. It also explained that Faldo had selected Ian Poulter and Paul Casey as his wild-cards. The rejected Scot had no problem with not being chosen because his golf that season had not been worthy of the top dozen players in Europe, but he still felt Faldo had erred in his selection.

Monty believed that Faldo had made a mistake in not picking the in-form Darren Clarke, the man around whom the 2006 triumph had been built. His passion for the Ryder Cup matched Montgomerie's own and the Scot knew Faldo would miss Clarke's influence out on the course and in the team room. His opinion was somewhat vindicated when it emerged that the omission prompted the American captain Paul Azinger to take out his wife for a celebratory dinner that Sunday night, such was his dread of the Ulsterman's positive influence on the European cause.

Monty was also stunned that he had not been asked to play a vice-captain's role. He was convinced that Faldo's message would end with a call to arms, albeit among Europe's back-room team. How could Europe go into a Ryder Cup without the talismanic Montgomerie being involved in some capacity?

As Europe fell to a 16½–11½ defeat at Valhalla, their first loss since 1999, Montgomerie watched the action unfold on television in his Perthshire home. On the evening of the final day singles he drove to London listening to his beloved continent's capitulation on BBC Five Live before readying himself to compete in the British Masters at the Belfry the following week. He had no idea at that stage that he would be the man charged with regaining the trophy two years later.

He also had no inkling that the period of his captaincy would coincide with uncomfortable questions being raised about the commitment to the Ryder Cup of some of Europe's best golfers. Just as disturbingly, there were also queries over Montgomerie's fitness to lead the team.

Monty's ability to attract headlines had been considered a genuine asset at the time of his appointment. He was going to be the man to reignite European golf, generate new interest and bring in sponsors' cash. As former Tour player Jay Townsend said: 'His appointment was nothing to do with his record in the Ryder Cup, money is what is foremost on the pros' minds.'

Nevertheless, at the time of his appointment in early 2009 Montgomerie seemed the perfect choice. He appeared to have put behind him the lowest point of his career – the controversy at the Indonesian Open – and off the course his sometimes turbulent home life now seemed the epitome of domestic bliss.

As an elder statesman of world golf, he had settled into an apparently happy second marriage to Gaynor Knowles, who had walked the fairways of the K Club to watch her new man play in the 2006 Ryder Cup. They had been introduced by a mutual friend, the television commentator Dougie Donnelly, and hit it off immediately. Montgomerie's then coach Pete Cowen commented: 'He's someone who doesn't like to be on his own.'

They married at Loch Lomond Golf Club on 19 April 2008 in a ceremony and reception said to have cost £1 million. Not that money would ever be a problem because, on top of Montgomerie's fortune, Gaynor brought her own as the widow of the wealthy Scottish furniture tycoon George Knowles. Ryder Cup team-mates Lee Westwood, Paul Casey and Padraig Harrington were guests and the joy of the occasion was there for all to see. Another of those in attendance was the *Daily Mail*'s Golf Correspondent Derek Lawrenson who reported: 'Over the past twenty years I thought I'd seen every emotion from this particular groom, from the magnificent Monty to the borderline psychopath. But I've never seen him in the state of rapture he reached on Saturday.'

As Ryder Cup captain, Montgomerie revelled in the authority and attention the role generated. At once he sought to make changes. He had seen how the American skipper Paul Azinger had benefited from being given four wild-card picks to add to eight automatic qualifiers. Indeed, Monty had always said the strongest team would come from making all twelve players the subject of a captain's pick, although even he could never envisage such a move becoming reality.

The selection policy was to take the leading five world ranking points accumulators and add the top five money-earners on the European Tour who didn't feature in the first list. These ten were supplemented by two captain's picks. This system had been introduced for the 2004 match to reflect the global schedules of so many of the continent's top golfers and it produced two record-breaking wins before the Valhalla defeat. Monty wanted to alter the formula, to have a bigger say in the make-up of the team. He went to the committee armed with statistics that had been worked out by the *Daily Telegraph*'s Mark Reason, although the skipper was happy to take the credit for the research. 'I looked at the percentage points won by the captain's picks over the last five years,' Montgomerie said. 'It is 70 per cent. Players eight, nine and ten from qualifying have won less than 50 per cent of the points. That was my argument to get the extra pick.'

When the Tournament Committee gave the captain his additional wild-card option it seemed it would be a boon. By the time it came into use it was more of a curse. Monty was confronted with the most difficult choice faced by any captain and made arguably the most contentious selections in the history of European golf. Furthermore, in keeping with most of his turbulent career, there was much more controversy and heartache to be endured before he came close to those key moments of finalising his team and leading them in Wales.

Such a malaise was not on the horizon when he began the job. In the early part of his captaincy Montgomerie was an emboldened and forthright figure ready to lay down the law. His immediate priority was to promote European golf and stem the flow of talent to the American PGA Tour. The new generation of leading European players like Paul Casey, Luke Donald, Ian Poulter and Justin Rose had built their homes in the United States. Their 'global' schedules are effectively determined by the more dominant US calendar and around that they fit in sufficient sanctioned events to allow them to retain their membership of the European Tour and so their eligibility for the Ryder Cup. They might hail from Europe, but they play precious few tournaments on European fairways. Excluding the Open Championship, this leading quartet mustered just ten appearances between them at European-staged tournaments played in the heart of the 2009 season. They made up the rest of their schedule at Tour events in Asia and the Middle East.

This trend doesn't sit easily with Monty, a loyalist who never took up the option of becoming a PGA Tour player. He decided to use his captaincy to try to convince the US-based stars to show more commitment to the continent. 'I feel that every European that is qualified should be playing in the BMW PGA Championship,' Monty said of the Wentworth tournament the Tour regards as its flagship event. 'I will be asking for that personally in my role. The second event would be the Wales

Open at Celtic Manor. I think it would do them no harm at all as a European if they were to win in Wales [at the home of the 2010 Ryder Cup].'

Montgomerie made this scheduling pronouncement at the Johnnie Walker Championship in August 2009, the event where he is Tournament Chairman. It was here that, twelve months on, he would announce his team at the completion of the final qualifying tournament. He went on to explain that he expected all contenders for his side to turn up at this event as well. 'I think this is an automatic, the last event under the spotlight. It will be an amazing event here next year.'

This was Monty the Tour ambassador, using his position to bang the drum for the European Tour. He reinforced the message a couple of weeks later at the revamped Seve Trophy, now named the Vivendi Trophy, presented by Severiano Balles-teros. It's the biennial match between a team from Great Britain and Ireland and one representing continental Europe. The event was in danger of being lost from the calendar until Montgomerie became involved in the rebranding negotiations. He installed Paul McGinley and Thomas Björn as non-playing captains and attended the match to run the rule over contenders for his team twelve months hence at Celtic Manor.

Among the fallen apples from the trees that line the fair-ways of the picturesque Saint-Nom-la-Bretèche course on the outskirts of Paris several players took the chance to impress the Ryder Cup captain, as did the skippers on duty – McGinley and Björn. But many of the big names stayed away. There was no Casey, Donald, Rose, Poulter, Harrington, Sergio García or Lee Westwood. The illustrious absentee list was largely because the event clashed with the American season-ending Tour Championship and Monty conceded that the Vivendi was an opportunity for the emerging talent in Europe to show their worth. But he couldn't resist criticising Poulter, with whom he had had previous run-ins. At what had been an otherwise routine pre-tournament news conference Montgomerie suddenly lit the blue touchpaper: 'I feel that not having qualified for the Tour Championship and having been picked for the last Ryder Cup team, a little more effort might have been made to come here,' he said.

This was the latest round in a continuing feud between the Tour's elder statesman and the game's most colourful and flamboyant character. They had clashed when Monty had skippered Poulter in an earlier Seve Trophy and a year before this latest exchange they had traded insults over Nick Faldo's Ryder Cup wild-card picks. They were rivals for Faldo's affections and Montgomerie suggested the Englishman had some kind of hotline to the captain. The implication was that he might get favourable treatment. Poulter retorted by saying that Monty should just concern himself with trying to qualify for the team. This in turn provoked a withering response from Monty, his voice quivering with anger and indignation: 'Oh, well, it's nice to be told what to do by one so young and one so inexperienced,' he fumed. 'Can you honestly believe he said that? The only reason we said he has a hotline to Nick Faldo is because he's the one saying it. No one else is. He did say he has spoken to Nick. Has anyone else said that? No. Right then. It is Nick Faldo's decision. Self-praise is no praise.' And with that he was gone with a full-on flounce that told us what he truly thought of his English rival.

That was thirteen months before this latest attack and Montgomerie is savvy enough to know that anything he said against Poulter would be seized upon by the golfing media. His follow-up plea, 'Please don't make an issue of this . . .' had predictably little effect. Here was the next controversy of his captaincy because he had had a pop at a player most likely to be one of his key men at Celtic Manor. As the press conference finished Monty turned to me ahead of our radio interview and said: 'Well, I'm bloody well right, aren't I? It's a compliment to him that we want him here. He should take it as such.'

Montgomerie went on to watch the GB and Ireland team thrash their continental brethren, discovering along the way that Rory McIlroy was a natural leader who enjoyed being sent out first. 'He's a very quick player and he likes that position already at twenty years old. There's a definite mindset there with Rory.' But this was a rather different environment from the rarefied atmosphere that would prevail a year later at Celtic Manor. Could a twenty-one-year-old rookie really be put out in the opening match of a Ryder Cup? 'Why not? Why not?' Monty stated. 'It's very rare that you actually play a rookie on a Friday morning, never mind out first. We have a very special case here.'

Monty was loving this role of captain-cum-pundit, spewing opinions that people wanted to hear because of the position he had been given. This one provided yet another headline – complimentary and positive – created by golf's greatest generator of news, a mantle he had worn throughout his career.

No one would have expected him to lose this tag, particularly in a year in which he was captain of the European Ryder Cup team, and especially to the rather taciturn Tiger Woods. But the golfing world was turned on its head when Woods drove his Cadillac Escalade on to a fire hydrant outside his Florida home in the middle of Thanksgiving night. The accident proved the precursor to an unprecedented fall from golfing grace as the world's top player became engulfed in scandal as a series of extra-marital affairs became public knowledge in the days and weeks that followed.

As Woods went into hiding and speculation grew about what the future might hold for the world's highest paid sportsman, Montgomerie was naturally consulted for his opinion. Europe's captain sought to avoid adding to the controversy but told me that he wondered how the spouses of the other American players might react if he were a member of the US team. 'The wives are a very important part of a Ryder Cup and many will be friends with Elin [Woods' now ex-wife],' Montgomerie noted. He later aired the same thought in his column for the sports pages of the *Daily Telegraph*. At the time it appeared an insightful and relevant observation. There was no indication that his words might return to haunt him.

The Woods scandal dominated golf's news agenda throughout the first half of the 2010 season. Where was he? How many girls were there? When would he return? Would he divorce? Would he be a weaker or stronger player? Was he a changed man? On 18 December 2009 his story was on the front page of the *New York Post* for the twentieth consecutive day, surpassing the previous record on the front cover of the same paper, which was nineteen days of unbroken reporting of the 9/11 attack on the World Trade Center. Not even Monty could compete with this level of fame or infamy.

Woods' return to public life and then to professional golf at the Masters in April left little room for anything else in golf to be discussed. Montgomerie kept, for him, a relatively low profile and was delighted to see almost every big name in European golf heed his call to play in May's BMW PGA Championship at Wentworth. Sergio García was absent, citing tax rules that limit the time he spends in the UK, but otherwise they were all there to play a revamped West Course. Had common sense prevailed, most would probably have stayed on the following week to play the Wales Open as well, but the European Tour inexplicably headed to Spain for the Madrid Masters before coming back to Britain for the tournament staged at the 2010 Ryder Cup venue. In that time most of the big names went stateside to play Jack Nicklaus's Memorial Tournament and to begin in earnest their preparations for the US Open.

Padraig Harrington committed to play at Celtic Manor but withdrew when it became clear that he needed minor knee surgery. The Wales Open was the most dispensable event in his schedule. Luke Donald, who had been runner-up at Wentworth and then won in Madrid, stayed on in Europe. 'It might get me some brownie points with the captain,' he said prior to finishing third behind Graeme McDowell, who shot rounds of 64 and 63 to win by three from the local youngster Rhys Davies, who fired a final round 62.

The previous week Montgomerie had been involved in twin pursuits. One was helping with his new family's move from a plush rented house on the Gleneagles estate to their newly rebuilt luxury property some five miles away in the delightful Perthshire village of Dunning. His other occupation was trying to damp down the growing disquiet about the absentee list at Celtic Manor. In his pomp as a new captain – call it his honeymoon period – he had demanded that his team show up but, largely, they hadn't bothered. 'No, I'm not disappointed. I'm actually quite happy,' he said, without convincing. 'The American Tour has a big event, the Memorial, that several of my potential team will be competing in the week before the US

Open. Of course I'd like all thirty candidates that I have to play, but that's impossible. If the Wales Open was the week after the BMW PGA Championship I think more people would have stayed on.'

Europe's captain continued to back-track in this way when he arrived at Celtic Manor, seeking to apply a positive spin at every opportunity. His own golf had been pretty wretched throughout the season and he was looking for four solid rounds to try to do his bit to bolster a tournament that had a significantly weaker field than the one he'd expected.

Montgomerie's hopes that his golf would provide the talking point for the week were dashed before he'd struck a ball in anger. The *Daily Mirror* of 4 June 2010, the opening day of the last tournament to be held at Celtic Manor before the Ryder Cup, contained a bombshell from the blue: 'Golfer Colin Montgomerie Cheats on Wife with Old Flame', said the page thirteen headline.

The story alleged that Monty had been involved in an affair with an ex-girlfriend with whom he had had a relationship after the end of his first marriage. The golfing world was stunned. Montgomerie and his second wife, Gaynor, had given the impression that they were blissfully happy. They'd been seen together regularly on the Edinburgh social scene and at occasions like the European Tour's Gala Dinner which had been staged just a fortnight earlier. The golfer had issued a statement to the paper saying: 'I have put my marriage under considerable strain but we are working through these problems. I am very sorry for the hurt I have caused to ones I love so much.'

On the day the story was published Montgomerie had a lunchtime start and looked the picture of happiness as he signed autographs on his way to the first tee. He even allowed one spectator to give him a pat on the back, something that might have prompted a 'don't touch me, don't touch me' in his more competitive days. On the tee he laughed with his playing partners Álvaro Quirós and Oliver Wilson, who were both keen to impress on the skipper their Ryder Cup credentials. The captain didn't seem to have a care in the world as he smote his opening drive straight down the middle of the fairway. It was the first shot in a highly respectable one under par round of 70 and he willingly spoke to reporters when it was completed. Had it been a difficult day given the revelation in the *Mirror* that morning? 'The crowd have been very supportive, everyone's been very supportive,' he said. 'It's up to Gaynor and I to work things out and continue and we are doing that and we look forward to welcoming everyone here in Wales in October with a win.' But I wondered whether the affair would have any impact on his captaincy. 'Not at all, not one bit,' he told me.

Except that it did. It is hard to quantify how much damage was done to Montgomerie's leadership of his continent; that's something we will never know. But there is no doubt that there was an adverse effect. Suddenly his captain's column in the *Telegraph* wondering about American wives' reaction to Tiger Woods' dalliances was being regurgitated for public consumption and this time the bitter taste was at Monty's expense. He also felt compelled to cancel his reconnaissance trip to Pebble Beach for the US Open where he had planned to give an out-of-form Sergio García a pep talk. Montgomerie had said of the trip: 'I think it is most important. It is in my interests, those of the European Tour and my team because, believe me, no stone will be left unturned in our quest to win back the Ryder Cup. Whatever the result I want to be able to look back and say I gave it 100 per cent, and if that means flying around the world to see someone for ten minutes I'll do it.' But now his priority was the family he had hurt. He needed to be with them rather than in California trying to reignite García's stalling career or watching one of his team, Graeme McDowell, become the first European in forty years to win the US Open.

Monty had not qualified for Pebble Beach, but the day after completing all four rounds at Celtic Manor he came through thirty-six holes at Sunningdale to become eligible for the Open Championship. He had fired a second round 62 to ensure his twenty-one-year run of playing consecutive Opens would remain intact at St Andrews a month later. However, although he played all four rounds at the Home of Golf, he never challenged for the title, finishing in a share of 68th place.

Another major had gone by and it was hard not to speculate that it might prove the penultimate one of his career given the way he was playing. As Ryder Cup captain he was invited to the US PGA Championship in August but after that it was increasingly difficult to see how he might make himself eligible for another of the top four events in the future.

Not that this was his primary concern. Damaging, unsubstantiated rumours were circulating again about his private life and there was Ryder Cup work to be done as well.

On the Tuesday that followed Open Champion Louis Oosthuizen, of South Africa, becoming the second successive European Tour player to win a major after McDowell's triumph at Pebble Beach, Monty was scheduled to announce his vice-captains. Given how well they had performed their respective duties at the Vivendi Trophy the previous year, and how poorly they had played in trying to qualify for the team, it was obvious that Paul McGinley and Thomas Björn would be among the appointments.

The third man was a surprise and the result of a brave and inspired piece of leadership from Monty that had taken place during Open week, when he decided to knock on Darren Clarke's door at the Old Course Hotel. The two men were not close, they hadn't been for years and Clarke was one of the most damning of the Tournament Committee men who sat in judgement on Monty after the 2006 ball-replacing incident at the Indonesian Open. But Monty knew what the Ryder Cup meant to Clarke and what Clarke could mean in a Ryder Cup. The Ulsterman said he still harboured hopes of playing his way into the team but was keen to help in whatever role he could. The previous week he had come close to winning the Scottish Open at Loch Lomond and he'd at last found some decent form. Monty said simply, 'I want you there in whatever capacity' and the pair shook on the deal. This was the most tangible sign yet that the captain was prepared to do whatever it took to win back the trophy.

So Björn, McGinley and Clarke were unveiled as vice-captains at the European Tour headquarters at Wentworth on a day that should have been a hugely optimistic one for Monty and his team. The announcement was screened live on Sky television, which seemed a tad excessive for mere assistants, but that's the nature of twenty-four-hour news. In revealing who he had chosen as his helpers, Montgomerie adopted his most serious tone, one that a prime minister might use to announce imminent war. 'These are the three that will hopefully help us regain the Ryder Cup. I'm very proud and honoured to have this opportunity here today to speak to you on their behalf,' Montgomerie said. 'This is very much a team, a European Ryder Cup team this particular year; the four of us are working towards the same cause and the same outcome, which is trying our best to regain the Ryder Cup in seventy-three days' time.' There was no room for José Maria Olazábal, the man the skipper had identified as an inevitable assistant on the day he beat the Spaniard to the top job. Monty said he needed people who were on tour and Olazábal had been unable to do this because of his ongoing health problems. He also said he only needed three assistants but within a month he had backtracked on that one as well.

Extolling the virtues of the right-hand men he had chosen gave grounds for European optimism, but it was undermined because the captain also had to deal with questions about rumours surrounding his private life that had been circulating at St Andrews. 'Everything is absolutely ideal at home and around so there's nothing to worry about,' he told me. 'My main task now and for the next six weeks is putting this together. This is what I am completely and 100 per cent behind and then the famous week. Everything is set fair and there's nothing else.'

There was more than a hint of desperation in his answer. He knew that we knew that something was up. The pressure was building and the stress of keeping a lid on whatever had prompted the situation was taking its toll.

Word spread across the Atlantic and his old nemesis David Feherty stepped into the fray in the days before the final major of the year, the US PGA at Whistling Straits in Wisconsin. Feherty had been a team-mate of Montgomerie's on his Ryder Cup debut at Kiawah Island. The Ulsterman then carved his successful career as a television commentator in America. His ready wit made him ideally suited for the job and it was he who was credited with giving Monty the nickname 'Mrs Doubtfire' after the character played by Robin Williams in the eponymous 1993 film. The sobriquet stuck among American golf fans, providing many a heckler with plenty of ammunition. Feherty thought that his former team-mate had a more than passing resemblance to the movie character in the rotund, blond, curly-haired days of his early thirties. Monty is now more mellow about being dubbed as a film character who was a man who dressed as a woman. 'It doesn't bother me at all. I would rather have played as a character than having played a little bit on the dull side,' he told the Golf Channel. Back when the jibes from outside the ropes were flying, he was less forgiving and he always blamed Feherty. He demanded the former Ryder Cup man be removed from Europe's team room after the 1999 defeat at Brookline but they eventually shook hands at the behest of Sam Torrance, a great friend of both men, after the 2002 match.

Now, just at the point that Montgomerie's captaincy was coming under increasing pressure, and with the match fast approaching, Feherty gave an interview that prompted more trouble for Europe's leader. The interviewer was Dan Patrick, the host of a popular sports radio show syndicated nationwide in the US. Patrick asked Feherty if he'd heard anything about a player 'filing an injunction against the *News of the World*'.

Feherty named Montgomerie and added this observation: 'The chances of this remaining secret until after the Ryder Cup are just zero.' This conversation across the airwaves tallied with some of the rumours that had been circulating since just before the Open Championship at St Andrews. The fact that it was now 'out there' also meant that Montgomerie would be liable to questioning from the American media not bound by any legal action that might have been taken in the UK. There was a Ryder Cup captains' news conference scheduled for the morning of the Tuesday of US PGA Championship week and it proved one of the most uncomfortable moments in Montgomerie's public life. Four questions into the Q and A session came this bombshell from Steve Elling, a colourful and robust scribe for CBSSports.com: 'Monty, I don't know if you're aware, your old friend Feherty went on a nationally syndicated radio show yesterday and talked about the existence of a super injunction in the UK.' He asked if Monty wanted to confirm this, and whether it might affect his captaincy.

'Yeah, obviously I listened to that radio show and I know a lot of you are having a lot of fun right now at my expense,' Montgomerie replied. 'Let me clear this up, though, that I can categorically say that there's no injunction against the *News of the World*. I'm really not going to discuss this any further. All I can say is categorically there is no injunction against the *News of the World* regarding anything. I apologise for this, that you have to bring this up, but at the same time, no further – no further comments from myself on this matter.'

Montgomerie had been careful with his words by stating there was no injunction against the *News of the World*, but he hadn't said that a legal action hadn't been taken elsewhere. When another question came in to try to clarify this he refused to answer and the American captain Corey Pavin felt obliged to step in to save his opposite number further embarrassment. 'Let's stick to golf subjects here. We'd appreciate that. Thank you,' Pavin said.

After the news conference ended Montgomerie, who usually

hangs around to do radio and television interviews, walked straight from the podium to the sanctuary of the officials' area in the lobby of the huge PGA media tent. Needing my own interview on matters golfing, I asked a European Tour official whether the captain would be willing to speak to me. Monty agreed and we stood together in the salubrious surroundings of the press centre's photocopier room. He made it clear he would only talk about golf but it was equally apparent from his distressed demeanour that Europe's captain was close to breaking point. It seemed obvious he'd been suffering sleepless nights and the pressures of the intense scrutiny that came with the role he had always coveted had almost become too much. When he spoke in the interview his voice was a couple of octaves higher than usual and the words were delivered at machine-gunfire pace compared with the more calm, measured way he normally speaks. At the end of our recorded chat I seriously wondered whether he would be able to see the job through.

Whispers were flying through the media tent and across the range where players, coaches and caddies gossiped and giggled. The rumours about his private life grew ever more exaggerated. The previous weekend's *Mail on Sunday* had already asked him whether he was on the verge of resigning. 'There is no way I have ever thought of doing anything like that,' he had told the paper. The European Tour's Ryder Cup Director Richard Hills issued a statement expressing full confidence in the captain, but back in the UK the newspaper for whom Monty wrote a regular column was preparing to make him front-page news.

The *Daily Telegraph* accompanied a picture of Monty with his wife Gaynor on their wedding day with a story stating that the golfer had 'become the latest sportsman to use an injunction to prevent the publication of a story about his private life'.

The man who was due to lead Europe on their quest to regain the Ryder Cup was now the centre of a story that had the potential to destroy his captaincy. He also had to try to play golf and that proved an equally miserable experience. Rounds of 79 and 83 left him in last position in what might prove the final major of his career. 'He played like a man with a lot on his mind,' commented Matt Kuchar, the American who'd been in the same group.

Montgomerie had reached the lowest point. There was no suggestion that he'd been involved in another affair, indeed it became apparent that this all stemmed from a relationship Montgomerie had been involved in with another woman while he was between marriages. But the exaggeration of what he was trying to prevent becoming public knowledge was out of control. There was a grave danger that it could have undermined his authority to lead his continent's golfers.

The only consolation from playing so poorly at the PGA was that he could make a quick exit. It was important for him not to provide the story with any more fuel and that meant keeping his mouth shut. If Montgomerie was going to continue as captain the serious work was about to start and he would need to be at the very top of his game to handle the awkward decisions that were about to head his way.

Montgomerie's wasn't the only big European name to be heading out of the PGA Championship early. Padraig Harrington, Luke Donald and Justin Rose all missed the cut and squandered the chance to add to their points tallies as they sought to qualify for the Ryder Cup. Furthermore, they had no intention of flying to the Czech Open or to Gleneagles for the last two events that would count towards making it into an automatic place in the team. The same applied to Paul Casey, who had finished in a share of third place at the Open. The Englishman then finished twelfth at the PGA and climbed into the ninth and last qualifying berth. He was in the team, but vulnerable.

Sure enough, Sweden's Peter Hanson did make the journey from Wisconsin to the Czech Republic and was duly rewarded with a victory that catapulted him above Casey in the standings. This meant a European ranked inside the world's top ten would now require a captain's pick if he didn't show up and play well at the Johnnie Walker Championship, the last counting event at Gleneagles. Casey had no intention of going to Scotland. His ambition was to make it to the American season-ending Tour Championship and that meant competing in the first play-off tournament, The Barclays, in New York the same week as Europe's Ryder Cup qualifying process ended. Furthermore, Harrington, Rose and Donald also preferred to chase dollars in this FedEx Cup series of play-off tournaments rather than trying to claim an automatic space in Monty's team. They weren't doing any favours for their beleaguered captain, who had only three wild-card options available to accommodate four world-class players.

Montgomerie's proclamation that anyone in contention for his team should make sure they were at Gleneagles now looked lame. His own weakened position because of the pressure he was under from influences outside golf made it difficult for him to pick fights with anyone, let alone four of Europe's top players. Speaking early in his captaincy about players on the cusp of earning a place in his team coming to Gleneagles, where he was Tournament Chairman, Monty had stated, 'I won't even have to ask them.' Well, he did have to ask and they said no.

The captain also had to contend with the politics of the European Tour. Most of the rank and file players felt let down by the big guns who had preferred to honour the American Tour with their presence rather than their native circuit. This meant there was growing pressure to select someone like Edoardo Molinari, an Italian who had put together an impressive string of results to climb close to the world's top twenty while playing a European Tour schedule.

Montgomerie arrived at Gleneagles two days before the tournament started. This was Tuesday and by Sunday evening he would be announcing the three names that would join the nine automatic qualifiers. The captain was a rejuvenated figure. He was relishing the prospect of taking the tough decisions that lay ahead. Suddenly the prospect of being back in the public eye didn't seem so daunting. It was as though the problems that had been so evident at Whistling Straits had been resolved for good and he could get on with being an authoritative captain. Reflecting on the scrutiny he had been under he said: 'It is difficult to put on one side. I've always had it in my life in the last twenty years. It hasn't really affected me; I just want to get on and do the job I was given and that's to try to win the Ryder Cup for Europe.'

Monty also told the *Daily Mail* that the real low point in his personal life had been having to admit to his affair around the time of the Wales Open in May. 'That was the worst by miles because I knew how much it would hurt Gaynor, but I'm thrilled to say we have worked at it and everything is good now.'

So Montgomerie was ready to revel in being the centre of attention. The man who couldn't leave the press tent quickly enough at Whistling Straits was now wondering whether the one at Gleneagles would be big enough to house all those who would want to see the announcement of his team on the Sunday night. 'We should go outside to do it,' he tried to tell one of the Tour's media managers, not that the idea had any chance of becoming reality.

On the eve of the tournament, Monty strode confidently into the interview room and in composed, measured tones handled all the questions fired at him. He was well-prepared, having spent the early part of the morning with the head of the Tour's media department, Mitchell Platts, who had run through with him the questions he was likely to face. They worked on responses that would not necessarily be answers because the questions naturally centred on who he might leave out from the list of illustrious players who had stayed away.

Montgomerie gave a command performance and was later able to reflect on having talked a lot without actually saying anything. Disgruntled reporters trudged away shaking their heads. For the first time they'd attended a Monty press conference and he hadn't given them a single line worth writing. The captain was rather pleased with himself, to say the least. He had exuded confidence and reasserted his authority. It was clear he was through the shaky time and could now concentrate, along with his vice-captains, on the task of picking his team.

The popular view was that Justin Rose was going to be the unlucky man and Monty would pick Harrington, Donald and Casey.

On the Saturday afternoon at Gleneagles, third-round day,

Montgomerie, who had missed the cut, came to the media centre to see me for a prearranged interview. When he arrived he surveyed the leaderboard, only to see steadily climbing it the name of Edoardo Molinari. 'There are a lot of people around here who would like to see him in the team, you know?' Monty said in half-statement, half-question. It was clear the conundrum was no longer four but five into three and he was dreading having to make the calls to the players he would leave out. 'Those who didn't come here made their own choice,' I reminded him and he seemed grateful for the observation.

By the end of the third round Edoardo had climbed to second place, trailing his younger brother Francesco by a single stroke. Victory for the elder sibling the next day would make him impossible to ignore. 'He's doing the same as Peter Hanson did at the Czech Open, coming to an event having to win to make my job even harder than it is,' he told reporters who ambushed him as he tried to leave the media centre. 'This is an extremely interesting situation that we find ourselves in . . . and it would happen to me!'

Edoardo Molinari duly overhauled his brother in the final round and did it in great style. The former US Amateur Champion was two shots behind the clubhouse leader, Australia's Brett Rumford, with three holes to play. He needed to birdie each of the closing stretch of holes. Molinari made four at the par fifth 16th and then holed a curling 35-foot birdie putt on the 17th that had at least ten feet of break. It was a putt of sheer genius and inspiration and so was the chip he produced at the last for a tap-in birdie that gave him a stunning victory and Montgomerie a huge headache.

The Johnnie Walker Championship finished at around 5 p.m. The captain, who had been holed up in the Gleneagles complex all afternoon along with his three assistants, was due to reveal his team an hour later. It was clear that whatever he decided it would be a dramatic announcement and to heighten the tension it was put back until 6.30. It had been a fraught afternoon that built to an evening climax when Montgomerie, in a voice wavering slightly with nerves, read out his team. After completing the nine automatic qualifiers he said: 'I would like to add three picks to that particular nine, and they are: from Ireland Padraig Harrington; from England Luke Donald; and from Italy . . .' By naming the country and before he'd said Edoardo Molinari, we knew Paul Casey, the world number nine, was not in the team and nor was Justin Rose, the winner of three out of four points in a losing European team two years earlier and two-time champion already in 2010.

'I've been a member of the Tour for twenty-four years, I don't think I've seen a finish of that quality under such pressure by anyone, ever,' Montgomerie said to justify Molinari's selection. He also said that Harrington had won three majors in the last three years so couldn't be left out (he neglected to note that the Irishman had won no tournaments in the last two years) and praised Donald for his dependability.

But leaving out a player ranked as highly as Casey was a huge gamble and highlighted a flaw in the selection system if Europe wanted to field its strongest team. Montgomerie dealt calmly with a barrage of questions to justify the decisions he had made in consultation with Björn, McGinley and Clarke. He did it in a way that accentuated the positive and he had words of praise for the players who had been left out. Only in his Radio Five Live interview afterwards was he in anyway critical, saying that Casey was more of a fourball player and so offered more limited options than Donald.

That dramatic afternoon he had left the meeting room to call Rose and tell him the bad news and it hadn't been easy because the Englishman was on the range preparing for the final round of The Barclays when he took the call. What had counted against him was the fact that his two wins had come in a condensed three-week period in early summer when his putter had been red hot. Was there any guarantee that he could rediscover such a touch on the slower greens of Celtic Manor in October?

Montgomerie also left a voicemail for Casey because he was already on the course, ironically paired alongside Harrington. They were mid-round when the Irishman's caddie, Ronan Flood, received a thumbs-up from his boss's wife Caroline after news of the selections broke. Casey noticed the exchange. He knew that Mrs Harrington would have told him he was in as well if he'd been picked and she didn't. Casey therefore knew he was out and did remarkably well to maintain his concentration for the rest of the round. Who knows whether the big-hitting Englishman would also have received a happy signal from Harrington's wife if Molinari had not birdied those closing holes at Gleneagles? The Italian certainly believed he had to win, saying that Monty had told him that he had needed victory to force his way into the team.

The captain also announced that Sergio García, who was taking a two-month break from the game to try to regain his appetite for tournament golf, would be his fourth vice-captain. Montgomerie had categorically stated that he would not be adding anyone to his trio of vice-captains, but García requested the role, such was his passion for the Ryder Cup. The skipper was keen to have him on board, though whether Harrington would be so enthusiastic was open to question given that the Irishman and the Spaniard have little time for each other.

That was of no concern to Montgomerie who acknowledged it had been the most stressful afternoon of his golfing career. 'Very much so, and I haven't hit a golf shot!' he told me. 'I don't think any captain has had the difficulty that I have had here in trying to select three out of a possible ten.' An insider who was in the room with the skipper and his vice-captains throughout the afternoon described the atmosphere as fraught as they debated the options and Montgomerie went through the painful process of telling hopeful players that they had missed out. At the end of his news conference on that chilly, breezy late-summer evening in Scotland, Monty heaved a huge sigh. Relieved he'd made his choices, he wondered how the media and golfing world would react to what he had decided. Leaving the press tent his vice-captains congratulated him on his performance in front of the television cameras, radio mics and massed reporters. 'Monty, you shot a 63 there, that was terrific,' said McGinley. Björn and Clarke were quick to agree and they were all smiles for the official photographs that had them standing next to a board containing name plates for the twelve players who would be charged with the task of winning back the Ryder Cup.

After the shutters stopped clicking Montgomerie moved away and stopped, muttering almost to himself: 'I've left out the world number nine here.' (Casey went to number eight the next morning.) The captain's comment bore no evidence of regret; it was more a statistical acknowledgement of how tough the decision had been.

As he drove the five miles or so back to his family home in

Dunning that evening he perhaps reflected on what a turbulent year it had been. Classic Monty – never out of the headlines with all kinds of attendant stresses and strains. In contrast to the week of hell he'd had at Whistling Straits, it had been a hell of a week at Gleneagles and in a positive sense because it had been all about the Ryder Cup. But as much as he protested that being able to leave out Casey and Rose was a sign of Europe's strength it was also a huge gamble, one that could easily return to haunt him. He had made his first decisions that could affect the eventual outcome of the match and choosing to leave out a player from the world's top ten undoubtedly left his judgement open to question. What had the winless Harrington done in the last year to earn selection ahead of both Casey and Rose?

This was the team who would determine whether Montgomerie's stellar Ryder Cup career would come to a glorious climax, but was it Europe's strongest possible line-up?

Lee Westwood: Aged thirty-seven, from Worksop, England. Six previous Ryder Cups. Overall record: played 29, won 14, lost 10, halved 5. Total points 16½. The continent's number one player and expected to be one of Europe's leaders on the course, having risen to number three in the world rankings, but facing a worrying race to recover from a leg injury in time for the Celtic Manor clash.

Rory McIlroy: Aged twenty-one, from Holywood, Northern Ireland. Ryder Cup debut. Monty said he would have no fears in sending out first this 'special talent'. He finished tied third in the Open and US PGA, the last two majors before the Ryder Cup. Had said the biennial clash with the Americans was 'more of an exhibition' but a mature PR strategy averted a damaging controversy. Earmarked to play all five series of matches.

Martin Kaymer: Aged twenty-five, from Düsseldorf, Germany. Ryder Cup debut. Monty's only worry about the dependable German was when he injured his foot in a karting accident a year before the selection date. Confirmation of his boundless potential came with his victory in a dramatic US PGA when he beat Celtic Manor rival Bubba Watson in a three-hole play-off thanks to magical putting touch under pressure. Another set to play in every session.

Graeme McDowell: Aged thirty-one, from Portrush, Northern Ireland. One previous Ryder Cup appearance. Record: played 4, won 2, lost 1, halved 1. Total points 2½. Took a giant step towards retaining his place with victory at the Celtic Manor Wales Open and confirmed his spot on the team when he became the first European for forty years to win the US Open by being last man standing at Pebble Beach. Great friends with McIlroy and expected to be paired with fellow Ulsterman.

Ian Poulter: Aged thirty-four, from Hitchin, England, but based in Orlando, Florida. Two previous Ryder Cups. Overall record: played 7, won 5, lost 2, halved 0. Total points 5. The great showman, who starred with four points out of five under Nick Faldo's captaincy at Valhalla. Secured his place with victory in the Accenture WGC Matchplay in February 2010 but subsequent form patchy. Would he pine for his great friend Justin Rose and would his tense relationship with Monty hold up under the pressure of Ryder Cup week?

Ross Fisher: Aged twenty-nine, from Ascot, England. Ryder Cup debut. Played his way on to the team with midsummer victory at the Irish Open, the fourth victory of his career. Ability in head-to-head combat was confirmed by his 2009 victory at the Volvo World Matchplay where he beat American Anthony Kim in the thirty-six-hole final. Unknown quantity under Ryder Cup pressure.

Francesco Molinari: Aged twenty-seven, from Turin, Italy. First Ryder Cup and became only the second Italian to qualify for Europe after Costantino Rocca. Had seven top four finishes while racking up the points to secure his place in Monty's team. No one more consistent from tee to green in the European game, but question marks over his putting, especially from ten feet and in. Shared in World Cup victory played over same fourball and foursomes format as used in Ryder Cup with elder brother Edoardo at the end of the 2009 season.

Miguel Ángel Jiménez: Aged forty-six, from Málaga, Spain. Fourth Ryder Cup. Overall record: played 12, won 2, lost 7, halved 3. Total points 3½. The winner of the Dubai Desert Classic and Alstom French Open, he cancelled plans to attend a nephew's wedding to shore up his position in the qualifying list by playing the Johnnie Walker Championship in the final counting event. Just the spirit Monty would have wanted from a few more illustrious figures in the European game. A great character for the team room, but with a poor playing record in his three previous Ryder Cups.

Peter Hanson: Aged thirty-three, from Svedala, Sweden. Ryder Cup debut. Forced his way into the team with victory in the Czech Open in the penultimate week of qualifying. It was his second victory in the 2010 season, the first having come in Mallorca in May. Another engaging character but untried at this level and with a poor record of played 14, won 4, lost 7, halved 3 from representing continental Europe in Seve Trophy and Vivendi Trophy matches.

Padraig Harrington: Aged thirty-nine, from Dublin, Ireland. Sixth Ryder Cup. Overall record: played 21, won 7, lost 11, halved 3. Total points: 8½. Rewarded with a wild-card selection courtesy of his stature in European golf following his wins in the 2007 and 2008 Opens and the 2008 US PGA Championship. Failed to win a match in his last two Ryder Cups and without a tournament victory since his 2008 PGA triumph. Many thought he was more likely to be omitted than Casey; is under immense pressure to deliver.

Luke Donald: Aged thirty-two, from Hemel Hempstead, England. Third Ryder Cup. Overall record: played 7, won 5, lost 1, halved 1. Total points 5½. Based in America but gained great credit in the captain's mind for playing the Wales Open at Celtic Manor where he finished third. It boosted his claims for a wild-card, as did his stellar Ryder Cup record, having been on the winning side in both his previous appearances. His 79 per cent success rate is the highest of anyone in Europe's team.

Edoardo Molinari: Aged twenty-nine, from Turin, Italy. Ryder Cup debut. A year earlier he was a mere Challenge Tour player but three wins at that level followed by victory in the Dunlop Phoenix Open in Japan showed his winning credentials. He rocketed up the world rankings and his win at the Barclays Scottish Open put a Ryder Cup place within touching distance. Arrived at Gleneagles knowing he could not automatically qualify but that a win would provide an irresistible case. In sensational style he duly obliged to force the captain's hand. Could he repeat such heroics in the game's most rarefied atmosphere?

15

THE US SELECTION

7 SEPTEMBER 2010, NEW YORK STOCK
EXCHANGE, WALL STREET, NEW YORK

*'It's great to be part of this team. I'm honored to
be selected and head over to Wales to represent
the United States in the Ryder Cup'*
Tiger Woods

While debate raged over the choices made by Colin Montgomerie, at least he could reflect that the process of
making his wild-card choices hadn't resulted in a heated row
played out in front of much of the world's golfing media. His
American counterpart, Corey Pavin, couldn't say the same.

The joint news conference the captains gave at the US PGA
Championship had been uncomfortable for Monty but it was
no stroll down the middle of the fairway for Pavin either. The
US skipper became embroiled in an unseemly squabble with
a Golf Channel reporter, Jim Gray, over whether Pavin had
said that he would definitely select Tiger Woods for the Celtic
Manor clash. The reporter is an experienced television man
who has worked across several sports for US networks and he
seized on a quote from Woods on the Tuesday of PGA week
saying that the world number one would accept a captain's
wild-card pick. Up to that point there had been some doubt

given his indifferent form following his return from the string of revelations that precipitated his divorce from his wife Elin.

After Woods had declared his availability for the Ryder Cup, Gray bumped into Pavin as he arrived in the players' registration area at Whistling Straits. According to Gray, he asked America's captain if he was going to pick Woods and Pavin replied: 'Of course I'm going to. He's the best player in the world.' Gray immediately took this juicy piece of news to the airwaves of the Golf Channel, an American cable broadcaster that does precisely what it says on the tin.

Then, in the joint news conference with Monty, Pavin said of Gray's report: 'His interpretation of what I said is incorrect. There's nobody that's promised any picks right now, it would be disrespectful to everybody that's trying to make the team.'

When these formal press conferences end it is usual for reporters to advance towards the podium to continue the quizzing in a bid to acquire a new line or something that has not been broadcast during the formal part of proceedings. These confabs are known as 'afters' and, as we know, on this occasion Montgomerie had his own reasons for being in no mood for any 'afters' and swiftly departed. Pavin was feeling more comfortable and was happy to stay and chat but he was quickly confronted by an irate Gray who was angry that his journalism had been called into question.

'You're a liar,' Gray is alleged to have said to Pavin. 'You're going down,' the reporter added, pointing his finger.

'I just said, "You're full of 'something',"' Pavin later recounted. 'I'm not going to let that happen. He got upset, his eyes were a little odd. He was just a little crazy.'

As arguments go it had all the sophistication of a pair of nine-year-olds yelling 'liar, liar, pants are on fire'. Neither party emerged with much credit, Gray for having no documentary or taped proof to back up his story; Pavin for rising to the bait and allowing himself to become embroiled in such an unseemly incident in the middle of a major championship media tent.

Juvenile as it may have been, the altercation also illustrated a defining trait in America's captain. He is a fighter and, when cornered, he will not back down. Not without justification is this diminutive figure known as 'Bulldog'. He may have been lightweight in stature but the 1995 US Open Champion was a heavyweight achiever, usually against bigger and stronger golfers who could propel the ball far further than he could. Pavin's 230-yard four wood to six inches on the final hole at Shinnecock Hills that won him his only major title and denied Greg Norman remains one of the greatest shots ever played. What would Monty have given for such accuracy from the final fairway at the 2006 US Open when the Scot had a mere seven iron in his hands? Had he replicated it, Montgomerie would have claimed the major that would have provided the pinnacle of his career.

There are times when you feel Monty talks up the significance of the Ryder Cup and his Orders of Merit because he can't do that with the majors. He never won one, but Pavin did and yet he shares Montgomerie's view that puts transatlantic clashes with Europeans ahead of individual glory. 'Comparing the Ryder Cup to winning the US Open, well, I can tell you I got far more nervous playing in the Ryder Cup,' he said. 'Compared to the Ryder Cup the last shot I hit into eighteen in the US Open was very easy. I am very proud to represent my country. That adds to the pressure.'

So taking over from Paul Azinger for the defence of the

trophy was Pavin's idea of a dream job. His wife Lisa often recounts how, during their early dates, her husband-to-be spoke obsessively of his pride in playing for his country in the Ryder Cup. In Pavin and Monty the 2010 match could not have featured two more passionate leaders.

The American captain's task was to become the first in that role to fire such a passion for the match in the world's top player because, regardless of what he might or might not have said to Jim Gray, it was inevitable that he would pick Tiger Woods. Equally certain was the fact that Pavin's four wild-card picks didn't stir as much controversy as Monty's three had done.

Amid the splendour of the New York Stock Exchange, Pavin's stock held firm as he announced that Woods, major winners Stewart Cink and Zach Johnson and the youngster Rickie Fowler were his four selections. The choice of Fowler raised most eyebrows. The twenty-one-year-old had enjoyed a fine rookie season and his colourful outfits and boyish enthusiasm had ensured plenty of coverage from the US networks throughout his first full year on tour. But in the months leading up to the Celtic Manor clash his form had tailed off and his selection was a gamble made possible only by the steady nature of the other three picks. The American line-up featured only five survivors from the dozen who had reclaimed the trophy at Valhalla as Pavin fielded this team:

Phil Mickelson: Aged forty, from Rancho Santa Fe, California. Playing his eighth Ryder Cup. Overall record: played 30, won 10, lost 14, halved 6. Total points 13. The reigning Masters Champion who squandered repeated opportunities to overhaul Woods as world number one throughout the 2010 season.

Hunter Mahan: Aged twenty-eight, from Plano, Texas. Playing in his second Ryder Cup. Overall record: played 5, won 2, lost 0, halved 3. Total points 3½. He was one of the stars to earn his stripes in Azinger's victorious team. His accuracy looks likely to be an asset at Celtic Manor, though a lack of overseas experience could undermine his contribution in 2010.

Bubba Watson: Aged thirty-one, from Bagdad, Florida. Rookie. A big-hitting left-hander who claims never to have received a golf lesson in his life. Lost a play-off to Martin Kaymer for the US PGA title and promptly told everyone he was happy because his main objective, to qualify for the Ryder Cup, had been achieved.

Jim Furyk: Aged forty, from West Chester, Pennsylvania. Seventh Ryder Cup. Overall record: played 24, won 8, lost 13, halved 3. Total points 9½. Fiercely proud to represent his country, the experienced 2003 US Open Champion closed out victory for Azinger at Valhalla. As methodical and respected as his swing is unorthodox, he has the potential to provide the spiritual heartbeat of the US team.

Steve Stricker: Aged forty-three, from Madison, Wisconsin. Second Ryder Cup. Overall record: played 3, won 0, lost 2, halved 1. Total points ½. Like Mickelson and Lee Westwood, he had a mathematical chance of going to the top of the world rankings in the summer of 2010 but failed to take the opportunity of leapfrogging Woods. Nevertheless, his brilliant putting makes him a danger man provided he can come to grips with the relatively sluggish Celtic Manor greens.

Dustin Johnson: Aged twenty-six, from Myrtle Beach, South Carolina. Rookie. This immense ball striker blew a three-shot lead heading into the final round of the US Open before suffering more heartbreak at the US PGA. Holding a one-shot advantage coming to the last, he grounded his club in a bunker he erroneously thought was a sandy waste on his second shot and was penalised two strokes that cost him a place in the play-off. Gained some solace by beating Paul Casey to the BMW Championship in the final FedEx Cup play-off series event.

Jeff Overton: Aged twenty-seven, from Bloomington, Indiana. Rookie. The player Europe know least about and the one, perhaps cruelly, held up to be the weak link in Pavin's team. Steady rather than spectacular performances throughout the season on the PGA Tour, including five top three finishes without forcing a win.

Matt Kuchar: Aged thirty-two, from Ponte Vedra Beach, Florida. Rookie. Although he first burst on to the scene as an ever-smiling US Amateur Champion in 1997, he took until 2010 before fully realising his potential in the pro ranks. His deadly putting touch enabled him to claim victory in The Barclays, the first tournament after confirming his place in the American team at the US PGA.

Tiger Woods: Aged thirty-four, from Cypress, California. Sixth Ryder Cup. Overall record: played 25, won 10, lost 13, halved 2. Total points 11. The Ryder Cup was the only golfing arena in which he has never truly excelled. Some question his desire to play for his country. Unbeaten in singles since his debut in 1997.

Stewart Cink: Aged thirty-seven, from Duluth, Georgia. Fifth Ryder Cup. Overall record: played 15, won 4, lost 7 halved 4. Total points 6. The third time he had been picked as a wild-card. He had not won a tournament since beating the fifty-nine-year-old Tom Watson to win his only major, The Open in 2009. Like his captain, he is a committed Christian and someone likely to provide a level head in the US team room.

Zach Johnson: Aged thirty-four, from Heathrow, Florida. Second Ryder Cup. Overall record: played 4, won 1, lost 2, halved 1. Total points 1½. Another regular attender at the Tour's Bible study classes, his one Ryder Cup was the 2006 match at the K Club. There he performed respectably despite America's record-equalling defeat. He lost his singles amid the memorably emotional scenes that greeted Darren Clarke's victory over him.

Rickie Fowler: Aged twenty-one, from Anaheim, California. Rookie. Pavin's joker in the pack identified to inject youthful verve in the way that Anthony Kim did in 2008. Kim failed to find post-injury form in time to force his way into Pavin's thoughts, so the skipper went with his gut feeling as he gambled on Fowler. The captain also took due note of seven points from a possible eight in the two Walker Cup matches the youngster has played.

There were five debutants compared with Europe's six, but Pavin's team seemed to have a healthy balance between youth and experience. Woods had needed a wild-card pick for the first time in his career, after finishing twelfth in the qualifying list, but even allowing for his winless year and lacklustre Ryder Cup reputation, it was impossible for Pavin to ignore a fourteen times major champion. The US skipper repeated his mantra that Woods was just one member of a team and that they would all be treated the same. He also said that there was no guarantee that Woods would play in all five sessions at Celtic Manor.

The world number one's inclusion in the American team was welcomed by Montgomerie. 'Any Ryder Cup is a better event when Woods plays in it,' he said, while he no doubt hoped that this would not become the contest that would provide the fallen star with his most effective road to redemption in the eyes of the American public.

Monty had enough to be worrying about with his own team to spend too much energy concerning himself with Woods anyway. Europe's top player, Lee Westwood, was in a race to be fit in time for Celtic Manor having not completed a tournament since the Open in July. The Englishman, who had risen to number three in the world rankings was suffering from a ruptured plantaris muscle in his right calf. 'This could go anywhere,' the laconic Westwood said as he lined up the opening drive in his comeback round at a corporate day at Lindrick Golf Club a fortnight before battle commenced at Celtic Manor.

Heading into the 2010 Ryder Cup, Europe remained strong favourites given that they had home advantage and boasted in their number the winners of two of the four majors, Graeme McDowell and Martin Kaymer, but it was now looking as if the match would prove a lot closer than had been anticipated earlier in the year.

And if it all went wrong, Monty knew which way the flak would fly. 'I do wonder if the role of the captain is overplayed, since we never hit a shot. You see it in football all the time. It is never the star player who gets it in the neck if his team loses, it is always the manager who gets the blame,' he said. 'I do think, though, the captain has an important role to play. I'll probably be called "Captain Useless" if we lose.'

16

*'His second shot was brilliant and his putt was
better'* – Colin Montgomerie, 4 October 2010

The days and nights that followed the announcement of
the two teams were long and restless for Colin Montgomerie. Europe's captain had a feeling of impatience that
equated to a fanatical amateur waiting for delivery of a brand
new set of clubs. He lay awake at night playing out in his mind
scenarios that might unfold over the three days of competition at Celtic Manor. He surfed the internet seeking inspiration for his speech at the opening ceremony, using YouTube
to look back at the efforts of Sir Nick Faldo at Valhalla and
Bernhard Langer at Oakland Hills. He was convinced that
when he stood at the podium the power of his words could
give his side an early edge.

Equally important was the first team meeting of Ryder Cup
week. Monty rehearsed and rehearsed in his head what he
would say to his players, their caddies and their wives on that
Monday night. This was where he intended to set the tone
for the week, stoke up the passion and inspire his men 'to
show the world and especially America how good they are'.
He even prepared his winner's speech before any of his players
arrived at Celtic Manor. There was a losing version written,

too, though he would not use the term 'losing' preferring 'runner-up' – a position with which he was already too familiar given his near misses in major championships.

Montgomerie wrestled with options over who he might pair together and more than ten days before the start of the match knew who would be sent out with whom on the vital first day. What is more, he claimed he had told each of the twelve players what to expect and that they would all be appearing on that first Friday. Even more surprising, he made this public knowledge when he gave a news conference in Paris at the Vivendi Cup, the last European Tour event before the Ryder Cup. 'We have nine days to go and it's getting close now. In fact, I know who is going to be on that first tee on the Friday morning barring, of course, accidents or illness,' he revealed. 'Everybody knows what's going on. I think it's important that they do know; that they understand that they are all going to be playing.'

Montgomerie was in his element. It was as though this public appearance was an opportunity to release the pent-up energy that was being stoked inside. The European Tour's Steve Todd, who was moderating the press conference, sought in vain to close it because one of Europe's players, Peter Hanson, was waiting to follow Monty into the interviewee's chair. The captain wasn't for budging. At one point he sat back, arms wide as if to say: 'Come on, guys, I'm enjoying this, got any more questions?' When Hanson went to sit behind the micro-phone, Montgomerie moved to the floor to sit among the reporters. He wanted to discuss further his bold policy of already having decided his opening-day pairings. Only after completing that conversation was he prepared to leave and let the journalists quiz a now somewhat bemused Hanson.

After playing the Wednesday pro-am in Paris, Monty headed to Celtic Manor to take up his captain's residency. Soon after arriving he went to the first tee of the Twenty Ten Course and stood in front of the empty grandstands that horseshoed around the spot where players would hit the most nerve-wracking tee shots of their lives later that week. Monty soaked up the silence, surveying the scene, imagining the din and passion that would scorch this tiny corner of Wales the following Friday, the first day of October 2010, the opening day of the Ryder Cup. He cast his mind back to the times he'd been centre of attention in such arenas; the tee shot that set the ball rolling in the singles at the Belfry in 2002, the first drives of the 1995 and 2004 matches, and leading off again for Europe on the final day in 2006. He wondered whether he would ever play another Ryder Cup and conceded to himself, perhaps for the first time, that there was, at best, merely an outside chance.

Montgomerie also pondered what the next few days would mean for him. The whirlwind of news conferences, interviews, team meetings, dinners and other pomp and ceremony. He wondered whether this Ryder Cup was bigger than any he had experienced; or was it just that it felt this way because he was at the centre of the maelstrom?

Probably a bit of both. Europe were bidding to regain the trophy rather than continue a run of ritual thrashings of America; this provided an edge and appetite lacking two years earlier at Valhalla. Monty, of course, hadn't been in Kentucky for that match. In his *Daily Telegraph* column he claimed missing that Ryder Cup was a bigger disappointment than failing to land the 2006 US Open. 'Of course I would have loved to have won a major and the ones that narrowly got away, such as Winged Foot, will always haunt me,' he wrote. 'However, hand on heart I wouldn't swap my eight Ryder Cup experiences, even if it were an option.' He went on to say: 'If I had to pinpoint the worst moment of my career, it wouldn't be the duffed approach to the 18th at Winged Foot, as many might expect, but rather the moment that I found out I wasn't on the 2008 team.'

He wasn't in the 2010 side either, but he was in charge of Europe's quest to regain the trophy. This was the stuff of his dreams: to be the man to whom the trophy would be handed after masterminding an inspiring victory in the arena that most defined his career. Would it be the victory that would fit so much of the success? Or would he come up short and suffer agonising defeat that would drag the Ryder Cup towards the other main characteristic of his career – being a nearly man when it truly counted? For his golfing reputation this amounted to the highest of stakes and he wouldn't hit a single ball to influence the outcome.

What Monty described as 'the biggest week of my life' began with a trip to Cardiff airport to welcome the American team. They flew in from Atlanta where Jim Furyk had netted more than £7 million for winning the Tour Championship and FedEx Cup play-off series the previous evening. Furyk beat Europe's Luke Donald into second place. Somewhat incongruously, the American side used a British Airways charter that landed in Wales at 11.05 a.m. on the Monday before the match. Corey Pavin's team disembarked clutching the trophy they desperately hoped would accompany them on their return.

After a short joint news conference by both captains at the airport, they made their way to Celtic Manor where again the skippers appeared before reporters, this time in the venue's vast media tent. Montgomerie seemed less at ease when sharing the stage with his opposite number. The two men got along famously throughout their tenures, but Monty was less fluent and less inclined to go down the route of self-deprecation in front of America's captain. He ummed and erred and allowed himself to be trapped by questions over whether he had banned his team from using social networking sites like Twitter during Ryder Cup week. He said he'd asked his players to avoid tweeting but by the next day the captain was embroiled in 'Twittergate' because two members of his side, Ian Poulter and Graeme McDowell, tweeted that no such ban existed. It was a silly side story that might have blown into something bigger had not Monty conceded the next day that it was okay for his players to use these sites if they didn't betray any team-room secrets.

His priority, though, was neither Twitter nor the demands of the media but that agenda-setting Monday evening team meeting attended by the players, their wives, the caddies and their spouses. Montgomerie wanted them to know that they were all part of the team and to remind them of his passion for the Ryder Cup. He began by showing them a picture of Corey Pavin disembarking that morning with the trophy in his hands. It was as though someone had stolen his favourite toy and his team must get it back for him. Monty then introduced a video that catalogued Europe's greatest moments in these matches and moments of individual triumph enjoyed by the players on duty.

It had the desired effect on everyone in the room. 'It made the hairs on the back of my neck stand on end,' admitted Rory McIlroy.

McIlroy's Northern Ireland compatriot Graeme McDowell

was also greatly impressed. 'Everyone got pretty fired up,' said the US Open champion. 'We got a big buzz from it. Colin has been a phenomenal captain so far. He's been meticulous in his preparation. We are absolutely wanting for nothing this week.' McDowell was also keen to praise the selections of Darren Clarke, Paul McGinley, Thomas Björn and Sergio García as vice-captains. 'I talked about not having the X factor in the team room two years ago in Valhalla. I really feel we have that this time and we really want to win the Ryder Cup back this week.'

The players' caddies were also thrilled to be treated as integral cogs in the set-up. 'He made us part of the team meeting and told us exactly what our jobs were for the week,' recalled Martin Kaymer's bagman, Craig Connolly. 'He made sure we would have no expenses at all, we were given everything we needed and a lot more, so he made us very, very comfortable. Every year you get a standard pass when you are on tour, but with Colin they were "access all areas" passes to allow us to go wherever we needed or wanted to go. This was very important to us because in Ryder Cups our jobs are multiplied tenfold. The week is so intense with a lot of walking, two rounds a day. He made sure we had access to physios. Anything we needed we could get.'

Montgomerie maintained the impetus the following evening. While his opposite number, Corey Pavin, returned to his military instincts by recruiting Major Dan Rooney, a fighter pilot veteran, to inspire his players, Monty chose sporting legends to do the job. Most movingly he turned to Seve Ballesteros, the ailing former captain who provided the spiritual heartbeat for European golf. It was Paul McGinley's idea because he had been in regular contact with Ballesteros throughout the Spaniard's long battle with the brain tumor that prevented him from attending the Ryder Cup. McGinley felt it would be inspirational for the players to converse with the Spanish legend via speakerphone and Monty readily agreed. 'The whole team spoke to Seve for about ten minutes and that was very motivational, very passionate,' Montgomerie revealed. 'The passion is still very, very strong within Seve for us as a team.'

It was also important to maintain a relaxed mood and the players enjoyed a lighthearted quiz on that Tuesday evening, culminating in a tie-breaker which asked the team to name the players who had failed to beat Montgomerie in the final-day singles of his eight Ryder Cups. Banter flew around the room, some of it at the skipper's expense, the consensus being that the singles opposition hadn't actually been particularly strong and it wasn't as great a record as it had been cracked up to be.

Anything to make the time go quicker had to be beneficial, especially for professional golfers who ordinarily don't turn up until two days before a Thursday start. Here they would have to wait an extra day and go through all the ceremony that forms such a big part of Ryder Cup week.

On the Wednesday evening they were whisked to Cardiff for dinner with His Royal Highness Prince Charles in the city's castle, before crossing to a spectacular Welcome to Wales show staged at the Millennium Stadium. Performances from classical singer Katherine Jenkins and Dame Shirley Bassey raised the roof in the famous arena and the event was an undoubted success, watched by a crowd of more than 13,000 people.

The caddies of both teams had functions laid on as well. Montgomerie's regular bagman, Jason Hempleman, had been put in charge of the European caddies with the specific role of making sure there would be no fractures in team unity. 'I made sure that with me and my assistant Julian Phillips, all fourteen of us attended those functions,' Hempleman revealed. 'On the Tuesday night I think three of the Americans turned up and on the next evening two of them. That was a good start from my point of view, keeping us as a unit and keeping us all together. The Americans didn't quite get it, I don't think, on the team aspect.

'I'd listened to Gareth Edwards in an interview on the radio when I was driving up, talking about how they kept the Lions together, and it was just like that because everything was done as a team and that's what the Ryder Cup is about.'

Edwards, the Welsh rugby legend, had also addressed the European side, along with cricketer Sir Ian Botham and former captains Ian Woosnam and Sam Torrance. Montgomerie was determined to promote the team ethic in any way that he could.

Enjoyable and inspirational as the build-up was, the clock was ticking ever more slowly for Monty and his team because they could not wait for the match to begin. The eve of the 2010 Ryder Cup was chilly but dry. The Europeans played only eight holes on the back nine before heading to the range to fine-tune their games. They were used to the course, one that didn't appear to have been set up to particularly favour the home team. This was a surprise because previous captains had used this prerogative to good effect: Torrance at the Belfry and Paul Azinger at Valhalla had both taken steps to counter the strengths of the opposition. The obvious move for Montgomerie would have been to narrow the fairways after 310 yards to restrict the driving prowess of Dustin Johnson and Bubba Watson, the two longest hitters in either side. Monty assumed the moral high ground, saying that he wanted the course to be set up so that the better team won and didn't see any need to 'trick it up'. One former European Tour player, however, told me the approach was less to do with this Corinthian spirit than Monty was letting on. 'I have it on very good authority that at the time when he had to decide on the lines of the fairways he believed his team would probably include Álvaro Quirós, Sergio García and Paul Casey. He didn't want to narrow the fairways for the big hitters with them in the side. Once he knew the make-up of the teams it was too late,' the source said.

The time had not yet passed, though, to decide on what order to send out the players for the first day. Lee Westwood approached Monty ahead of the opening ceremony and told him that he wanted to hit the first ball for Europe, to show the world that he was his continent's number one. 'I want to push out my chest and be a leader,' Westwood said. Montgomerie heeded his top player's call, disregarding the fact that injury had prevented him from completing a competitive tournament for more than two months in the run-up to the Ryder Cup.

As he was making this decision the media were stoking up the rivalry between Tiger Woods and Rory McIlroy. The Northern Ireland youngster had suggested this would be a good time to take on the world number one because of Woods' indifferent form in 2010. He made his remarks immediately after Woods had finished in next to last position at the Bridgestone WGC Invitational in August, but naturally those quotes were revisited in Ryder Cup week. This was emphasised because Woods later warned McIlroy 'to be careful what you wish for'.

At Woods' Ryder Cup news conference I asked him what he thought about McIlroy saying he fancied the prospect of taking him on. Woods replied with two words: 'Me too.'

'Care to elaborate?' I wondered.

'Nope.'

The stare said it all and upped the ante to such an extent that both captains then faced questions over whether they would be prepared to do a deal to pit together the two players for a match that everyone wanted to see. The answer was an emphatic no from both skippers.

We had to wait until the opening ceremony to find out the opening pairings. Monty felt this event could get his team off to a flier. 'It's funny the number of times the team led by the captain who makes the best speech goes on to make the best start,' he noted. When it came to it, Pavin made the biggest gaffe by failing to include Stewart Cink in the list of players he introduced to the watching thousands in Wales and millions viewing around the world. It was a howler, but the American captain recovered quickly, turning it into a moment of comedy thoroughly enjoyed by his team. It didn't do any damage and nor did Montgomerie's effort which began with him stating in a voice choking slightly with emotion: 'This is without question the proudest moment of my golfing career.'

The game of poker as each captain tried to guess and second-guess his rival was revealed when they were asked to say which pair of players had been put into the four slots for the opening fourball matches. Montgomerie had originally planned to open with Rory McIlroy and Graeme McDowell, but Westwood's intervention meant he went with the Englishman in partnership with the newly crowned US PGA champion Martin

Kaymer. They faced Phil Mickelson and big-hitting Dustin Johnson. McIlroy and McDowell dropped down to second in the batting order and were up against Matt Kuchar and the forgotten man, Cink.

Corey Pavin decided to 'hide' Tiger Woods. As expected, he was put together with Steve Stricker, with whom he had enjoyed a 100 per cent record at the Presidents Cup the previous year, but it was the first time since 1999 that Woods wasn't sent out first. The Americans were put third and faced the English duo of Ian Poulter and rookie Ross Fisher, both of whom relished the prospect of taking on the world number one. When the pairing was announced Poulter, sitting on the stage, turned and winked in the direction of five-times former Ryder-Cup player Ken Brown.

Montgomerie combined two of his wild cards, Padraig Harrington and Luke Donald, in the often pivotal bottom match. The big surprise was that they would face two Ryder Cup debutants – the highly strung Bubba Watson and the unheralded Jeff Overton, a player with zero victories on the PGA Tour. Surprisingly, there was no room in the opening American line-up for the £7 million man Jim Furyk or for Hunter Mahan, who had been unbeaten on debut two years earlier.

Day One – Friday 1 October 2010

Colin Montgomerie had spent nearly two years consumed by the preparation for this day and before first light he knew it would prove to be long and wet. Very wet. Sir Nick Faldo hadn't got much right at Valhalla two years earlier but his in-famous advice to 'bring your waterproofs' delivered at the closing ceremony proved to be spot-on. Rain lashed the windscreen of the 2010 captain's courtesy BMW as it transported him in pitch-darkness from the Celtic Manor Resort hotel to the practice ground. The journey involves a steep climb before an even steeper descent into the Usk Valley, but at least it was smooth. Monty had been annoyed by the speed humps that had been put in place and figured they would also upset his team, so he had requested their removal.

Nevertheless, the skipper felt helpless as he watched his players warm up on the floodlit range. 'Look at them; so strong, so strong,' he had commented earlier in the week when they had been pounding away at balls. Now all he could do was hope his assessment would prove correct.

Spectators streamed to the stand that surrounded three sides of the first tee and huddled beneath umbrellas that were only discarded when the 7.45 a.m. tee-off time approached. By then they were belting out chants of 'Europe, Europe, Europe'. Stamping their feet to create a thunderous din, they sang: 'There's only two Molinaris' and 'We love you, Monty, we do'.

One by one the European vice-captains arrived on to the tee, each receiving rapturous applause to stoke up the atmosphere. Then came the players. Phil Mickelson and Dustin Johnson for the Americans, wearing navy blue waterproof suits with white flashes at the bottoms of their legs and, garishly, their surnames across the backs of their jackets. They looked like members of a college basketball team. Mickelson had also taken the unusual precaution of wearing a golf glove on each hand to try to counter the effects of the rain.

It was thought the Masters champion would assume the role of hitting the first tee shot, but, a little like Montgomerie had done at Brookline, he hung back and allowed his rookie partner the opportunity of hitting the most nerve-wracking shot in professional golf. In Monty's case it had been a tactical move to suit the foursomes format, but this was better-ball golf so the American batting order was harder to fathom.

The big-hitting Johnson struck the first ball of the 2010 Ryder Cup. He blasted a driver into the crowd down the right side, while Mickelson found the fairway, just as Westwood and Kaymer did as they began Europe's campaign. Water was lying as the rain pounded the course and a local rule was invoked to allow players to place the ball within a club's length of where it lay on the fairway.

Even though Johnson had found the rough, it was sufficiently trampled to allow him a straightforward approach to the green and the young American hit the most impressive of the second shots, but he missed his birdie chance and the opening hole was halved. At the second he missed again, but Westwood didn't. Europe were ahead, just as they were in the match behind as McDowell sank a three-footer for par. Blue was on the board from the off as the pandemonium continued on the first tee when each European pair was introduced by the silver-haired official starter, Ivor Robson.

Montgomerie and his opposite number Pavin saw off the players in all four matches amid a partisan and carnival atmosphere that defied the atrocious conditions. The question was, how long would the course remain playable? The answer was one minute short of two hours. Chief referee John Paramor called both captains on to the same radio frequency to tell them that he thought it was unfair to continue. Fairways and greens were under water and the course staff were fighting a losing battle. Both skippers indicated that they couldn't argue with the official's decision and at 9.44 a.m. Paramor officially suspended play.

The timing could hardly have been worse for the home side. Westwood had made a fine start and singlehandedly had built a two-hole lead in five holes. McDowell and McIlroy were one up after four holes against Cink and Kuchar, and Poulter and Fisher were also a hole ahead against Woods and Stricker. Only Donald and Harrington trailed. They were two down after a blistering start from Overton and Watson.

Besides halting Europe's early home momentum, there was another reason why the interruption favoured the Americans. Their waterproofs were proving useless. Instead of repelling the rain they were soaking it up. One US player claimed that it was like cloaking yourself in a towel that had been dipped in a bath of cold water. Furthermore, the retro-style golf bags Pavin had commissioned were also letting in the rain. Tiger Woods' caddie Steve Williams had stuffed the world number one's bag with towels to try to protect the grips of his clubs. The atrocious weather was no great surprise and this inability to provide adequate protection was a devastating indictment of America's preparations.

They were in stark contrast to those made by Europe. Montgomerie had included his caddie Hempleman in the process of making sure his team would be properly protected from the elements. 'We were designing all the equipment, from the golf bags to the shoes to the waterproofs to the mittens,' Hempleman revealed. 'Everything was done. We put a year and half's work into it and it paid off. We were definitely one step in front.'

No one knows better how to stay dry on a golf course than a caddie and Monty had cannily tapped into that expertise. America's rain suits were designed by Corey Pavin's wife. Humiliatingly, a PGA of America official was dispatched to the merchandise tent to make alternative arrangements with

Proquip, the company that supplied the European team with their waterproofs.

Rain continued to fall and it became clear that the 2010 Ryder Cup was slipping hopelessly behind schedule. The event has to use every second of daylight over the first two days, especially when staged as late as early October, and here the delay was stretching into hours. The organisers knew that they would have to alter the schedule to have any chance of finishing on time. Officials of the European Tour and the PGA of America met to discuss what could be done. Chief referee John Paramor, European Tour Chief Executive George O'Grady and Kerry Haigh from the American side gathered to bounce around ideas. They were loath to shorten the contest; it had to remain the best of twenty-eight points. The only way to do this and have a chance of finishing on time was to turn it into a match of four rather than five sessions.

Both captains were summoned to a secret meeting. It took place in the boiler room in the bowels of the Twenty Ten clubhouse, a surreal setting to discuss an unprecedented change to the Ryder Cup format. 'It was like the scene where the reporter met Deep Throat in the Watergate affair,' said one eyewitness. Amid the myriad pipes and the concrete an initial proposal was made to the captains. The idea was for the second session to become six foursomes matches, to be followed by six fourball contests. Montgomerie instantly agreed to the reduction in the number of sessions but Pavin was more cautious. He wanted to see it written down. The American skipper soon saw the sense of having all the players on the course simultaneously to help make up the lost time and agreed to the change. Before it was announced, though, there was to be one more alteration. Montgomerie suggested that two of the matches in the later fourball session should be played as foursomes. That way the Ryder Cup would still be decided by the usual number of matches in each of the formats. Furthermore, Monty felt it played into his hands because he was convinced his team, with its strength in depth, was more adept at the more exacting discipline of foursomes.

'One of the captains left that meeting with more of a bounce in his step,' revealed a source. It was not hard to guess which one it was.

'I think he knew what he was doing when the new format was offered to him,' commented Jason Hempleman. 'He was happy to go with that.'

It was by now mid-afternoon and Montgomerie stated that the changes were a 'brilliant option'. He called together his team to gain their approval and he used the meeting as another opportunity to provide a rallying call. 'All of you are going to play. I can give you no greater compliment,' he told them.

There was still the opening sequence of matches to be completed and that would not happen by the end of the scheduled first day. The rain relented at around 3.30 p.m. and a resumption in play was announced for 5 p.m. Some seven and a quarter hours on, could Europe maintain their encouraging start?

Monty assigned a vice-captain with each match and through their walkie-talkies they informed the captain of every shot played. The messages were less upbeat that Friday evening. No longer clad in their duff waterproofs but instead sporting light-coloured sweaters bearing giant Ryder Cup motifs, the Americans seemed reborn. Dustin Johnson still could not putt accurately, which helped keep Lee Westwood and Martin Kaymer ahead in the first match, but their lead was whittled away by a resurgent Phil Mickelson. Elsewhere it was an even greater struggle for the home pairings.

In the now glorious evening sunshine, Stewart Cink set the tone, holing a monster putt to win the fifth against McIlroy and McDowell and the match was all square. Then, at the seventh, he holed another to go one up.

The top match was turning into a classic. Johnson hit two massive blows to finish just to the side of the monstrous par five ninth and Kaymer needed to ram home a tricky right-to-left ten-footer to force a half in birdies. Back at the sixth, Luke Donald's putt to cut the arrears from two down in the bottom match defied logic and gravity, stubbornly refusing to budge from the very edge of the hole. Each development was being relayed into the ear of Europe's captain and his furrowed brow became ever more creased. What with the weather, the changed schedule and now this slump in Europe's fortunes, it was turning into one of the most stressful days of his golfing career.

When the pairings had been announced many experts believed they had fallen perfectly for Europe. Predictions of 3-1 or even 4-0 leads abounded in Radio Five Live's preview show the previous evening, but the reality was telling a different story. By the time darkness fell on that first evening Europe were indebted to the tenacity of Ian Poulter after he holed a birdie putt from 25 feet at the tenth to level the third match against Steve Stricker and Tiger Woods. Montgomerie was crouched low greenside watching the Englishman in the gathering gloom. 'Do I have to play?' Poulter asked his captain.

'No, you can stop now if you want to,' Monty advised, but Poulter, who never lacks confidence, sensed he could hole it and give Europe some overnight momentum. He duly obliged, to deafening roars from the home crowd.

Had he missed, Europe would have been down in three of the four opening fourballs. As it was, the position still wasn't encouraging. Westwood and Kaymer were only one up after twelve holes against Mickelson and Johnson, the McDowell/McIlroy combination trailed two down after twelve holes against Cink and Kuchar, and Donald and Harrington were one down on the inspired rookies Overton and Watson. Donald had decided it was too dark for him to attempt a six-foot birdie putt for a half on the ninth, so he was facing the toughest of resumptions come Saturday morning.

'That two hours of play was obviously in the Americans' favour,' Montgomerie conceded during his evening news conference. 'This will ebb and flow for the next two days. I always said this was going to be a very close contest and it is proving that right now.'

Once he had departed the 320-seater interview room he was ready to be quizzed by me for Radio Five Live. The arrangement was that the chat would take place as we rode on his captain's buggy back up the steep hill to the Twenty Ten clubhouse. As we sat on the back seats it was clear from the higher pitch of his voice and the rapid delivery of his words that he was stressed and impatient. This became even more apparent when Montgomerie realised the driver could not start the vehicle because the electronic starting PIN he was using was not being recognised. Monty had no time for this and waved me off the buggy. The interview would continue in an ever more breathless fashion as we marched at pace up the slope. Halfway up, another buggy stopped to collect us, and the captain had the presence of mind to apologise to the listeners that there would be background noise from its petrol engine. The substance of what he had to say was that there was no need for panic, it was still early days. He was right because, although darkness had fallen hours earlier on what felt like an interminable day, it was in playing terms only eleven o'clock on the first morning.

Day Two – Saturday 2 October 2010

At least it wasn't raining. The course, however, was saturated. Water splashed with every step down the fairways, but up above there was no threat of more rain on that Saturday morning. With the new format in place, the players of both teams knew that they would be involved in every sequence of matches until the end of the 2010 Ryder Cup. They steeled themselves for golf's longest day and it began with the resumption of the Friday fourball clashes in which America had the edge.

Wearing a dark woolly hat to protect him from the early morning chill, Luke Donald opened up by converting the six-foot putt he'd abandoned the previous evening. The first cheer of the morning belonged to Europe as the Englishman ensured he and Harrington did not fall two holes behind against the rookies Overton and Watson. Rory McIlroy helped the home team cut the arrears to one in the second match when he birdied the 13th, and Lee Westwood sent an imperious drive into the heart of the green at the short par four 15th to help Europe go two up with three to play in the opening contest. But America hit back as Steve Stricker hopped, skipped and holed a chip at the 12th for a birdie to put the away side ahead in the third match.

Europe claimed the first point of the contest when Phil Mickelson failed to get up and down from the side of the 16th green. Westwood played the lead role in this 3 and 2 victory in partnership with Martin Kaymer and the Englishman had fully vindicated his request to be sent out first. Montgomerie watched as handshakes were exchanged, but he was tense because red was on the board in the other three games.

McIlroy came up with a stunning birdie at the 17th to level the second contest against the inspired Stewart Cink and Matt Kuchar, but the Northern Ireland youngster then followed Cink into the water that guards the final green. 'I've got you covered, you're all right,' Graeme McDowell told his crestfallen young partner. The US Open champion then hit what appeared a fantastic third shot that spun back to the very front of the green. One more revolution and his ball would have joined McIlroy's in the drink. Both McDowell and Kuchar missed their birdie putts and the match ended all square.

Back on the 15th, Donald's brave putt kept alive the bottom match but the wild-card pick, Padraig Harrington, had done nothing to justify his captain's faith. They were three down with three to play and it was all over one hole later. Monty's handpicked pair fell to a couple of raw rookies. Overton – the only man ever to qualify for an American Ryder Cup team without winning a tournament and regarded as a potential weak link – amassed six birdies in the 3 and 2 victory.

Tiger Woods' duffed chip on the 18th didn't matter as Stricker saw the Americans to another point and the opening session belonged to Corey Pavin's side as they went into a 2½ to 1½ point lead. Europe were only a point behind, but the fretful Montgomerie knew that his team had failed to wrest the momentum that he had so craved in the build-up to the match. The side that wins the first session rarely fails to win the cup, and he knew that as well. He had fielded what he thought were his strongest fourball partnerships and they had come up short.

Monty needed his team's strength in depth to come to the fore in the unprecedented sequence of six foursome matches that would immediately follow on that now gloriously sunny Saturday morning.

This was the intended order of the matches:

Miguel Ángel Jiménez & Peter Hanson
v Tiger Woods & Steve Stricker
Edoardo Molinari & Francesco Molinari
v Zach Johnson & Hunter Mahan
Lee Westwood & Martin Kaymer
v Jim Furyk & Rickie Fowler
Padraig Harrington & Ross Fisher
v Phil Mickelson & Dustin Johnson
Ian Poulter & Luke Donald
v Bubba Watson & Jeff Overton
Graeme McDowell & Rory McIlroy
v Stewart Cink & Matt Kuchar

From Colin Montgomerie's point of view the only problem with having six matches on the course was that he didn't have enough vice-captains to accompany all the matches. But he had a ready-made solution because José Maria Olazábal, the man who had rejected his overtures on the day of his appointment, was at Celtic Manor doing promotion work for a coffee machine company. 'Not the best use of his talents,' was Monty's assessment. This time Olazábal didn't say no to the captain and Monty swiftly arranged for him to be kitted out with European colours and walkie-talkie. Olazábal brought knowledge, respect and passion and was a more than welcome addition.

With Woods and Stricker still completing their fourball clash when the foursomes were due to start, the batting order needed to be rejigged. The crowds around the first tee burst into a rendition of 'There's only two Molinaris' as the Italian brothers arrived to begin the foursomes sequence against Hunter Mahan and Zach Johnson. They began what proved a tense and dramatic session in which Europe strove to wrest back the initiative but America stood firm.

In the first incident of note the youngest player in the match, Rickie Fowler, committed a schoolboy error. On the fourth his partner Jim Furyk drove into the mud that lined the par four hole and the US pair were awarded a free drop. The twenty-one-year-old Fowler took from his pocket his own Titleist ball and dropped it into play, thus breaking the rule that states you have to finish the hole with the same ball with which you started. This error put the American pair two down on Westwood and Kaymer.

The opening exchanges were tight in all matches. By the time the bottom game reached the turn there were no more than two holes in any of them. Europe were ahead in three, the USA led in the remaining three. Montgomerie watched, chewing his fingernails and the antenna on his walkie-talkie. He was a study in solitary and helpless anxiety. At one point he asked me whether a Dustin Johnson tee shot at the seventh had been struck by 'this boy Overton' – Overton was playing in a completely different match. There wasn't much clarity of thought as he watched his side struggle to gain any kind of momentum.

As the series of matches progressed from late morning into early afternoon it was clear that a rejuvenated Padraig Harrington and an inspired Ross Fisher were the most secure of Europe's partnerships. Harrington had been told by Monty to take more responsibility after his poor showing in the four-balls. His initial contribution did not bode well because he left a ball in a fairway bunker at the first. Then the Irishman drove into the rough on the second. Fisher could only hack out, but from 220 yards out Harrington dispatched a brilliant approach that proved the big turning point. He gained a massive injection of confidence from that one shot. The Irishman read his partner's putts to great effect, nursing Fisher back from the disappointment of his earlier loss to Woods and Stricker. Harrington played faultless golf and secured his first full Ryder Cup point since 2004 when Fisher drained a birdie putt on the 16th to inflict a second defeat on the luck-less Mickelson/Johnson partnership. On being given that extra responsibility of being paired with a rookie, Harrington said: 'It was good for me and it was an excellent idea by Monty and the vice-captains.'

Just as those two were winning their match, the Jiménez/Hanson combination succumbed to a barrage of brilliant putts from Stricker as he and Woods notched up a 4 and 3 win. The Molinaris manfully tried to stay with their opponents, but Mahan's excellent tee shot at the 17th and the Italians' inability to birdie the par five last meant that America claimed another precious point. Furthermore, Martin Kaymer's putting was not of its usual accuracy on the back nine and the early initiative he and Westwood had gleaned from Fowler's carelessness was in danger of being frittered away. At the last Furyk struck a superb third shot over the water that clinched an important and unlikely half from a match that Europe had led throughout. Westwood came up short with his putt to win the match. An errant photographer's click didn't help and caddie Billy Foster was heard to call out witheringly: 'Nice camera work there, lads, brilliant.' Westwood stared angrily and Europe trailed 5-3.

Luke Donald had a 100 per cent record in Ryder Cup foursomes and was in no mood to surrender it against Watson and Overton. The Englishman hit the shot of the day over the water from the left rough on the 14th to ten feet, but the left-handed Watson put his partner even closer. Poulter missed the Europeans' birdie chance and the rookie Overton pounced to put his side one up. A birdie at the next for the English pair levelled it and a par at the 16th was enough to put them one ahead. Montgomerie was desperate for them to convert this hard-earned advantage and was thrilled to see Donald – a modern-day Bernhard Langer if ever there was one – nail his tee shot to the long par three 17th. High fives abounded with the ball nestling less than three feet from the flag. Moments later Poulter closed out a vital win.

The bottom match was all square by the time it reached that 17th hole. Stewart Cink found the green but had only a distant birdie chance. For Europe, McDowell launched a superb tee shot that finished within five feet of the flag. Advantage Europe, but not for long. Kuchar showed the putting touch that had become his hallmark on the PGA Tour in 2010 as he drained his unlikely birdie chance. It was a hammer blow that visibly rocked McIlroy, who missed from five feet. Suddenly the best the European pair could manage was a half and to gain that they had to win the closing hole. McIlroy recovered sufficiently to dispatch a decent drive and McDowell laid up short of the water. Cink found the green with an unspectacular third shot that offered only an outside birdie opportunity. It was up to McIlroy to put his wedge close enough for his partner to win the hole, but again the Northern Ireland youngster's nerve failed him. His pushed approach bounced level with the pin and spun sideways. It caught the slope and tumbled frustratingly into the greenside bunker. From there they could not get up and down and America had the full point that meant they had won their second session running. The watching Sam Torrance called it 'A calamitous end.' Europe were in trouble, they trailed 6-4 and their captain was not impressed.

Montgomerie did not think the players were using the raucous support generated by the Welsh fans as their thirteenth man to best effect. 'We have the motivation because we lost the cup two years ago, but we need more passion.' He could not address his players en masse because of the rapid turnaround of matches, but each member of the team received the message to seize the moment, gee up the crowd and make home advantage count.

'I've given them a bit of a bollocking, not that you can use that term on the radio. Call it a pep talk,' Monty told me soon after the beginning of the next session. It was one that Europe could not afford to lose.

Here is how they lined up:

Foursomes
Luke Donald & Lee Westwood
v Steve Stricker & Tiger Woods
Graeme McDowell & Rory McIlroy
v Zach Johnson & Hunter Mahan

Fourballs
Padraig Harrington & Ross Fisher
v Jim Furyk & Zach Johnson

Peter Hanson & Miguel Ángel Jiménez
v Bubba Watson & Jeff Overton
Edoardo Molinari & Francesco Molinari
v Stewart Cink & Matt Kuchar
Ian Poulter & Martin Kaymer
v Phil Mickelson & Rickie Fowler

If Europe were to regain the Ryder Cup these would have to be the matches to provide the bedrock of the triumph. The home side had lost each of the first two sessions, they trailed by two points and could not afford to be behind going into the final session of singles. Every one of Montgomerie's players was expected to deliver.

The transformation as they embarked on this crucial sequence of matches was astonishing. In Donald and Westwood, Monty put his two best players together for the foursomes and – despite their crushing disappointment at the end of the last session – he was sure McIlroy and McDowell must come good eventually. Each of his pairings for the session made absolute sense. There were no surprises in the combinations the captain fielded.

Donald and Westwood set the tone from the moment Donald struck a stunning fairway bunker shot into the first green. It piled pressure on Woods and Stricker and they buckled. The previously unbeaten Americans failed to make par and Europe were one up at the first opportunity. Westwood then rolled in a birdie from 12 feet at the second. Two up. At the fourth Woods missed from four feet; Westwood was closer and made no mistake. Three up. Two holes later Woods hacked the Americans' second shot into the water. Four up. At the next Donald chipped to within inches of the hole; Woods missed from 15 feet for par. Five up. The roars echoed all over Celtic Manor and matches ahead and behind this contest tapped into the electricity being generated. As darkness began to fall, Stricker finally made an impact on the ninth with a birdie that cut the arrears to four holes, but the momentum was still irresistibly with Europe.

'I had been disappointed the passion wasn't there,' Montgomerie admitted. 'But by God we have it now and it is fantastic for the crowd to leave tonight on a hugely positive note.' Europe held the advantage in all six matches. McIlroy and McDowell were three up after seven, Fisher and Harrington one up after eight, Hanson and Jiménez two up after six, the Molinari brothers were one hole ahead of Cink and Kuchar after five and Poulter and Kaymer were two up after four holes against Mickelson and Fowler.

Yes, the scoreboard still read 6-4 to the USA but the force was most definitely with the home team. 'I am going to have to preach into them tonight that we must maintain this tomorrow,' Montgomerie noted. After his duties in the media tent we had our usual rendezvous for his journey back up the hill to the clubhouse. Gone was the defective buggy of the previous evening. Instead, our mode of transport was a plush people carrier. 'You have upgraded,' I remarked to Monty.

'Yes, I have, and more importantly my team has upgraded its position too,' Montgomerie replied. He knew his job was to inspire his players to make sure that these positions of superiority would ultimately be reflected on the scoreboard ahead of the final-day singles. It had been a long and glorious day; and the golf had matched the much improved weather. The organisers still hoped to end the 2010 Ryder Cup on time, but worryingly in the evening darkness as we headed towards the clubhouse raindrops were starting to splash on the captain's windscreen.

Day Three – Sunday 3 October 2010

Already at saturation point from Friday's deluge, the Celtic Manor course could not take much more, but that Saturday night the most torrential rain of the week hit the Newport area of South Wales. More than 15 millimetres fell on the course. The 18th fairway became a river of running water and there was no way that play could resume on time. For the first time in its eighty-three-year history the Ryder Cup would spill over into a fourth day. Both teams arrived at the Twenty Ten clubhouse before dawn, but with the rain still hammering down the decision to delay the start was swiftly taken and the players retreated to their bedrooms in the Celtic Manor resort. 'More sleep, that's what I'm going to do,' stated Ian Poulter as he boarded his courtesy car. 'It's been an exhausting week already and the more rest you can get the better.'

Montgomerie travelled back to the hotel with his wife, Gaynor. He knew that whenever play resumed he must put his players in the correct frame of mind to make the most of their excellent starts from the previous evening. Europe could not afford to be behind going into the singles matches that would now be played on the Monday morning.

Momentum, momentum, momentum. That is what it was all about. Europe had had it early on the Friday morning but lost it when play was halted. It had taken them until late on the Saturday afternoon to recover and now they must pick up from where they left off. Just after lunchtime, a fleet of cars ferried the players out to the furthest reaches of the course and upon the restart Zach Johnson signalled America's intent with his very first blow. It was a putt across the 8th green that rattled home to cut the arrears to two holes against McIlroy and McDowell. Up ahead on the tenth, though, Westwood was sending his own message for Europe. With his captain standing at the side of the green, the Englishman holed a sensational 40-foot putt for a birdie that put Woods and Stricker five down again. 'Good boy,' Monty told Westwood as he patted him on the back en route to the 11th tee.

These opening exchanges set the tone for the most spectacular golf played in the 2010 Ryder Cup. The rains had departed and conditions were ideal. The greens were as soft as rice puddings and the players could indulge in target golf that thrilled the vast galleries. Donald and Westwood went six up at the 11th and one hole later Donald followed in Stricker for a birdie that ensured the Europeans could not lose the top match.

Behind them Jeff Overton spectacularly holed his second shot at the eighth for a winning eagle two. 'Boom, baby, yeah, baby come on,' the American rookie yelled as he exchanged high fives with his partner, Bubba Watson. As each match developed the intensity grew. Both sides knew the importance of these exchanges and Europe continued to stay ahead in all six matches. Montgomerie had called for an overnight change to the design of the electronic scoreboards to increase the presence of blue and to emphasise Europe's ascendant position. Of course, this would only be effective if his team could stay in front.

At the par three 13th Westwood holed from Donald's delicate bunker shot to seal victory over Tiger Woods and Steve Stricker. It was the seventh time Westwood had beaten the then world number one in Ryder Cup matches and overall

Europe now only trailed by a single point. 'We knew the Americans would come out fired up and we had to make sure we were even stronger,' Donald said. Then he was off to support his team-mates because, although Europe remained ahead in all six matches, the margins were diminishing. In three of the remaining contests the lead was down to a single hole. Montgomerie was going through more and more batteries in his walkie-talkie as his vice-captains continued to relay the outcome of each shot into his earpiece.

Graeme McDowell holed from 15 feet for a birdie at the 15th to remain three up with three to play after Zach Johnson threatened to snatch the hole back for the Americans by chipping stone-dead. Europe had a guaranteed half at the very least from that match, but in the fourballs the Molinari brothers were pegged back to all square by Cink and Kuchar. Fisher was keeping Harrington's head above water with some inspired putting, but the Irishman could not repeat the brilliance of his foursomes play the previous day. 'Not the man he was,' noted the watching Peter Alliss in the BBC Television commentary booth.

McIlroy and McDowell lost the 16th and, having been beaten at the last a day earlier, were showing signs of anxiety until McDowell's tee shot, struck with a hybrid club, landed on the back of the 17th green 18 feet from the flag. The opposition tee shot had skipped through the back and Johnson then charged his chip. It left McIlroy with the simple task of rolling the birdie putt up to the side of the hole. The youngster has never lacked a sense of occasion, though, and his putt tumbled into the hole to seal victory in style. It was now 6-6 and Europe had won both foursomes matches in this third session.

Momentum was undoubtedly with the home team who were

ahead but only by a single hole in the remaining matches apart from the one involving the Molinaris. That was all square until, on the 13th, Kuchar holed with his ball's last revolution to put American red on the board for the first time in the session as he and Cink went one up on the Italians.

One hole ahead Dustin Johnson three-putted with a jabby stroke that charged the ball through the right-to-left break and suddenly Fisher and Harrington were two clear. It was a huge moment that offered much-needed breathing space and they maintained their two-hole advantage until the par three 17th where Fisher found the heart of the green with a long iron tee shot. He'd missed a chance to close out the match on the previous green but, with Harrington reading the line of his birdie putt, the Englishman made no mistake to seal Europe's third win of the session. A carnival atmosphere broke out around the green with the victorious pair orchestrating a raucous chorus of 'Ole, Ole'. Europe were ahead 7-6 and were leading for the first time since Westwood and Kaymer had landed the very first point of the 2010 Ryder Cup.

Fortunes continued to ebb and flow in the way Montgomerie had predicted at the outset. The Molinaris levelled their match at the 15th and up ahead Miguel Ángel Jiménez birdied to go one up on Watson and Overton with two to play. Poulter birdied the 15th to go two up with three holes left and Monty began to breathe more easily. He even managed a rare smile as the scoreboards reflected European domination. But then Francesco Molinari was too timid with his short putt for a half at the 16th and the brothers were one down with two to play.

Jiménez was proving to be a real star and he and Hanson held their nerve coming down the last where neither Watson nor Overton could birdie the par five and Europe had another point in the bank. They were now 8-6 ahead.

Two up with two to play, Kaymer struck a superb tee shot into the 17th while both Phil Mickelson and Rickie Fowler missed the green. The German had two putts to close out yet another European win and cosied the ball up to the side of the hole. Now Monty's side were leading 9-6 with one match left on the course. They had already exceeded the captain's expectations; they would be leading going into the final day of singles matches and the Molinaris might just grab something from the only match left on the course.

They were one down playing the final hole but hit the best approach shots, wedges over water to the plateau green. Each set up his own birdie chance. Edoardo put his to ten feet; Francesco brilliantly landed his three feet from the hole. Kuchar had only a distant birdie chance to win the match, but his attempt came up short and Cink was out of the reckoning.

So now the brothers had the chance of giving Europe an unbeaten sequence of matches, but Edoardo's putt never threatened to drop. Now it was up to Francesco to convert his short birdie putt. From tee to green his game is as strong as any other player on the European Tour. His weakness is putting, particularly from short range like the one he'd underhit on the 16th. Putts like the one he was now facing. The grandstand behind the green was packed, so was the banking all around the putting surface. Europe held its breath, Monty watched on. This half-point might make all the difference. It had to drop. The stocky but diminutive Italian settled over his putt. Assistant captain Thomas Björn could not watch. He lay back on the damp grass and pulled the peak of his cap over his eyes. Francesco Molinari drew back the putter head, made the forward movement striking the ball sweetly in the middle of the blade. The little white sphere moved purposefully towards the hole and fell into the middle. Pandemonium. Francesco fell into the arms of his brother, the captain was there to offer his thanks and congratulations. America had been limited to a mere half-point out of a possible six and the 2010 Ryder Cup had been sensationally turned on its head. A two-point deficit had been turned into a three-point lead. Europe were ahead 9½-6½.

'Quite phenomenal,' Montgomerie said. 'All credit to the Molinaris; two brothers and two rookies. They have not been in that position before and to come through in the way that they did was a fantastic performance.'

Sundays at Ryder Cups always treat Montgomerie well. Even though the match had not been decided, this one had been true to form. He had set the tone beautifully with a calm and measured call to arms. He had reminded his side to avoid complacency on the resumption and they had followed his lead to the letter. Sam Torrance, the 2002 European captain, called it 'The best day in European history that I have seen.'

The day's work had not yet been done for the leader in 2010, though. Colin Montgomerie now had to make what would prove his most telling contribution to the match. The pairings for foursomes and fourballs had been relatively easy. All of Europe's partnerships had come naturally. It made sense to put together the Molinaris, the Macs from Northern Ireland. Jiménez and Hanson were a perfect fit, so were Westwood and Donald for the foursomes. Harrington enjoyed playing the senior role to inspire Fisher. The new improvised format also spared Monty awkward decisions over who to leave out after the initial sequence of fourballs. Now, though, the captain's job was to come up with a batting order for the twelve singles to maximise Europe's chances of securing the five more points they required to reach the magic number of fourteen and a half that would mean they had regained the Ryder Cup.

Monty headed straight for the clubhouse to consult with his five vice-captains, Darren Clarke, Paul McGinley, Thomas Björn, Sergio García and José Maria Olazábal. Has there ever been a gathering of more informed golfing brains in the European game? Unanimously they agreed that Lee Westwood, who would wake the next morning as golf's official world number two, should lead off for Europe. They wanted heavyweights to follow to try to maintain the momentum that had been gained on that extraordinary Sunday afternoon. McIlroy, Donald, Kaymer and Poulter were the next four names, then Fisher, Jiménez and the Molinari brothers. Peter Hanson was placed tenth, Harrington in the penultimate slot and the anchor match would be played by the US Open champion Graeme McDowell.

The European brains trust were convinced they'd decided on a winning line-up. Strength at the top and bottom of the order should provide the five points out of twelve required. The names were submitted and Corey Pavin handed in his American line-up. Top of Monty's list would play the top of Pavin's and so on down the order. These were the match-ups that would decide the 2010 Ryder Cup:

Lee Westwood v Steve Stricker
Rory McIlroy v Stewart Cink
Luke Donald v Jim Furyk
Martin Kaymer v Dustin Johnson
Ian Poulter v Matt Kuchar

Ross Fisher v Jeff Overton
Miguel Ángel Jiménez v Bubba Watson
Francesco Molinari v Tiger Woods
Edoardo Molinari v Rickie Fowler
Peter Hanson v Phil Mickelson
Padraig Harrington v Zach Johnson
Graeme McDowell v Hunter Mahan

Europe were now overwhelming favourites thanks to their three-point lead, but the older heads in the team room were guarding against any kind of complacency. Montgomerie, Harrington, Westwood, Jiménez, Clarke, García and Olazábal were all Brookline veterans. Westwood had been a leader on the course throughout the week at Celtic Manor and it was now time to be one off it as well as he backed up his captain's plea for no let-up from the European team. 'I said in the team room that I'd seen grown men cry in a locker room only once, when we had lost a 10-6 lead at Brookline in 1999,' Westwood said. 'I told them we couldn't let that happen again.'

Day Four – Monday 4 October 2010

The rain was long gone, replaced by a drifting mist that gave a ghostly and ethereal backdrop to the start of what proved as dramatic a day of golf as has been seen at any Ryder Cup. Ahead of the first match Montgomerie marched on to the tee to rapturous applause and he responded by politely clapping above his head while tightly hanging on to his ever-present walkie-talkie. He was grateful for the support, having the previous night offered to be Dr Monty ready to sign sick notes to ensure as many of Sunday's ticket holders could skip work and return again on the Monday. Throughout the week the captain had paid tribute to the patience and passion of the fans who had endured atrocious conditions, tramping through liquid mud that brought a touch of Glastonbury to South Wales. How were those fans to be rewarded on that unprecedented fourth and final day?

Westwood completed the first part of his task in no time at all, taking an early lead over Steve Stricker to put blue on the board (Monty-style) from the word go. The Englishman missed good chances on the sixth and seventh holes to turn it into a commanding lead. As the match progressed, Stricker grew in authority and piled pressure on to Westwood's shoulders as he tried to stay in front. Behind, Rory McIlroy and Luke Donald also made fast starts and the scoreboards had a healthy European glow in the glorious autumn sunshine. The waterproofs and brollies, so essential in the first few days, had been replaced by shirtsleeves and sun visors.

Stricker knew that he had to wrest the initiative if the United States were to stand any chance and began to play mesmeric golf. A stunning chip at the 11th forced a half in birdies and Westwood made a mess of the next two holes to slip from one up to one down. At this point Europe were up in five matches, the Americans up in five and two were all square, a scenario that could provide a comfortable European win. Stricker then eagled the short par four 15th to go two up with three to play and, although Westwood took him to the 17th, the American secured the first point with a hole to spare. At the same time Dustin Johnson was completing a 6 and 4 thrashing of Martin Kaymer and the overall score was now 9½-8½. Europe's lead was down to one. The picture on the course was still encouraging for the watching Montgomerie, though, because his team were ahead in six of the remaining ten matches.

Spectacular golf was being played all over Celtic Manor. Miguel Ángel Jiménez had chipped in at the eighth to take the lead in his match against Bubba Watson, Poulter pitched in for eagle at the par five 11th and Stewart Cink and Rory McIlroy were embroiled in a ding-dong clash just behind the Westwood match. Cink missed a short putt at the 15th to allow the match back to all square and one hole later McIlroy holed a lengthy par putt to retain parity.

Donald and Furyk were going at it hammer and tongs as well and, despite a brilliant tee shot to the 17th, the Englishman couldn't convert the birdie chance that would have brought victory. They headed to the last, just like McIlroy and Cink up ahead. The Northern Ireland youngster had 255 yards over water to the green for his second shot. Most players had been laying up all week, but McIlroy thought he could get there in two. He struck the three wood superbly but it drifted right into a greenside bunker. Cink, who'd missed from six feet and so halved the 17th, pitched on and gave himself a 15-footer for birdie. The advantage was with McIlroy, his ball was lying well in the deep trap. There wasn't much green to work with; all he had to do was pop it up far enough on to the putting surface and allow the ball to trundle down to the side of the hole. His bunker shot was a fraction undercooked. It made it to the green, but not far enough on and, sickeningly, it rolled back into the sand. Now the initiative was with Cink. McIlroy didn't make the same mistake second time round, splashing out to four and half feet. The American had a putt to win the match but it was always on the low side and shaved the left edge. Darren Clarke, standing greenside, relayed the situation on his radio to his increasingly worried captain. McIlroy stood up and showed extraordinary nerve to knock in the par putt for a crucial half. 'Great match, well done,' the youngster said to the former Open champion as he shook hands with Cink before being embraced by the relieved Clarke.

Any result that prevented America cutting their deficit further had to be welcomed and Ian Poulter provided that and more as he played sensationally to end Matt Kuchar's unbeaten record. Now Europe led 11-9. They were ahead in four of the remaining matches, still on course, but the situation was getting tighter by the moment.

Donald, one up, safely found the final green in three and watched his opponent Furyk, who had beaten him into second place at the Tour Championship eight days earlier, push his approach into McIlroy's bunker. The American splashed out rather clumsily and Donald unflappably used the two putts he had for victory to put Europe 12-9 in front. Just two and a half more points were required. But Ross Fisher was falling apart, having led against Jeff Overton, and Tiger Woods was playing fabulous golf, including holing his second shot at the 12th for an eagle to take control against Francesco Molinari. America was fighting back. Mickelson was in charge against Hanson, Zach Johnson was well ahead against Harrington and something was stirring inside young Rickie Fowler even though he trailed Edoardo Molinari.

Jiménez played an extraordinary bunker shot at the 15th, standing outside the hazard to address a ball that lay well below his feet. Watson couldn't find the birdie he needed and the Spaniard tapped in to win the hole and his match 4 & 3. Europe were edging ever closer; they needed just one and a half points while America, now 13-9 down, needed five points to force the draw that would mean they would keep the Ryder Cup. At this stage Europe were only ahead in two matches.

Edoardo Molinari was three up on Fowler after thirteen holes and McDowell led by the same margin with six to play. They were healthy leads but there was no wiggle room because America were comfortably ahead in the remaining contests. A succession of American wins duly followed. Overton beat Fisher in a match where emotions threatened to spill over when BBC Radio summariser and former captain Bernard Gallacher became involved in a row with Overton's father after the American questioned the validity of a free drop awarded to Fisher: 13-10. Woods was nine under par by the time he completed his demolition of Francesco Molinari on the 15th: 13-11. Mickelson accounted for Hanson 4 and 2 to record his first point of the week: 13-12.

And Fowler was making his move against Molinari. Three down with three to play after Edoardo had left short his eagle putt to win the match at the 15th, Fowler beautifully fed his approach to the long par four 16th. Molinari pitched on to eight feet, but missed his par attempt and his lead was down to two holes. Worse still, McDowell was in the process of losing the 15th to Hunter Mahan. The Portrush man's previous three-hole advantage was now down to one.

Fowler then struck his tee shot at the 17th to the heart of the green and when Molinari missed his birdie attempt the American youngster calmly holed out; the Italian was now only one hole ahead going to the last tee. Corey Pavin was with Fowler every step of the way. Montgomerie was hanging back to encourage McDowell, especially now that Harrington had succumbed to Zach Johnson to level the match at 13-13. McDowell crunched a fabulous drive down the 16th after Mahan had tugged his into the left rough. 'When he hit the middle of that fairway I felt a lot more comfortable,' Montgomerie recalled. 'The left-hand rough on that sixteenth is awful.'

At this stage McDowell still thought half a point from him would be enough to win back the Ryder Cup, but up ahead Fowler had other ideas. The American found the home green in three, as did Edoardo Molinari, even though the Italian had laid up into the rough down the right side of that final hole. Molinari hit a decent birdie attempt but it didn't drop, allowing Fowler the chance to snatch an unlikely half. Stroking from the shade into the sunlight, the youngster judged to perfection the putt from 12 feet that borrowed from right to left and dropped into the hole.

Sergio García watched on. Molinari was aghast. He'd been four up in this match, three up with three to play, and all he could manage was a miserable half-point: 13½-13½. One match left. Before Molinari could be consoled by the Spanish vice-captain, García was radioing news of this savage blow to Europe's hopes to his captain. Montgomerie saw McDowell in the middle of the fairway. 'Do you want to know what's happened up ahead?' Monty asked the last man on the course who could deliver the elusive winning point.

'Yeah, what's happened?' McDowell replied.

'Edoardo only got half a point. You are going to have to win.'

'Oh, shit,' replied the US Open champion.

McDowell had been disappointed to have been put out last. He thought he would miss out on the moments of European glory on this final day. Not any more; now it was down to him.

From the middle of the fairway he struck a beautifully crisp long iron feeding into the green. Mahan muscled his second shot from the rough down the fairway before hitting a well-judged pitch that kept alive his hopes of a par. Thousands of fans were gathered on the steep banking to the left of this most atmospheric green. There had been an ear-splitting cacophony as the players arrived on to the green, but now it was dead silent. McDowell was settling over his putt from 15 feet. This for birdie, this to go two up with two to play in a match he had to win. It was delicate, downhill. He didn't need to hit it hard, just set it off on the right track. These were the hands that had won a US Open; they should be steady. He had never felt this nervous on a golf course before, though. The ball set off on its journey starting to the left of the hole, then drifting right towards it. Had it drifted too far to the right? It might, it might. No! It grabbed the very right edge and disappeared.

Lift-off.

The hillside popped, sending thousands of people into an upward motion, roaring, cheering, shaking their fists in utter delirium. McIlroy and García leaped from their buggy, Montgomerie stood up and marched towards the next tee; he had to get to his man who was roaring 'Come on!' at the top of his voice, shaking both fists simultaneously as he stood in the middle of the green. Two up with two to play. Almost there. Almost.

'His second shot was brilliant and his putt was better,' Montgomerie said.

'I had to remind Graeme there was so much adrenaline running through him at that moment, he must take account of it with his tee shot. That seven iron could go much further than he might have been thinking' was the captain's recollection of the conversation he had with McDowell ahead of his tee shot on the 17th.

This hole had been good to Europe that week. Four times they closed out victories on this par three ahead of the last match on the course. A fifth would take Europe to the precious trophy. The vast majority of the 35,000-strong crowd gathered around this 211-yard hole wondering if this would be that moment. McDowell hit first and it flew just to the right of the green and settled on the fringe. Mahan went with a six iron and came up short. As the players made their way to the green, Montgomerie went on ahead in his buggy and was there in time to start thanking individually each member of his team as they stood at the side of the green.

Then the captain settled down next to his assistant Darren Clarke as Mahan prepared to chip. It had been a glorious day but the fairways remained damp and his ball was sitting on a tightly mown patch of grass. In such circumstances contact has to be as crisp as it is precise, but under the greatest pressure any golfer will ever face Mahan's stroke crumbled. The ball leapt forward abjectly and failed to make the green. He'd duffed it like an eighteen-handicapper might. It was purely the result of the overpowering circumstances. 'I've never been happier to see a player duff a chip,' McDowell admitted. Montgomerie leaned forward and muttered to Clarke: 'It's okay, we've done it.'

McDowell tentatively chipped up to five feet before Mahan attempted the par putt from the front of the green that had to drop for the USA to have any chance of retaining the trophy. It was a brave effort but it didn't drop. All the tearful American could do was take his cap from his head and offer a congratulatory handshake that signalled that Europe had won the Ryder Cup by 14½-13½ points.

Caddies, players and fans charged on to the green to embrace

McDowell, the hero. Montgomerie wanted to get to him, but couldn't fight through the crowds. Amid the euphoric melee McDowell's caddie, Ken Comboy, received a bash on the head from a television camera that drew blood. Montgomerie embraced Ross Fisher, then found Westwood and gave his on-course leader the biggest of bear hugs, an action that said so much about the contribution the Englishman had made on his return from injury. Champagne rained on them; some went in Monty's eyes. People thought he was crying. Not quite yet he wasn't.

'Monty's won his major,' Sam Torrance told BBC Television viewers. Andrew Coltart, a veteran of 1999 at Brookline, said exactly the same thing on Radio Five Live. Newspaper head-lines around the world made the same proclamation the following morning as they carried pictures of Europe's captain clutching his favourite trophy.

Before it was presented to him, Montgomerie and the team had to return to the clubhouse. The captain embarked on a march down the 18th fairway. The players and thousands of fans followed him, trying desperately to match his purposeful speed-walking. His head was up, chest out, left-right, left-right. Field Marshal Montgomerie was marching but he wasn't talking. He couldn't. He just wanted to get into the clubhouse. The job had been done, Europe had won and his players had helped him deliver on the promise he had made so long ago on the day of his appointment in Dubai in February 2009.

'It was relief more than anything else. It's two years in the making. It's a very, very difficult, stressful time and when it was won it was more a relief than anything else,' Montgomerie later told me. Once he reached the clubhouse he disappeared into the locker room. He left his players to go straight to the balcony to sing, dance and spray champagne on the gathering thousands of cheering fans below.

'I went through those doors, I tried to regain my composure, to be honest,' Monty told me of his disappearing act. 'It was going, well, completely gone. I realised I had to get composure because I was going to have to make a speech in front of a hundred million people. A very important speech.'

He had no idea whether he would be able to deliver it in the way that he wanted, such was the emotion coursing through his body at that stage. Recounting what happened next, Montgomerie needed several deep breaths to tell his story to me as those emotions resurfaced. 'I got my speech out, had a quick shower, changed and tried to compose myself to make that very important speech. I couldn't get through it when I was in the locker room, no chance. I was all over the place. I was so emotional because I had to mention my players, my vice-captains who had helped me so much. Those were the best decisions I made, getting the five of them to come on board. Then, when you start mentioning family, you get emotional. I didn't think I could do it, I had to read it a few more times to prepare myself for what was due to happen.'

This was the closing ceremony of which he had dreamed. Carwyn Jones, the First Minister for Wales, handed over the trophy that had been given to the game of golf by the St Albans seed merchant Samuel Ryder in 1927. The eighty-three-year-old match hadn't seen a contest quite like the one that had been played out over four long and extraordinary days in South Wales. Montgomerie demonstrated that he'd fully regained his composure when he executed his best line with perfect timing: 'This is one of the finest moments in my golfing career,' said Monty. Then he examined his notes and delivered the punchline: 'Hang on . . . this was *the greatest* moment of my golfing career.'

It was an epic match and how could it have been anything other with Colin Montgomerie playing such a leading role? Nothing is ever straightforward when it comes to this unique character from Troon in Scotland. It never has been. He is a man of many contradictions. No one can strive harder for and desire victory more than Monty, yet once it is achieved he has never been one to celebrate until all hours. It is always time to move on to the next challenge. Few golfers possess the warmth and charm of which he is capable and there are fewer still who can be as rude or boorish when things go against them. There are even fewer golfers as talented as he has been who have not won at least one major championship. In that regard he remains, probably for ever more, golf's nearly man, its ultimate enigma. But in the Ryder Cup he has always been a different animal. This is the part of the game that always provided his fulfilment. It's his patch, his manor. Whenever an American arm tried to rip his hand from this trophy the grip never faltered in the way it did with the majors.

It was only fitting that Corey Pavin's brave team took Europe to the limit in this Ryder Cup. And it was so appropriate that Europe held firm in the shape of Graeme McDowell, the man Monty had hand-picked to make sure his team wouldn't be beaten. 'It was getting ugly out there, horrible,' Montgomerie told me. 'It all changed the wrong way and it was left to Graeme, but he was put there for a reason. He won the Wales Open at Celtic Manor and he's won the US Open. He's got guts. He was put there for a very big reason.'

The stakes could not have been higher for Europe's captain

because the eggs of his career lie so firmly in the Ryder Cup basket. It is why he was so stressed when the opening exchanges went against the home team. Montgomerie knows golfing statistics as well as anyone. He will have been aware that on only one occasion previously, back in 1985, had Europe come back to win after losing the opening session. It had never happened in his time as a Ryder Cup player. His team felt that stress and his well-timed wrath when the second session was lost as well. 'Colin really rallied the troops,' McDowell remembers. 'That period between the second and third sessions, with Monty giving us the gee-up in the team room, just trying to get everybody charged up, was vital. He said, "Come on lads, we really need to do something here. I don't care how disappointed you are, you need to go back out and get the job done. Get out there and do it." It was a semi-hairdryer moment.'

Monty had called it 'a bit of a bollocking'. The result was the pivotal session in which Europe dropped only half a point from six matches. It was the only session they won, but it was enough. 'That's when we won the Ryder Cup,' Montgomerie admitted. 'Not in the singles. It was on that Sunday afternoon when we won five and a half points out of six.'

The morning after victory was completed, he acknowledged just how high the stakes had been for him. 'I had set myself up here for a very big fall,' the victorious captain said. 'I had accepted the captaincy after a reasonable playing record and all I would be remembered for would be as a losing captain, not for the playing record I had. Not having lost in eight singles would have gone by the wayside.'

Now that 'reasonable' record looks prouder than ever. In the nine Ryder Cups in which Montgomerie has had involvement (eight as a player, once as a captain) he has been on the winning side six times. His captaincy sits alongside the leadership of Sam Torrance in 2002, Bernhard Langer in 2004 and Ian Woosnam two years later. The two biggest elements he brought to the European team were his raw passion for victory and the five vice-captains. His willingness to let bygones be exactly that was the key. Darren Clarke had been more a critic than a friend down the years, Monty had had his dust-ups with Thomas Björn as well and José Maria Olazábal had not taken kindly to the presumptuous way Monty treated him in the aftermath of his appointment. Yet all three came on board to show that the European cause was paramount.

Clarke summed it up beautifully when he spoke to the *Scotsman*'s John Huggan: 'It's clear that Monty and I have not always seen eye-to-eye on certain issues,' the vice-captain said. 'But in terms of what he did as captain, he has my utmost respect. Inside the Ryder Cup "bubble", if you like, he has always had my respect. And he was so good as captain, he deserves no hassle from anyone. In fact, the first thing I did when we won was to give Monty a big hug. He was standing right beside me. I was genuinely delighted for him. He has been a Ryder Cup legend. I was so pleased for him.

'He was relaxed and quite amusing all week. He really is a funny guy. He can obviously be very difficult too. But off the course he is actually very good. And I think all the guys wanted to win for him. Everyone wanted to help him. He was meticulous in his preparation. He had it all worked out. And he got nothing wrong.

'This is how much I would praise him: if you were to publish a textbook on what to do at the Ryder Cup and how to do it, he should write it. I can't say more than that.'

Montgomerie was the arch-pragmatist, happy to change his

mind throughout his captaincy. Sometimes it was because he was making things up as he went along, like his Twitter ban that wasn't. Another example came with an early pronouncement that there would be no need for him to identify any on-course 'leaders' in a team captained by him. By the time the match came around he had encouraged and entrusted Padraig Harrington and Lee Westwood with just those roles. Westwood told me: 'Monty was a big character in the team room. I'd seen him play a lead role when he wasn't captain before and he was always very vocal. He's had a lot of experience. If he speaks you are going to listen. I thought he did a great job.

'It's difficult to quantify how much help and input captains give to a team in the week of a Ryder Cup but I would say that if they get it wrong it can be disastrous and it can stop the team from winning. I think he pretty much got most things right. If you wanted a blueprint of Ryder Cup captaincy then you would look at how Monty did it and then give it your own little fine touches and tweaks here and there.'

As the controversial wild-card pick, Padraig Harrington played under more pressure than any other player in the European team. He contributed two points and only played his best golf in one match, the foursomes in which he partnered Ross Fisher. But as a leader in the locker room he fulfilled his captain's orders and at the closing team news conference he repaid further his skipper's faith in him. 'I know Colin says that it was all about the team and it is very much that way and that's what he kept us thinking. But I think we all knew in the team how much this meant to Monty,' Harrington said. 'He's done so well as a player it is only fitting that he should win as a captain.

'But, you know, at the end of the day, things don't always work out like that. You don't automatically get guaranteed to be a winning captain just because you're a winning player. I think everybody in the team was aware that this was the one opportunity you would get to really cap off an unbelievable Ryder Cup career and we didn't want to let him down. I think as much as he didn't play on that, it was very obvious to the team members that he deserved it. We wanted to deliver that for Monty.'

One of the challenges the captain faced was balancing the needs of the experienced men like Harrington and Westwood with those of the six rookies for whom the Ryder Cup was a brand new experience. 'He might have his eight Orders of Merit, but he is Mr Ryder Cup,' commented one of those debutants, Rory McIlroy. 'You could see that at Celtic Manor. He was just under the most fierce amount of pressure and he could not do a thing about it. All he could do was watch and see how we played.

'Before the singles on Sunday night he just said to us we're nine and a half to six and a half up and reminded us what happened at Brookline. "We cannot be complacent, we have to go out and fight for every point, don't care what anyone else is doing, don't look at boards, just care about winning your match" is what he said,' McIlroy added. 'We got there in the end and you could see just how much he wanted it. He was fantastic. He took a leading role in the team room but when it got out on to the golf course he just let us do our thing. He was great.'

There was no shortage of praise for the captain in the week that followed the greatest moment of his golfing career. The way that he embraced the influence of figures such as Seve

Ballesteros and José Maria Olazábal, standing a life-size poster of these European legends in the locker room, was an inspired and selfless piece of captaincy. But if the result had gone the other way the critics would have been sharpening their pens. And it might have gone in America's favour had Rickie Fowler not dropped the wrong ball on the Saturday, or if McIlroy had missed his four-footer on the closing green on that extraordinary final day. The margins were that close and there were a thousand more ifs, buts and maybes in this amazing match. Many of them were left to swim around the head of the beaten captain, Corey Pavin.

This is the way of the sporting world when it involves an event that captures so much of the public's attention. Montgomerie knew it only too well and it took the hardest of hearts not to share in his joy at the outcome.

The fluctuations, drama and tumult of the 2010 Ryder Cup were all in keeping with the man who played the lead role. The Full Monty, indeed – not least the result. It was a truly fitting end to an extraordinary Ryder Cup career for the forty-seven-year-old Scot. He once said in a press conference, 'I am the Ryder Cup, I suppose.' He didn't mean it to sound as presumptuous and conceited as perhaps it did, but the fact is there is no one better qualified to say it.

As for the future? 'I want to be the first European captain ever to return as a player to a Ryder Cup team.'

Onwards to the next challenge.

AFTERWORD

BY GRAEME McDOWELL

Colin Montgomerie is one of my golfing heroes. Anytime I think about him I think of the Ryder Cup; he is synonymous with this great competition. I've been watching these matches since I was a kid and the one that really sticks out for me is at the Belfry in 2002 where he led from the front. How he went out there against Scott Hoch and put blue on the board to set the tone was phenomenal and the importance of doing just that was something he tried to instil in all of us throughout the week at Celtic Manor.

Colin's unbeaten history in singles is incredible. He tries to be modest when he says he has a 'reasonable' record but it is obvious to everyone that Monty's Ryder Cup career is very impressive. I have a much better appreciation now, having played in two matches myself. They are very, very special events. There is nothing quite like the pressure you feel at a Ryder Cup. I'd say it is like what I felt on the back nine at Pebble Beach when I was winning the US Open, multiplied by twelve. I say twelve because that takes account of my eleven team-mates and my captain.

Monty kept saying the 2010 match didn't mean anything to

379

him personally, that it was all about the players and the European Tour. To be honest, that was a smokescreen and I could see through it. He wanted to win the Ryder Cup so badly. Colin wears his heart on his sleeve and I could see that the pressure was on him big time that week. He badly, badly wanted to win that Ryder Cup for himself, his team and the European Tour. It must have been intense pressure because spectating is so much more stressful than actually doing it yourself. There was nothing he could do after putting his pairings together and sending us out. He must have felt helpless even though he put together an amazing backroom team with his five vice-captains.

On the Sunday evening Monty read out our order of players for the final day singles. I had said I was happy to go out anywhere. When he got down to numbers six, seven and eight I started to wonder when my name would be mentioned and at what stage I would be getting my game. Then came ten, then Padraig Harrington at eleven and only then did I know I was in the anchor match. My first reaction was actually to be a bit disappointed because I wanted to be in the mix when the Cup would be won, and I thought the other boys in the team would probably get the job done with me being a bit of a sideshow. Then I thought: 'Wow, it could come down to me', and I felt excited. It felt great that Monty and his vice-captains had such faith in my game. And, of course, it did come down to that final match and we needed a full point and not just a half.

Monty met me on the 16th fairway and asked me if I wanted to know the situation. I said yes and he told me that Edoardo Molinari had halved up ahead with Rickie Fowler. Somehow, having Colin there at that moment was a real comfort because

I knew that he knew how I would be feeling. After I holed that putt to win the 16th to go two up with two to play on Hunter Mahan, I made my way to the 17th tee and Colin was there again. He was telling me, 'Keep calm, keep calm' and I was saying, 'I am calm, I am calm.' I was so delighted that I was able to close out victory, but it would not have been possible without my team-mates. We all contributed to those magic 14½ points.

It was such a great team effort that week and that's what I take most pride in and I'm sure Monty does, too. It would have been a travesty if we had not won with him in charge. It just would not have been appropriate and our victory was a fitting end to another extraordinary chapter in his Ryder Cup career.

Graeme McDowell
October 2010

Appendix

Home team players appear first

1991 **Ocean Course, Kiawah Island, South Carolina,
27–29 September**
Captains: United States **Dave Stockton**
Europe **Bernard Gallacher**

Foursomes
P. Azinger & C. Beck lost to S. Ballesteros & J. M. Olazábal
(2 & 1)
R. Floyd & F. Couples beat B. Langer & M. James
(2 & 1)
**L. Wadkins & H. Irwin beat D. Gilford & C. Montgomerie
(4 & 2)**
P. Stewart & M. Calcavecchia beat N. Faldo & I. Woosnam
(1 hole)

Fourballs
L. Wadkins & M. O'Meara halved with S. Torrance &
D. Feherty

P. Azinger & C. Beck lost to S. Ballesteros & J. M. Olazábal
(2 & 1)

C. Pavin & M. Calcavecchia lost to S. Richardson &
M. James (5 & 4)

R. Floyd & F. Couples beat N. Faldo & I. Woosnam (5 & 3)

Foursomes

H. Irwin & L. Wadkins beat D. Feherty & S. Torrance (4 & 2)

M. Calcavecchia & P. Stewart beat M. James &
S. Richardson (1 hole)

P. Azinger & M. O'Meara beat N. Faldo & D. Gilford
(7 & 6)

F. Couples & R. Floyd lost to S. Ballesteros & J. M. Olazábal
(3 & 2)

Fourballs

P. Azinger & H. Irwin lost to I. Woosnam & P. Broadhurst
(2 & 1)

**C. Pavin & S. Pate lost to B. Langer & C. Montgomerie
(2 & 1)**

L. Wadkins & W. Levi lost to M. James & S. Richardson
(3 & 1)

P. Stewart & F. Couples halved with S. Ballesteros &
J. M. Olazábal

Singles

R. Floyd lost to N. Faldo (2 holes)

P. Stewart lost to D. Feherty (2 & 1)

M. Calcavecchia halved with C. Montgomerie

P. Azinger beat J. M. Olazábal (2 holes)

C. Pavin beat S. Richardson (2 & 1)

W. Levi lost to S. Ballesteros (3 & 2)

C. Beck beat I. Woosnam (3 & 1)

M. O'Meara lost to P. Broadhurst (3 & 1)

F. Couples beat S. Torrance (3 & 2)

L. Wadkins beat M. James (3 & 2)

H. Irwin halved with B. Langer

S. Pate halved with D. Gilford*

(*match not played: Pate withdrew with injury, Gilford named in envelope)

United States 14½ Europe 13½

**1993 The Belfry, Sutton Coldfield, England,
24–26 September**
Captains: Europe **Bernard Gallacher**
United States **Tom Watson**

Foursomes
S. Torrance & M. James lost to L. Wadkins & C. Pavin
(4 & 3)

I. Woosnam & B. Langer beat P. Azinger & P. Stewart
(7 & 5)

S. Ballesteros & J. M. Olazábal lost to T. Kite & D. Love III
(2 & 1)

N. Faldo & C. Montgomerie beat R. Floyd & F. Couples
(4 & 3)

Fourballs
I. Woosnam & P. Baker beat J. Gallagher Jr & L. Janzen
(1 hole)

B. Langer & B. Lane lost to L. Wadkins & C. Pavin (4 & 2)

**N. Faldo & C. Montgomerie halved with P. Azinger &
F. Couples**

S. Ballesteros & J. M. Olazábal beat D. Love III & T. Kite
(4 & 3)

Foursomes

**N. Faldo & C. Montgomerie beat L. Wadkins & C. Pavin
(3 & 2)**

B. Langer & I. Woosnam beat F. Couples & P. Azinger
(2 & 1)

P. Baker & B. Lane lost to R. Floyd & P. Stewart (3 & 2)

S. Ballesteros & J. M. Olazábal beat D. Love III & T. Kite
(2 & 1)

Fourballs

**N. Faldo & C. Montgomerie lost to J. Cook & C. Beck
(2 holes)**

M. James & C. Rocca lost to C. Pavin and J. Gallagher Jr
(5 & 4)

I. Woosnam & P. Baker beat F. Couples & P. Azinger (6 & 5)

J. M. Olazábal and J. Haeggman lost to R. Floyd &
P. Stewart (2 & 1)

Singles

I. Woosnam halved with F. Couples

B. Lane lost to C. Beck (1 hole)

C. Montgomerie beat L. Janzen (1 hole)

P. Baker beat C. Pavin (2 holes)

J. Haeggman beat J. Cook (1 hole)

M. James lost to P. Stewart (3 & 2)

C. Rocca lost to D. Love III (1 hole)

S. Ballesteros lost to J. Gallagher Jr (3 & 2)

J. M. Olazábal lost to R. Floyd (2 holes)

B. Langer lost to T. Kite (5 & 3)

N. Faldo halved with P. Azinger

S. Torrance halved with L. Wadkins*

(*match not played: Torrance withdrew injured, Wadkins named in envelope)

Europe 13 United States 15

**1995   Oak Hill Country Club, Rochester, New York,
        September 22–24**
Captains: United States **Lanny Wadkins**
            Europe **Bernard Gallacher**

Foursomes
**C. Pavin & T. Lehman beat N. Faldo & C. Montgomerie
  (1 hole)**
J. Haas & F. Couples lost to S. Torrance & C. Rocca (3 & 2)
D. Love III & J. Maggert beat H. Clark & M. James (4 & 3)
B. Crenshaw & C. Strange lost to B. Langer &
  P-U. Johansson (1 hole)

Fourballs
B. Faxon & P. Jacobsen lost to D. Gilford & S. Ballesteros
  (4 & 3)
J. Maggert & L. Roberts beat S. Torrance & C. Rocca (6 & 5)
**F. Couples & D. Love III beat N. Faldo & C. Montgomerie
  (3 & 2)**

C. Pavin & P. Mickelson beat B. Langer & P-U. Johansson
(6 & 4)

Foursomes

C. Strange & J. Haas lost to N. Faldo & C. Montgomerie
(4 & 2)

D. Love III & J. Maggert lost to S. Torrance & C. Rocca
(6 & 5)

L. Roberts & P. Jacobsen beat I. Woosnam & P. Walton
(1 hole)

C. Pavin & T. Lehman lost to B. Langer & D. Gilford
(4 & 3)

Fourballs

B. Faxon & F. Couples beat S. Torrance & C. Montgomerie
(4 & 2)

D. Love III & B. Crenshaw lost to I. Woosnam & C. Rocca
(3 & 2)

J. Haas & P. Mickelson beat S. Ballesteros & D. Gilford
(3 & 2)

C. Pavin & L. Roberts beat N. Faldo & B. Langer
(1 hole)

Singles

T. Lehman beat S. Ballesteros (4 & 3)

P. Jacobsen lost to H. Clark (1 hole)

J. Maggert lost to M. James (4 & 3)

F. Couples halved with I. Woosnam

D. Love III beat C. Rocca (3 & 2)

B. Faxon lost to D. Gilford (1 hole)

B. Crenshaw lost to C. Montgomerie (3 & 1)

C. Strange lost to N. Faldo (1 hole)
L. Roberts lost to S. Torrance (2 & 1)
C. Pavin beat B. Langer (3 & 2)
J. Haas lost to P. Walton (1 hole)
P. Mickelson beat P-U. Johansson (2 & 1)

US 13½ Europe 14½

1997   Club de Golf Valderrama, Sotogrande, Spain, 26–28 September
Captains: Europe **Severiano Ballesteros**
                United States **Tom Kite**

Fourballs
J. M. Olazábal & C. Rocca beat D. Love III & P. Mickelson
    (1 hole)
N. Faldo & L. Westwood lost to F. Couples & B. Faxon
    (1 hole)
J. Parnevik & P-U. Johansson beat T. Lehman & J. Furyk
    (1 hole)
C. Montgomerie & B. Langer lost to T. Woods &
    M. O'Meara (3 & 2)

Foursomes
C. Rocca & J. M. Olazábal lost to S. Hoch & L. Janzen
    (1 hole)
B. Langer & C. Montgomerie beat M. O'Meara & T. Woods
    (5 & 3)
N. Faldo & L. Westwood beat J. Leonard & J. Maggert (3 & 2)

J. Parnevik & I. Garrido halved with T. Lehman &
P. Mickelson

Fourballs

**C. Montgomerie & D. Clarke beat F. Couples & D. Love III
(1 hole)**

I. Woosnam & T. Björn beat J. Leonard & B. Faxon
(2 & 1)

N. Faldo & L. Westwood beat T. Woods & M. O'Meara
(2 & 1)

J. M.Olazábal & I. Garrido halved with P. Mickelson &
T. Lehman

Foursomes

**C. Montgomerie & B. Langer beat L. Janzen & J. Furyk
(1 hole)**

N. Faldo & L. Westwood lost to S. Hoch & J. Maggert
(2 & 1)

J. Parnevik & I. Garrido halved with J. Leonard & T. Woods

J. M. Olazábal & C. Rocca beat D. Love III & F. Couples
(5 & 4)

Singles

I. Woosnam lost to F. Couples (8 & 7)

P-U. Johansson beat D. Love III (3 & 2)

C. Rocca beat T. Woods (4 & 2)

T. Björn halved with J. Leonard

D. Clarke lost to P. Mickelson (2 & 1)

J. Parnevik lost to M. O'Meara (5 & 4)

J. M. Olazábal lost to L. Janzen (1 hole)

B. Langer beat B. Faxon (2 & 1)

L. Westwood lost to J. Maggert (3 & 2)

C. Montgomerie halved with S. Hoch

N. Faldo lost to J. Furyk (3 & 2)

I. Garrido lost to T. Lehman (7 & 6)

Europe 14½ United States 13½

**1999   The Country Club, Brookline, Massachusetts,
24–26 September**

Captains: United States **Ben Crenshaw**

Europe **Mark James**

Foursomes

**P. Mickelson & D. Duval lost to C. Montgomerie &
P. Lawrie (3 & 2)**

T. Lehman & T. Woods lost to S. García & J. Parnevik
(2 & 1)

D. Love III & P. Stewart halved with M. Á. Jiménez &
P. Harrington

J. Maggert & H. Sutton beat D. Clarke & L. Westwood
(3 & 2)

Fourballs

**D. Love III & J. Leonard halved with C. Montgomerie &
P. Lawrie**

P. Mickelson & J. Furyk lost to S. García & J. Parnevik
(1 hole)

J. Maggert & H. Sutton lost to M. Á. Jiménez &
J. M. Olazábal (2 & 1)

D. Duval & T. Woods lost to D. Clarke & L. Westwood
(1 hole)

Foursomes

**C. Montgomerie & P. Lawrie lost to H. Sutton & J. Maggert
(1 hole)**

J. Furyk & M. O'Meara lost to D. Clarke & L. Westwood
(3 & 2)

T. Woods & S. Pate beat M. Á. Jiménez & P. Harrington
(1 hole)

P. Stewart & J. Leonard lost to J. Parnevik & S. García (3 & 2)

Fourballs

P. Mickelson & T. Lehman beat D. Clarke & L. Westwood
(2 & 1)

D. Love III & D. Duval halved with J. Parnevik & S. García

J. Leonard & H. Sutton halved with M. Á. Jiménez &
J. M. Olazábal

**S. Pate & T. Woods lost to C. Montgomerie & P. Lawrie
(2 & 1)**

Singles

T. Lehman beat L. Westwood (3 & 2)

H. Sutton beat D. Clarke (4 & 2)

P. Mickelson beat J. Sandelin (4 & 3)

D. Love III beat J. van de Velde (6 & 5)

T. Woods beat A. Coltart (3 & 2)

D. Duval beat J. Parnevik (5 & 4)

M. O'Meara lost to P. Harrington (1 hole)

S. Pate beat M. Á. Jiménez (2 & 1)

J. Leonard halved with J. M Olazábal

P. Stewart lost to C. Montgomerie (1 hole)
J. Furyk beat S. García (4 & 3)
J. Maggert lost to P. Lawrie (4 & 3)

United States 14½ Europe 13½

2002   **The Belfry, Sutton Coldfield, England,**
         27–29 September
Captains: Europe **Sam Torrance**
              United States **Curtis Strange**

Fourballs
D. Clarke & T. Björn beat T. Woods & P. Azinger (1 hole)
S. García & L. Westwood beat D. Love III & D. Duval
   (4 & 3)
C. Montgomerie & B. Langer beat S. Hoch & J. Furyk
   (1 hole)
P. Harrington & N. Fasth lost to P. Mickelson & D. Toms
   (1 hole)

Foursomes
D. Clarke & T. Björn lost to H. Sutton & S. Verplank (2 & 1)
S. García & L. Westwood beat T. Woods & M. Calcavecchia
   (2 & 1)
C. Montgomerie & B. Langer halved with P. Mickelson &
   D. Toms
P. Harrington & P. McGinley lost to S. Cink & J. Furyk (3 & 2)

Foursomes

P. Fulke & P. Price lost to P. Mickelson & D. Toms (2 & 1)

L. Westwood & S. García beat J. Furyk & S. Cink (2 & 1)

C. Montgomerie & B. Langer beat S. Verplank & S. Hoch (1 hole)

D. Clarke & T. Björn lost to T. Woods & D. Love III (4 & 3)

Fourballs

N. Fasth & J. Parnevik lost to M. Calcavecchia & D. Duval (1 hole)

C. Montgomerie & P. Harrington beat P. Mickelson & D. Toms (2 & 1)

S. García & L. Westwood lost to T. Woods and D. Love III (1 hole)

D. Clarke & P. McGinley halved with S. Hoch & J. Furyk

Singles

C. Montgomerie beat S. Hoch (5 & 4)

S. García lost to D. Toms (1 hole)

D. Clarke halved with D. Duval

B. Langer beat H. Sutton (4 & 3)

P. Harrington beat M. Calcavecchia (5 & 4)

T. Björn beat S. Cink (2 & 1)

L. Westwood lost to S. Verplank (2 & 1)

N. Fasth halved with P. Azinger

P. McGinley halved with J. Furyk

P. Fulke halved with D. Love III

P. Price beat P. Mickelson (3 & 2)

J. Parnevik halved with T. Woods

Europe 15½ United States 12½

2004   Oakland Hills Country Club, Bloomfield Township, Michigan, 17–19 September

Captains: United States **Hal Sutton**
Europe **Bernhard Langer**

Fourballs
T. Woods & P. Mickelson lost to C. Montgomerie & P. Harrington (2 & 1)

D. Love III & C. Campbell lost to D. Clarke & M. Á. Jiménez (5 & 4)

C. Riley & S. Cink halved with P. McGinley & L. Donald

D. Toms & J. Furyk lost to S. García & L. Westwood (5 & 3)

Foursomes
J. Haas & C. DiMarco beat M. Á. Jiménez & T. Levet (3 & 2)

D. Love III & F. Funk lost to P. Harrington & C. Montgomerie (4 & 2)

P. Mickelson & T. Woods lost to D. Clarke & L. Westwood (1 hole)

K. Perry & S. Cink lost to L. Donald & S. García (2 & 1)

Fourballs
J. Haas & C. DiMarco halved with S. García & L. Westwood

C. Riley & T. Woods beat D. Clarke & I. Poulter (4 & 3)

C. Campbell & J. Furyk lost to P. Casey & D. Howell (1 hole)

S. Cink & D. Love III beat P. Harrington & C. Montgomerie (3 & 2)

Foursomes

J. Haas & C. DiMarco lost to D. Clarke & L. Westwood
 (5 & 4)

P. Mickelson & D. Toms beat M. Á. Jiménez & T. Levet
 (4 & 3)

J. Furyk & F. Funk lost to L. Donald & S. García (1 hole)

D. Love III & T. Woods lost to P. Harrington & P. McGinley
 (4 & 3)

Singles

T. Woods beat P. Casey (3 & 2)

P. Mickelson lost to S. García (3 & 2)

D. Love III halved with D. Clarke

J. Furyk beat D. Howell (6 & 4)

K. Perry lost to L. Westwood (1 hole)

D. Toms lost to C. Montgomerie (1 hole)

C. Campbell beat L. Donald (5 & 3)

C. DiMarco beat M. Á. Jiménez (1 hole)

F. Funk lost to T. Levet (1 hole)

C. Riley lost to I. Poulter (3 & 2)

J. Haas lost to P. Harrington (1 hole)

S. Cink lost to P. McGinley (3 & 2)

United States 9½ Europe 18½

**2006   The K Club, Straffan, Co. Kildare, Ireland,
        22–24 September**
Captains: Europe **Ian Woosnam**
              United States **Tom Lehman**

Fourballs
**C. Montgomerie and P. Harrington lost to T. Woods &
  J. Furyk (1 hole)**
P. Casey & R. Karlsson halved with S. Cink & J. J. Henry
S. García & J. M. Olazábal beat D. Toms & B. Wetterich
  (3 & 2)
D. Clarke & L. Westwood beat P. Mickelson & C. DiMarco
  (1 hole)

Foursomes
P. McGinley & P. Harrington halved with C. Campbell &
  Z. Johnson
D. Howell & H. Stenson halved with S. Cink & D. Toms
**L. Westwood & C. Montgomerie halved with P. Mickelson
  & C. DiMarco**
L. Donald & S. García beat T. Woods & J. Furyk (2 holes)

Fourballs
P. Casey & R. Karlsson halved with S. Cink & J. J. Henry
S. García & J. M. Olazábal beat P. Mickelson & C. DiMarco
  (3 & 2)
L. Westwood & D. Clarke beat T. Woods & J. Furyk (3 & 2)
H. Stenson & P. Harrington lost to Z. Johnson &
  S. Verplank (2 & 1)

Foursomes

S. García & L. Donald beat P. Mickelson & D. Toms (2 & 1)

C. Montgomerie & L. Westwood halved with C. Campbell & V. Taylor

P. Casey & D. Howell beat S. Cink & Z. Johnson (5 & 4)

P. Harrington & P. McGinley lost to T. Woods & J. Furyk (3 & 2)

Singles

C. Montgomerie beat D. Toms (1 hole)

S. García lost to S. Cink (4 & 3)

P. Casey beat J. Furyk (2 & 1)

R. Karlsson lost to T. Woods (3 & 2)

L. Donald beat C. Campbell (2 & 1)

P. McGinley halved with J. J. Henry

D. Clarke beat Z. Johnson (3 & 2)

H. Stenson beat V. Taylor (4 & 3)

D. Howell beat B. Wetterich (5 & 4)

J. M. Olazábal beat P. Mickelson (2 & 1)

L. Westwood beat C. DiMarco (2 holes)

P. Harrington lost to S. Verplank (4 & 3)

Europe 18½ United States 9½

2010   The Celtic Manor Resort, City of Newport, Wales,
       1–4 October
Captains: Europe **Colin Montgomerie**
          United States **Corey Pavin**

Session 1
Fourballs
L. Westwood & M. Kaymer beat P. Mickelson & D. Johnson
  (3 & 2)
R. McIlroy & G. McDowell halved with S. Cink &
  M. Kuchar
I. Poulter & R. Fisher lost to S. Stricker & T. Woods
  (2 holes)
L. Donald & P. Harrington lost to B. Watson & J. Overton
  (3 & 2)

Session 2
Foursomes
M. Á. Jiménez & P. Hanson lost to T. Woods & S. Stricker
  (4 & 3)
E. Molinari & F. Molinari lost to Z. Johnson & H. Mahan
  (2 holes)
L. Westwood & M. Kaymer halved with J. Furyk &
  R. Fowler
P. Harrington & R. Fisher beat P. Mickelson &
  D. Johnson (3 & 2)
I. Poulter & L. Donald beat B. Watson & J. Overton (2 & 1)
G. McDowell & R. McIlroy lost to S. Cink & M. Kuchar
  (1 hole)

Session 3
Foursomes

L. Donald & L. Westwood beat S. Stricker & T. Woods (6 & 5)

G. McDowell & R. McIlroy beat Z. Johnson & H. Mahan
(3 & 1)

Fourballs

P. Harrington & R. Fisher beat J. Furyk & D. Johnson
(2 & 1)

P. Hanson & M. Á. Jiménez beat B. Watson & J. Overton
(2 holes)

E. Molinari & F. Molinari halved with S. Cink & M. Kuchar

I. Poulter & M. Kaymer beat P. Mickelson & R. Fowler
(2 & 1)

Session 4
Singles

L. Westwood lost to S. Stricker (2 & 1)

R. McIlroy halved with S. Cink

L. Donald beat J. Furyk (1 hole)

M. Kaymer lost to D. Johnson (6 & 4)

I. Poulter beat M. Kuchar (5 & 4)

R. Fisher lost to J. Overton (3 & 2)

M. Á. Jiménez beat B. Watson (4 & 3)

F. Molinari lost to T. Woods (4 & 3)

E. Molinari halved with R. Fowler

P. Hanson lost to P. Mickelson (4 & 2)

P. Harrington lost to Z. Johnson (3 & 2)

G. McDowell beat H. Mahan (3 & 1)

Europe 14½ United States 13½

ACKNOWLEDGEMENTS

When you are in the fortunate position of earning a living by travelling the globe watching golf, there are always offers of help. 'Do you need anyone to carry your bags?' is perhaps the question I am most frequently asked. But nothing quite prepared me for the level of willing assistance I received in writing *Monty's Manor*. I owe a debt of gratitude to so many people who helped make possible this book.

At the opening ceremony of the Ryder Cup, Monty announced his team in alphabetical order because, in his eyes, they were all equally valuable to the European cause. It was a sensible policy and it feels only right to (loosely) follow the skipper's example here. By happy coincidence it means I can begin with my heartfelt thanks and best wishes to Severiano Ballesteros for his time and effort in providing the Foreword. Thanks also should go to Guy Pelham and his wife, Maria Valcarcel Reyes, for translating Seve's Spanish into English.

To Ken Brown for his time and insights into Monty's character at Brookline in 1999 many, many thanks. My Five Live colleague Alastair Bruce-Ball spent ages at the US PGA along with our own radio G-Mac checking and double-checking Ryder Cup results dating back to Monty's debut in 1991. On the subject of checking, thanks are also due to the copy editor Richard Collins and proof reader Myra Jones for their diligence under the huge time pressure of making the book available for sale so soon after Europe's victory.

The technical genius that is Ian Cockett must be thanked

for his recording skills in making it possible for me to see more than just the matches I walked with at the 2010 Ryder Cup. Other local friends, Gordon Barker, David Best, Dave Pinder (pub Dave), James Clark, Mark Garnish and Warwick Brown, have inspired me with their interest in the project.

To Andrew Cotter, a man from the same Troon roots as Monty, a big thank you for the insights, gossip and impersonations of the captain that so entertained us throughout 2010 and apologies for the limited opportunities you had to beat me at golf while the laptop took precedence over the clubs. Normal service will be resumed in 2011.

A group of Fleet Street's finest scribes comes next. I'll begin this group with the *Independent*'s James Corrigan and add the *Guardian*'s Lawrence Donegan, the *Sun*'s David Facey, Derek Lawrenson from the *Daily Mail* and the *Daily Telegraph*'s Mark Reason. They are great pals on the golfing road but they are also hugely talented journalists who were a constant source of inspiration, encouragement and knowledge throughout this project. Special mention also to Paul Mahoney who had so many good ideas as we drove across Florida from The Players Championship.

Moving to the letter E enables me to thank all the staff at the European Tour and in particular everyone working in the media and public relations department. They are the best in the business.

Bernard Gallacher deserves special mention for the time and patience he afforded me in discussing his captaincy of Monty in the early part of his Ryder Cup career. To Ken Jackson, many thanks for taking my mugshot and for his interest in the project. Guy Kinnings is Monty's manager and was a constant source of encouragement and news throughout the writing of this book. To Guy and his IMG staff, including Michele Mair, very many thanks.

This book would never have happened without the help of my literary agent Melanie Michael-Greer. She was the first to hear the idea, and for recognising its potential and securing Yellow Jersey Press as publishers I am hugely grateful.

To Graeme McDowell, I speak on behalf of all European golf fans when I simply say THANK YOU! Not just for holding your nerve to put the Ryder Cup into Monty's hands, but also for taking the time to provide the Afterword for this book. I am very, very grateful.

The radio G-Mac is Graham McMillan, my golf producer at Five Live. Thank you for all your help and support. The same message goes to my unflappable editor at Five Live, Graeme Reid-Davies, and especially to the BBC's Head of Radio Sport, Gordon Turnbull, the man who gave me my job and was so encouraging in allowing me to write this book.

To my sister-in-law, Julie Parrish, thank you for sharing writing experiences and to Stuart, Emily and Jamie for their support. Julie's Mum and Dad, Cathy and Bill, as always, could not have been more encouraging. While we're on the subject of family, thanks should also go to my dad for introducing me to the game of golf, and to Stewart, Edel, Ellen, Niamh and Caitlin for their love and support.

The editor of this book is Matt Phillips. In commissioning it he had the foresight to recognise that the 2010 Ryder Cup would become an extraordinary story. Thank you, Matt, and all your staff at Yellow Jersey, including Bethan Jones in publicity and Phil Brown in production, for nursing me through my first book.

P is also for players. To all those who gave time to be interviewed for *Monty's Manor*, including, among others, Padraig Harrington, Rory McIlroy, Ian Poulter, Jamie Spence, Henrik Stenson, Hal Sutton and Lee Westwood, I am very grateful. Jay Townsend is a former player and my colleague at all the major championships. No one has contributed more to my knowledge and understanding of the game. All he has to do now is sort out my chipping. Thanks also to Denis Pugh for our enlightening conversation as we crossed the Atlantic.

There are three people I've exempted from an alphabetical listing because they are just too important. My wife, Sarah, had the original idea for this book, but probably didn't realise how much more time it would mean me spending away from household life. Sorry – but I'm back now. This is good news, I hope, for our amazing son, Ollie, who has had to put up with Dad being away from home far too much. Thank you.

The final word has to go to the man about whom this book was written. They broke the mould when they made Colin Stuart Montgomerie. He is a unique figure, far more intriguing than your usual run-of-the-mill sporting super-star. His relationship with the Ryder Cup has fascinated me from the moment I first saw him in the 1993 match at the Belfry. As BBC Radio Golf Correspondent I have recorded chats with him on countless occasions and he has always been extraordinarily helpful and accommodating. Quite simply, he is the best interview in sport.

Iain Carter

October 2010